J. Benjamin Marsden

**The Influence of the Mosaic Code Upon Subsequent Legislation**

J. Benjamin Marsden

**The Influence of the Mosaic Code Upon Subsequent Legislation**

ISBN/EAN: 9783744717717

Printed in Europe, USA, Canada, Australia, Japan

Cover: Foto ©Lupo / pixelio.de

More available books at **www.hansebooks.com**

THE

# INFLUENCE OF THE MOSAIC CODE

UPON

## SUBSEQUENT LEGISLATION.

BY

J. BENJ. MARSDEN,

SOLICITOR.

LONDON:
PUBLISHED BY HAMILTON, ADAMS, & CO.,
PATERNOSTER ROW; AND
HATCHARD & CO., 187, PICCADILLY.

1862.

LONDON:
PRINTED BY C. F. HODGSON,
GOUGH SQUARE, FLEET STREET.

# PREFACE

THE following pages can claim but slender pretensions to original research, still less to theological learning: opportunity was wanting for the one; the author's pursuits precluded the other. Materials for the work were chiefly furnished by the investigations of other writers, who, in pursuit of different objects, had already travelled over some portions of the same ground. Since, however, the authority of the Old Testament has been called in question, even by those whose profession bound them to defend it, to trace its influence upon the principles of jurisprudence as a moral science, presented itself as a subject of interest. It was one, at least, that not unnaturally would claim the attention of a person engaged in the practice of the law. Upon this inquiry, therefore, the author employed such leisure as he could spare from his professional pursuits. As it progressed, each step in the investigation confirmed the conclusions that are now submitted to the reader. Indeed, had the compass of the volume permitted, many resemblances in the laws of the Hindùs and the Chinese might have been added, in illustration of their origin from Hebrew sources. The laws of the Mohammedans have not been mentioned, because their source from the Mosaic Code has long since been placed beyond question. But should the demand for this Work ever justify the publication of another edition, the author hopes hereafter to enlarge it by the addition of some coincidences to be found in the Chinese and Hindù institutions.

To avoid the inconvenience of incumbering the text with notes, a list of the chief authorities that have been referred to upon the subjects to which they relate, is here added. They are as follows:— Gale's Court of the Gentiles.—Spencer de Legibus Hebræorum.—Selden de Jure Naturali et Gentium juxta Hebræorum.—Selden on Tithes (History of).— Sir Matthew Hale's History of the Common Law.— Fortescue de Laudibus Legum Angliæ.—A Learned Commendation of the Laws of England; translated by R. Mulcaster (1567).—Eden's Jurisprudentia Philologica. 4to. Oxon (1744).—A Compendious View of the Civil Law; by Arthur Browne (1798).— Blume's Lex Dei sive Mosaicorum (1833).—Savigny's History of the Roman Laws (1829). (Cathcart's

Edition).—Histoire de la Legislation; par M. Pastoret. 8vo. Paris (1817).—Cicero de Legibus. (Bohn's translation.)—Cicero de Naturâ Deorum. (Bohn's translation.)—Plato de Legibus, &c. (Bohn's translation.)—Plato in Timæum. (Bohn's translation.)—Diodorus Siculus. (Booth's edition.)—Sir G. M. Wilkinson's History of the Ancient Egyptians.—Petit's Leges Atticæ.—Potter's Greek Antiquities.—Adams's Roman Antiquities.—A New Pandect of Roman Civil Law; by John Ayliffe. (1734.)—Elements of Civil Law. 4to. London. (1769.)—Bacon on English Government.—Reeves' History of the Law.—Warburton's Divine Legation of Moses.—Niebuhr's History of Rome.—Dr. Thorpe's Anglo-Saxon Laws.—Bishop Butler's Sermons on Natural Law.—Sir J. Macintosh on the Law of Nature.—Blackstone's Commentaries.—Spence's Equitable Jurisdiction.— Esprit, Origine et Progrès des Institutions Judiciaires des Principaux Pays de l'Europe; par J. D. Meyer. (1818.)—Ellis's Introduction to Domesday Book.—Lord Bacon's Tracts.—Paley's Moral Philosophy; edited by Archbishop Whately.—Grotius de Jure Belli et Pacis; with Barbeyrac's Notes.—Ancient Laws and Institutes of England; printed by command of William IV., and compiled by the King's Commissioners.—Guizot's History of Civilization.—Gibbon's Rise and Fall of the Roman Empire.—Goguet on the Origin of Laws.—The Works of Josephus.—Selden's

Discourse on the Laws and Government of England; by N. Bacon. (1689.)

With this acknowledgment, it is hoped that the facts stated will be found capable of sufficient authentication without exposing the Author to the charge of pedantry. The conclusions must speak for themselves.

3, Crown Court,
Old Broad Street, London;
*October*, 1862.

# CONTENTS.

### CHAPTER I.
On the Law of Nature: ..................................... Page 1

### CHAPTER II.
On the Sources of Ancient Jurisprudence. ......... 28

### CHAPTER III.
On Laws Relating to Religion. ..,..................... 48

### CHAPTER IV.
On the Principles and Construction of the Hebrew Laws. ..................................................... 83

### CHAPTER V.
On the Influence of the Roman Laws, the Ancient Laws of England. ...................................... 110

### CHAPTER VI.
On the Laws of Retribution.—Homicide; Violence; False Witness. ........................................... 142

## CHAPTER VII.
Laws of Restitution.—Theft; Trespass; Pledges; Redemption. ............................................. 167

## CHAPTER VIII.
On Adulteries. ............................................. 209

## CHAPTER IX.
Laws relating to Marriage and Divorce. ............ 232

## CHAPTER X.
Laws relating to Parents and Children. ............ 266

## CHAPTER XI.
The Constitution of the Supreme Courts of the Greeks and Egyptians. ................................. 273

## CHAPTER XII.
Conclusion ..................................................... 281

ON THE

# PRINCIPLES AND LIMITS OF LEGISLATION

AND THE

# ORIGIN OF LAWS.

## CHAPTER I.

### ON THE LAW OF NATURE.

It is admitted universally, that when God created the world, He established certain rules, in accordance with which all things created are regulated and governed. So, when He created man, and endued him with free will to conduct himself in all the relations of life, He laid down certain immutable laws of human nature, whereby that free will is in some degree regulated and restrained, and gave him also the faculty of reason to discover the purport of those laws.

It is not, therefore, a matter of surprise that the political authors of antiquity should have come to the conclusion that all people who are governed by laws use partly those principles of justice which are adapted to their peculiar circumstances, and partly those which are common to all mankind.

It is with the latter only that we are now concerned. By most writers upon Jurisprudence they are defined as "the law of nature," and being coeval with mankind, and dictated by God himself, are of course superior in obligation to any others. Among our own writers, we have the authority of Blackstone and Sir James Mackintosh for supposing that this law is binding over all the globe, in all countries, and at all times; that no human laws are of any validity if contrary to this; and such of them as are valid derive all their force and all their authority, mediately or immediately, from this original. For it is founded in those relations of justice that existed in the nature of things antecedent to any positive precept. It springs from the everlasting and irrevocable principle of good and evil to which the Creator Himself, in all His dispensations, conforms, a knowledge of which he imprinted on the human intellect at the creation of man, so far as it was necessary for the conduct of human actions.

Those institutions which belong to the peculiar circumstances of mankind are less directly connected with the first principles of justice, being for the most part founded on human reason or convenience; and are consequently attributed to what is called the compact of society. But being thus self imposed, it is evident that they are revocable, as the right of imposing them implies also the power of revoking, rescinding, and modifying them at will. These are denominated municipal laws, although they are sometimes applicable to communities in general as well as to particular societies. These are simply the subject of convenience, inasmuch as they are obligatory only so long as the compact lasts. While natural law comprises also the duties of obedience to a principle which is eternal and universal. To the exaction of this, it is obvious, a supreme power is essential; and as the universe, taken collectively, is accountable to the Deity alone, no one can deny to them a divine obligation. Comprehending therefore, as it does, not only the rules, but the principles of right conduct, it is to be distinguished from that instinct which is sometimes called the law of nature, inasmuch as it is designed for the guidance of intelligent beings, and is indeed the object of reason, while instinct is only the object of sense, in obedience to which the brutes move as well as mankind.

As man is entirely a dependent being, he must necessarily be subject to the laws of his Creator, and consequently, as man depends absolutely upon his Maker for everything, it is necessary that he should in all points conform to his Maker's will.

Law, in its general signification, is a rule of conduct dictated by some superior being; and such laws must be invariably obeyed, so long as the creature itself subsists, for its existence depends on that obedience. (See Blackstone's Com. vol. i.)

This natural law, then, for its due fulfilment, requires a moral sense of right and wrong; and the necessity for observing the distinction between that which is morally right and that which is morally wrong depends wholly upon the existence of a Supreme Being, who has the power to bestow future rewards and punishments. For by these considerations alone can be determined the motives of any action; and its morality depends in a great measure upon its motives, while at the same time the motive is exercised by the reason. And upon this account the inculcation of those truths, upon which a right perception of the nature of moral obligations depends, formed so prominent a feature in the Hebrew jurisprudence. The conscientious principles of this natural law not only constitute the elements of all jurisprudence, but they also prescribe the principles upon which good laws must be founded, and furnish at once the purpose and the limits of such institutions. It is true that Tacitus says of the Germans, that good customs supplied there the place of good laws: But good customs can never long subsist without the support of good principles, and these only can be found in a system which acknowledges its obligations to that which is right in itself as well as beneficial in its consequences. The difference between divine and human laws is this: in the divine laws, that which is lawful is discerned because it is good; in human laws, that which is lawful is only to be distinguished from that which is unlawful, because it is prohibited. The one is positive law, the other is but a negative restriction. The consequence of this is, that the latter can only be effectual in a community where there is a temporary and immediate punishment. The other prevails with independent communities which acknowledge the supremacy of no human powers. To this, therefore, are referred the principles of international law, by which the relations of independent communities towards one another are sought to be regulated. Hence writers on these subjects, feeling the futility of human obligations, where there is no power to enforce them, take so much pains to seek their principles at the fountain-head, and endeavour to persuade by arguments of mutual advantage, where they cannot compel by the application of a superior force. Upon this account, some learned writers have confounded natural obligations with the law of nations. Yet it is very plain, that the duties of individuals towards each other differ as much from the relative duties of communities, as do the municipal laws of different states. What may be destructive to the welfare of one state may be suffered with impunity by another, whose prosperity depends upon different conditions. So one may be compelled to resent with arms what another may endure without dishonour. In fact, if carefully examined, the law of nations will be found to be nothing else than a compact entered into between communities for their reciprocal advantage. Hence it is revocable at pleasure. And for this very reason, that however just and right in themselves may be the principles upon which such arrangements are founded, when they exist amongst independent communities there is no superior power to enforce them. If a superior power should interfere, it abrogates that very law which omits to provide for its intervention. By a compact, is understood an agreement of societies, or between communities, of which there is only presumptive evidence; while a contract is an agreement between individuals, of which there is positive evidence. That this natural law, or moral obligation, must form an essential ingredient in every system of jurisprudence, is amply attested, not only by the writings, but by the customs of those who are esteemed the wisest of the ancients. And since the breach of moral laws is presumptively attended by a future as well as a present punishment, they enforced their authority in imitation of the Hebrews, by testifying their conviction that such principles were derived from the Creator of all things.

We now proceed to adduce some evidence that this law of nature, or sense of moral obligation, formed an essential element in the systems of ancient lawgivers. It is referred to under various terms, as each defined the principle and source of justice in accordance with the scheme of his own ethical system. But all unite in ascribing to it, directly or indirectly, a divine origin, and attribute to it the universal obligation due only to a supreme and overruling power. This conclusion will be the more readily conceded, when it is considered that the nature of the deity, or the supreme cause, forms the basis of those systems of metaphysics which have been handed down to us by such philosophers as have treated of the nature of laws and the sources of their obligation. Indeed, the philosophy of Plato and Pythagoras, so far as it concerns human institutions, has for its foundation the existence of a divine or natural law. The necessity for this they not only recognized, but spared no pains to enforce, both by argument and illustration. Plato (in Phœd.), shows that without some such standard it would be impossible to find any measure of right. Of this he gives a striking example. "By the names of silver or iron, he says, all men understand precisely the same things. But, if you call any thing just or good, not only does each man differ from another in his idea of what is just and good, but even amongst ourselves the precise meaning which is conveyed to our minds by the use of such terms, changes from time to time, and differs according to circumstances." Cicero, who adopted so many of Plato's opinions, that in quoting the one you repeat the other, in treating of the subject of laws, constantly refers to the authority of a similar principle.

" It is not, he says, in the edict of the magistrate, as

the majority of our modern lawyers pretend; nor in the twelve tables, as the ancients maintained; but in the sublimer principles of philosophy, that we must seek for the true source and obligation of juriprudence." "For, he proceeds, the true nature of moral justice must be traced back from the nature of man." "And those, he adds, who do not go to the fountain head, or treat civil laws in any other manner, are not so much pointing out the paths of justice as those of litigation."

In his treatise *De Legibus*, he begins by taking it for granted that the entire universe is regulated by the power of the immortal gods; "that by their nature, energy, mind, divinity, or some other word of clearer signification (as he here expresses himself), if there be such, all things are governed and directed." Unless this is admitted, he tells us it "is impossible to establish the principles of justice in that supreme law which has existed from all ages, before any legislative enactments were drawn up in writing, or any political governments constituted; and that this law constitutes the first principles of right." And afterwards, adopting the definition that law is the highest reason implanted in nature, prescribing those things which ought to be done, and forbidding the contrary, he maintains this doctrine in these words:—"For there is but one essential justice by which society is bound together, and one law which has established this justice. This law is right reason, which is the true rule of all commandments and prohibitions. Whoever neglects this law, whether written or unwritten, is necessarily unjust and wicked."

He then argues, that "if right and justice consisted only in submission to written laws and national customs, it might become right to rob and to commit adultery, if such conduct were sanctioned by the legislative power. And that if the opinions of foolish men had sufficient weight to counterbalance the nature of things, why should they not establish that what is essentially bad and pernicious should henceforth pass for what is good and beneficial. Or why, since law can make right of injustice, should it not also be able to change evil into good? And the consequence," he adds, "is that real justice has really no existence if it have not one by nature." But he concludes, "We have no other rule by which we are able to distinguish a bad law from a good one, than that of nature. Nor is it only right and wrong which are discriminated by nature; but generally all that is honourable is by this means distinguished from all that is shameful; for common sense has impressed on our minds the first principles of things, and has given us a general acquaintance with them by which we connect with virtue every honourable quality, and with vice all that is disgraceful."

There is nothing, he contends, more important thoroughly to understand than this—that man is born for justice and equity, and that law and equity have not been established by opinions, but by nature. The truth of this becomes more apparent, when he adds,—"For to those to whom nature has given reason, she has also given right reason, and therefore also law, which is nothing else than right reason, enjoining what is good, and forbidding what is evil."

Upon the divine origin of reason Cicero constantly insists. He says: "This animal which we call man, full of reason, memory, and counsel, has been generated by the supreme God in a most transcendent condition;" and what is there, he demands, not only in man alone, but in all heaven and earth, more divine than reason, which, when it becomes right and perfect, is justly termed wisdom? This, then, he urges, "is a connecting link, which associates human nature with divine, constituting a law which is common both to God and man;. for the law of right and justice is the same both in heaven and on earth."

In the second book of this treatise he is still more explicit. Sec. 4 is to the following effect: "This, then, as it appears to me, has been the decision of the wisest philosophers,—that law was neither a thing contrived by the genius of man, nor established by any decree of the people; but a certain eternal principle which governs the entire universe, wisely commanding what is right, and prohibiting what is wrong. Therefore they called that aboriginal and supreme law the mind of God, enjoining or forbidding each separate thing in accordance with reason. On this account it is that this law, which the Gods have bestowed on the human race, is so justly applauded; for it is the reason and mind of a wise Being, equally able to urge us to good and to deter us from evil."

This power he describes as not only far more ancient than the existence of any state or people, but coeval with God himself, who beholds and governs both heaven and earth. A little farther on he thus proceeds to give an illustration of its necessity. "Though in the reign of Tarquin there was no written law concerning adultery, it does not therefore follow that Sextus Tarquinius did not offend against the eternal law of nature when he committed a rape on Lucretia, the daughter of Tricipitinus; for even then he had the light of reason deduced from the nature of things, that incites to good actions and dissuades from evil ones, and which does not begin for the first time to be law when it is drawn up in writing, but from the moment that it exists. And this existence of moral obligation is coeval with that of the divine mind; therefore the true and supreme law, whose commands and prohibitions are equally authoritative, is the right reason of the sovereign Jupiter."

Hesiod also says that Jupiter, or the supreme deity, appointed laws for mankind.

In common with Cicero, Seneca, Plutarch, and others use the expressions, *deum sequi*, and *secundum deum vivere*, for living according to nature and according to reason.

But Hierocles, in his comment upon the Pythagorean hymns, sets at rest all doubt as to what was meant by obeying reason; for he tells us in so many words that to obey right reason is the same thing as to obey God.

The Greek philosophers constantly refer to the divine laws, sometimes in those words, sometimes as τὸ συνειδες, or a conscientious principle.

Euripides speaks of the νόμιμα θεῶν, or the laws of God. Aristotle says, that which is just of itself, αὐτοδίκαιον, i.e. the principles of law, is changeable only at the will of the gods.

Plato maintains that law is the gift of mind, i.e. God; the word νοῦς being frequently used by him in that sense. He tells us, also, that the sceptre of Minos was nothing but the doctrine or system derived from Jove.

In his treatise on Laws, he says, the Cretans derived their laws from Zeus; the Lacedæmonians theirs from Apollo.

He makes virtue, under which head he includes prudence, temperance, fortitude, and justice, the end and object of law. "All laws, then," he says, "should be well ordained, and their authority beyond question, because the gods are the beings who gave them." He adds in the dialogue, "it is proper to assert that the laws of the Cretans are not vainly held in very great esteem by all the Greeks. For they are in a correct state, by making those who use them happy; for they impart every good. Now there are two kinds of good; one human, and the other divine; and the former hangs upon the divine. And if any State receives the greater, it possesses likewise the lesser; but if not, it is deprived of both."

Indeed, inasmuch as jurisprudence, so far as concerns the *jus naturale*, or moral sense of right and wrong, formed no small part of every system of ancient philosophy, we may well conclude that natural law with the old philosophers was justly held to be a branch of theology.

Iamblichus, speaking of Pythagoras' conception touching the providence of God, says,—"That we have need of such a government, as we ought not in anything to contradict, which alone proceeds from the Deity, who deservedly may challenge a sovereign dominion over all. For man, being shamefully variable and fickle in his appetites, affections, and other passions, needs such a government from which proceeds moderation and order." According to the same author, Pythagoras made the knowledge of God, the first most universal being, to be the centre of all his philosophy—which idea, indeed, was the foundation of Plato's natural theology, or metaphysics. (See Gale's Court of the Gentiles, pt. ii. b. 2, c. 8.)

Plutarch, in the life of Numa Pompilius, tells us that Numa forbad the Romans to believe that God had any form or likeness of beast or man; which agrees with the doctrine of the Pythagoreans, who thought the gods invisible, incorruptible, and intelligible beings only. So that in these days there was at Rome no image of God, either painted or graven, for nearly one hundred and seventy years.

The Pythagorean symbol, "Engrave not the image of God upon a ring," conforms to this doctrine, which Iamblichus explains to be an intimation that the gods are incorporeal.

In reference to education, Plato (*de Leg.*) defines it to be "the leading of youth to that which is called by the law right reason, and which has been decreed by the most reasonable and oldest men through their experience to be really correct."

And he more than once alludes to the law "that should rule according to nature."

Demosthenes also conforms to the opinions of the other philosophers in this respect. In his oration against Aristogeiton, he says that natural law is the invention and gift of God.

But, in short, from their own confessions, it is beyond question that the most celebrated legislators of antiquity, such as Minos, Solon, Draco, Lycurgus, and others, denied to their laws any obligation or validity whatever, except so far as they were of divine authority, and received from the gods.

When, therefore, we consider that Pythagoras and Socrates, to whose principles it was the opinion of the ancients that Plato owed the origin of his philosophy, made the knowledge of the supreme Being, or efficient cause of all things, the main subject of their investigations; and that thence each of their systems recognized what they supposed to be the law of nature; it can hardly be denied that obedience to this principle pervaded all the institutions which sprang from their systems of moral philosophy and politics. It was in the knowledge of the Supreme Being, and the laws by which the universe is governed, that they sought the standard as well as the measure of right and wrong. Hence we find Seneca, in his Epistle, inquiring "what else is philosophy but the law of life." When Plato, unaided by the light of revelation, could discover "that with God there is the most exact government, and that justice follows God as the vindicator of his law,"—when he makes "sin to consist in all excess or transgression of the law," which elsewhere he truly defines as acting against right reason,—how can we doubt that they recognized the law of nature as the foundation of all law, by reason only of its divine institution? How else could they have arrived at the conclusion that the principles of justice were "eternal and of universal obligation"? Indeed, Cicero goes so far as to deny that any but those which are divine deserve the name of laws. "Those obligations which are self-imposed," he tells us, "may be said to exist rather by the favour of the people than by right." It is, however, confessed by the ancients, and all others, that no law can prevail unless founded on justice; and that to ascertain what is just and right, we must refer to a divine standard, which is nothing else than the will of God, the consciousness of which, in some essential particulars, is implanted naturally in all men. As Plutarch expresses it, in the life of Alexander, "God does not will a thing because it is just; but it is just, that is, it lays one under an indispensable obligation, because God wills it." St. Paul refers to this where he says, "Since the Gentiles, which have not the law, do by nature the things contained in the law, these, having not the law, are a law unto themselves, as showing the work of the law written in their hearts, their conscience also bearing witness, and their thoughts the mean while accusing or else excusing one another." So he appeals again to the same principle, "Doth not nature itself teach you that if a man have long hair it is a shame unto him." The foregoing opinions concerning natural law were adopted by the early christian writers, both of the eastern and western school. A few quotations from the Fathers, however slender may be their authority upon matters on which their sentiments were chiefly derived from the earlier philosophers, will nevertheless suffice to show how much importance was in their days attributed to this doctrine of natural law.

Tertullian goes so far as to discover the germ of natural law in the prohibition given to Adam not to eat of the forbidden fruit. In this he affects to trace all the precepts subsequently included in the decalogue, comprehending a man's duty both towards God and his neighbour. But it must be confessed that the reasons he gives for this conjecture are not conclusive, although the supposition might perhaps be better supported.

After calling this the primordial law, or mother of all precepts, before the law of Moses was written on tables of stone, he contends that there was an unwritten law which was naturally understood and kept by the patriarchs. For, he asks, whence was Noah found just, if the justice of natural law did not precede him, and whence was Abraham called the friend of God, if not from the equity and justice of natural law.

Origen also terms that the law of nature which God has appointed for the human race.

Isaiah xxiv. 5, says,—"The earth also is defiled under the inhabitants thereof, because they have transgressed the laws, changed the ordinance, broken the everlasting covenant." By this covenant Jerome understands the natural law which, he says, "all nations at first, and the whole world received; and the terms of this law were afterwards more explicitly declared by Moses, because the first law was weakened and dissipated by the perversity of mankind."

St. Chrysostom avers, that from the beginning of things, when God formed man, he imposed upon him natural law for the guidance of his conduct. "And what," says he, "is natural law, conscience has explained to us, and by itself made known to us, the perception of what things are honest, as well as those which are of a contrary sort." So he contends that the Hebrew legislator imported into the decalogue the interdictions against murder, adultery, and theft, under those terms, for the sake only of brevity and simplicity, reducing to those heads only what before had prevailed as a part of natural law.

St. Ambrose also plainly appears to think that the knowledge of what is honest in itself, is by God implanted in the conscience of mankind. True law, he says, is right reason. "True law is not written on tables, or carved in brass, but impressed on men's minds and infixed in the senses; wherefore a wise man is not under law, but is a law unto himself, containing in his heart the operation or effect of a law inscribed there by nature."

Jerome says, that by this natural law Cain knew that he had sinned; saying, "My punishment is greater than I can bear," or, as it is otherwise rendered, mine iniquity is greater than that it may be forgiven. By this also Adam and Eve knew they had sinned, when they concealed themselves in the garden. Pharaoh also, before the law of Moses was given, prompted by the law of nature, confessed his crimes, saying, "God is just, but I and my people are wicked."

So Job also, whose history is held to be more ancient than the laws of Moses, must have referred to some acknowledged precepts of divine obligation, when he says: "My foot hath held his steps, his way have I kept and not declined, neither have I gone back from the commandment of his lips."

Theologians consider divine law to be twofold, the one natural and coeval with human nature, the other positive and subsequently imposed by God. The first they describe as a participation of eternal law in the rational creature, and so far divine; and the second, those statutes which are comprised in the decalogue. Ludovicus Molina upon this point well remarks: "When nature was instituted by God, he impressed upon our minds the law of nature, by which we discern good from evil, and therefore we may consider that a divine law which was given by God himself."

Alphonsus a Castro says, "Natural law is that which

proceeds from the institution of nature herself, and this is common to all; and this also is a *jus divinum*, because God himself, who founded nature, is the author and institutor of natural law. If, then, you refer that law to its author, you must call it divine. But if you wish to compare it to the time of its origin, you call it natural, because it sprang into existence with nature itself, and not afterwards by any human or divine institution."

To these opinions, that God is the author of natural law, the writings of the jurisconsults conform. Fernandius Vasquius says: "All natural law is divine, although, on the other hand, all divine law is not natural." And Joachim Mynsinger explains that the natural law of mankind may be thus defined: "Natural law consists in those first precepts and rules of righteousness, which nature, and, so far, God himself, taught all men at the Creation."

So Stephen de Werbewcz, in his work upon the Laws of Hungary, says that the origin of natural law is to be traced to the beginning of created nature, and that it was instituted by God alone.

Gaius, speaking of natural law as *jus gentium*, describes it as of equal antiquity with the creation of mankind.

Justinian, speaking of civil and natural law, says, "it is very plain that natural law is that which the nature of things produced with the human race." And, reverting to its divine origin, he proceeds to observe, "that natural laws indeed, which amongst all nations and races are equally observed, being constituted by a certain divine providence, remain always firm and immutable. Such, among others, are these principles, that we should live honestly, should hurt nobody, and should render to every one his due." To these three general precepts Justinian has reduced the whole doctrine of law. But if we may adopt the opinion of those who define natural law as nothing else but right reason, we have the authority of Seneca in support of its divine origin. "Reason," he says, "is nothing else than a part of the Divine Spirit merged in the human body." To abide, then, by this natural law, implies obedience to God; and as it is the property of law to exact obedience to some superior power, where there is no superior power there can, properly speaking, be no law, but a mere compact resting on, and determinable by, convenience. Yet no moral obligation can exist in the absence of a duty, and cannot therefore arise by the simple consent and reason of mankind, except so far as it is in accordance with the will of, and subject to the supremacy of, a power to which obedience is due.

In the Scriptures we have illustrations of such obedience to the divine law, or law of nature, where the patriarchs are related to have walked with God, and in the fear of God. Hence Cain's fratricide, and the adultery of others before the time of Moses, are held to have been unlawful and wicked.

However, it cannot be denied that many learned writers hold that natural law is derived from human reason. But the reason they give for this is not inconsistent with the contrary conclusion; for they say that it is only binding so long as it is just, and consistent with reason and equity. Yet if it be divine, it can never be otherwise.

Again, it is held by some, that natural laws are partly

imperative, and partly permissive; and that the obligation of the latter may be controlled and restrained, amongst communities, by consent, for the sake of convenience. Yet this is only partly true; for natural laws contain rather the germ and principle of what is just and right, than the ordinances by which right and justice are to be observed. Some of these latter, though founded on natural or divine law, are of human institution, and therefore subject to modification. As, for instance, natural law forbids theft; it also punishes theft; but the method and measure of punishment are not prescribed, and may depend upon circumstances, as indeed it did with Jews.

Grotius, in speaking of the obligations of natural law, maintains that sociability is the fountain of right. But he qualifies this opinion by stating that there is another original of right besides that of nature, being, he says, "that which proceeds from the free will of God, to which our understanding infallibly assures us we ought to be subject. And even the law of nature itself, whether it be that which consists in the maintenance of society, or that which in a looser sense is so called, though it flows from the internal principles of man, may notwithstanding be ascribed to God, because it was his pleasure that these principles should be in us."

Barbeyrac, in a learned note upon this passage, observes, that the maxims of the law of nature are not merely arbitrary rules, but are founded on the nature of things, on the very constitution of man, from which certain relations result between such and such actions and the state of a reasonable creature. But he adds, "the duty and obligation, or the indispensable necessity, of conforming to these ideas and maxims, necessarily supposes a superior power, a supreme master of mankind, who can be no other than the Creator, or supreme Divinity."

Grotius defines natural right to be the rule and dictate of right reason, showing the moral deformity or moral necessity there is in any act according to its suitableness or unsuitableness to a reasonable nature; and consequently that such an act is either forbidden or commanded by God, the author of nature.

Law, he says, is that which obliges us to what is good and commendable. And in the assertion that it is a crime against natural law for one man to act to the prejudice of another, he includes under this head most of the precepts contained in the decalogue. To the same principle he refers the duties of obedience which children owe to their parents. Under the obligations of natural law he also includes the fulfilment of contracts and covenants, from which, he says, spring civil laws. This is manifest enough. Consequently natural law is the foundation of civil laws. Though civil laws, arising by consent, are instituted to secure some profit or advantage, while obedience alone constitutes the obligation of natural law, advantage being quite collateral. As this writer truly remarks, right has not merely interest for its end. For the moment we recede from right, we can depend upon nothing.

Puffendorf, in his Law of Nature and Nations, refers to this principle the breach of those duties in regard to himself which are enjoined upon man by the very frame of his nature. But amongst modern writers upon this subject, there are few whose opinions are entitled to greater respect than Sir James Mackintosh, whose beautiful discourse upon the Law of Nature and

Nations is almost too well known to justify quotation. He expresses his views thus:—"The science which teaches the rights and duties of men and of states has in modern times been called the Law of Nature and Nations. Under this comprehensive title are included the rules of morality, as they prescribe the conduct of private men towards each other in all the various relations of human life; as they regulate both the obedience of citizens to the laws, and the authority of the magistrate in framing laws and administering government; as they modify the intercourse of independent commonwealths in peace, and prescribe limits to their hostility in war."

The illustrious Bacon acknowledges the same principle in language quite as explicit, if not quite as elegant, where he says:—"For there are in nature certain fountains of justice whence all civil laws are derived; but as streams and like as waters do take tinctures and tastes from the soils through which they run, so do civil laws vary according to the regions and governments where they are planted, though they proceed from the same fountains." (Bacon's Dig. and Adv. of Learning.) "It is called," says Mackintosh, "the Law of Nature, inasmuch as it is the supreme, invariable, and uncontrollable rule of conduct to all men, of which the violation is avenged by natural punishments, which necessarily flow from the constitution of things, and are as fixed and inevitable as the order of nature. It is received and reverenced as the sacred code promulgated by the great legislator of the universe for the guidance of His creatures."

Of modern divines few have been more distinguished for their learning and sagacity than Bishop Butler.

In his sermon upon the law of nature, preached at the Rolls' Chapel before an audience of lawyers, this subject is handled in his masterly manner. The conclusion, that the law of nature, as distinguished from the instincts of nature, is of divine origin and of universal obligation, is here supported by a chain of reasoning close enough to dispose of such objections as would deny to it this supreme authority. In like manner, Sir James Mackintosh, speaking of the important relation between subject and sovereign, (or, in other words, between citizen and magistrate,) treats the supposition, that it could arise from compact, as an absurdity. And as the obligations which arise from this relation necessarily involve obedience to the laws, so far we shall avail ourselves of his authority in our favour, though at the same time we hesitate to adopt the conclusion at which he arrives. "The duties," he says, "which arise from this relation I shall endeavour to establish, not upon supposed compacts, which are altogether chimerical, which must be admitted to be false, in fact, which if they are considered to be fictions will serve no purpose of just reasoning, and to be equally the foundation of a system of universal despotism and of universal anarchy, but on the solid basis of general convenience." And he adds,—" If our principles be just, the origin of government must have been coeval with mankind."

In the Arab metaphysics, a divine origin is attributed to human reason, as well as with the Jews, amongst whom Philo Judæus says, "Natural law is impressed by immortal nature in mind immortal." Aben Tybon and the Talmudic writers, who abound in such definitions, describe natural law as intelligent precepts which are manifest amongst all nations. Much in the same sense, Chrysippus and the Stoics said that the original of right is to be derived from no other than Jupiter himself; from which word, it has been surmised by some, the Latins gave it the name of *jus*. Chrysippus expresses himself thus:—"For it is not possible to find any other principle or origin of justice than Jupiter and universal nature; for there we must always begin, when we design to treat of good and evil."

Epicharmus says that human reason itself is sprung from divine reason.

So Antoninus the emperor declares that mind and reason are particles of the divine nature; while Plato and Aristotle speak frequently to the same effect.

Cassiodorus remarks, that to teach men the duties of justice is indeed a work of some difficulty; but not impossible, because the Divinity has been so indulgent to all, that even they who are unacquainted with the principles of law are yet sensible of the consequential truths derived from them.

To the same purpose are the sentiments of Marcus Antoninus, where he says, every man who commits an act of injustice renders himself guilty of impiety.

Various indeed are the definitions of right and justice which different writers have given, but they almost all seem to spring from the same source.

Apuleius says that when justice is advantageous to the possessor of that virtue, it is to be termed benevolence; but when it extends to the interests of others, it is properly called justice. In this he follows Aristotle, whose words are: " The just man acts for the benefit of others; and it is for this reason we say justice is a good belonging to others." In like manner, Cicero, in his Republic, affirms that "justice regards what is without us; it is diffused and extensive."

But the existence of every community must depend on the recognition of some sort of right or justice; as Aristotle proved by his illustration of the robbers; whose association would inevitably be dissolved unless certain rules of justice were observed in the division of the spoil. Of this necessity Cicero gives a similar example. But the justice of a cause is so universally appealed to for its success, that it is utterly unnecessary to multiply illustrations in order to show that right and justice, or, in other words, natural law, has been perpetually recognized by mankind as the guiding principle of all virtuous actions.

Selden, in his learned work "De Jure Naturali et Gentium," gives innumerable examples of the divine obligation of natural law, to which those who care to investigate the subject further can refer. He divides natural law under seven heads, all of which, it will be manifest, are included in the tables delivered to Moses. The first, concerning the formal worship of the Creator. The second, of blasphemy, and cursing the name of God. The third, of bloodshed or homicide. The fourth, of adultery, incest, and uncleanness. The fifth, of theft and fraud. The sixth, of judgment and civil obedience. The seventh, the prohibition to eat the flesh of a living animal. The first six of these precepts Tertullian calls the primordial law of nature. The Fathers and the Rabbinical writers agree in supposing that these were observed by Adam and his posterity before the flood, and afterwards by Noah and his descendants.

St. Ambrose distributes natural law into three classes. 1. That which relates to the worship of the Creator. 2. That which relates to the duties of mankind towards themselves and their neighbours. 3. That which relates to the duty of teaching the knowledge of the Creator to others; which last, however, partakes partly of the nature of the two former.

The Jewish Rabbins maintained that the seven precepts to which we have referred were imposed upon the posterity of Noah before the time of Moses, although they were afterwards embodied in the decalogue; and they considered that these, being matters of manifest rectitude and duty, were understood as statutes of divine appointment before any written law existed. Yet the Rabbins differ slightly in the arrangement of these precepts; and some treat them as statutes which Noah taught his children, others as commands given by God himself to Noah and his posterity. Some define these precepts as follows:—1. Not to worship idols; 2. To bless God; 3. To abstain from incest; 4. To avoid every other sin of the flesh; 5. Not to shed human blood; 6. Not to steal; 7. Not to take a limb from any living creature. Whilst others maintained that the seven precepts which Noah gave to his sons were, 1. To observe the *Jus gentium;* 2. To eschew idolatry; 3. To avoid incest, adultery, and unlawful lust; 4. Not to kill; 5. Not to blaspheme the name of God; 6. Not to steal; 7. Not to cut off a member from any living animal. Others again enumerate these precepts thus:— 1. To abstain from idolatry; 2. Blasphemy; 3. Bloodshed; 4. Adultery; 5. Theft; 6. To obey civil ordinances; 7. Not to eat flesh that is cut off a living animal. But it will be observed, that these several versions contain the elements of the same ordinances somewhat differently expressed.

We may observe here, regarding the distinctions which the Doctors have made between precepts and statutes, that although the law concerning bloodshed, which was given to Noah, is primarily rather in the nature of a declaration than a command, yet, if we consider that a declaration by God of what is right is a declaration of the will of God, and that to obey His will is constantly commanded in other parts of Scripture, we may thence conclude that this is as much a command as any other declaration given in Scripture in more compulsory terms.

We trust we have now succeeded in showing that, in the opinion of the wisest both of ancient and modern jurists, the obligation of all laws depends upon their accordance with the will of God, leaving to man the power no more to vary than to annul the principles upon which they are founded. It will, therefore, hardly be necessary to refute those worshippers of human reason, who, despising the light of revelation, would seek in the arbitrary changes of convenience and utility the origin of the immutable principles of justice imposed by the Creator for the governance of the universe. The principle of justice and of truth is one which pagan philosophers did not presume to limit. Pagan philosophers used human reason as the means of ascertaining what was obscured by time, and yet unrestored by revelation. We conclude, then, that the obligation of all laws depends upon their conformity to the will of God. For from this they spring. And this consideration naturally leads us on to the contemplation of the revealed laws of God. For, to supply the deficiency, the imperfection, and the blindness of human reason, in applying the laws of nature to the particular exigencies of mankind, the interposition of Divine providence has been pleased to discover, and enforce by precepts which are to be found only in the holy Scriptures, not only the statute but the spirit of the law.

We hope, also, to furnish some reasons for concluding that the legal institutions of antiquity were not only founded upon the same principles, but derived, directly or indirectly, from the Hebrew laws.

## CHAPTER II.

ON THE SOURCES OF ANCIENT JURISPRUDENCE.

BEFORE proceeding to inquire into the remarkable resemblance between the laws of Pagan antiquity and those of the Hebrews, we propose now to adduce some evidence to show that the ancient legislators derived their systems, directly or indirectly, from Jewish sources.

And if we should succeed in producing satisfactory reasons for supposing that the Greeks derived the elements, and indeed a great part of the details, of their judicial institutions from the Hebrews, it will hardly be necessary to prove that the Romans must refer theirs to the same origin. For, that they imported their primary laws from the Greeks, is confessed by their own writers, and is, indeed, a fact universally acknowledged. That to the Roman laws the civil institutions which prevail over the greater part of Europe owe their foundation, is a question beyond dispute, inasmuch as they are avowedly based upon the codes of the later emperors, into which were embodied the earlier laws of Rome; so that to determine their source, nothing will remain but, in some essential particulars, to establish their identity.

Cicero, de Leg., lib. ii. § 25, says that the Decemvirs translated the laws of Solon almost word for word in the Ten Tables. Strangely enough, the example he gives is evidently of Hebrew extraction. For he proceeds:—"Our rule respecting the three suits of mourning, and other customs, were thus derived from Solon's regulations; and that edict respecting the mourning is expressed in his precise words. Let not women tear their cheeks, nor indulge their wailing at funerals." The very definition which Cicero gives of the origin of the term law is sufficient to show that it was never regarded as an original science. And so far, at least, as the Roman institutions were concerned, their foundation is attributed to a foreign source. His words are:—"The Greek name for law (νόμος) is derived from νέμω, to distribute, implying the very nature of the thing, that is, to give to every man his due. Whilst the Latin word *lex* conveys the idea of selection, *à legendo*. According to the Greeks, therefore, the name of law implies an equitable distribution; according to the Romans, an equitable selection." It is equally plain, that the use of the word selection implies the previous existence of institutions out of which the selection was to be made.

If, however, only the subject of these institutions, illustrated by fragmentary traditions, had reached us, we should still have quite enough to show that their purport and effect accorded with the judicial system of the Greeks.

But it is a matter of history, that these ancient laws, in another shape, and explained by the interpretations of long usage, were imported into, and indeed form the elements of, the subsequent codes of the Roman lawyers, in which they can be specifically traced, without our being obliged of necessity to resort to the supposition of accidental coincidence in support of this part of our proposition, or to attribute to them a subordinate position in the principles of Roman jurisprudence.

In the first place, we find it stated in Scripture, that the wisdom of their laws should make the Hebrew system the admiration of the world. (Deut. iv. 5, 6.) "Behold, I have taught you statutes and judgments, even as the Lord my God commanded me. Keep therefore and do them; for this is your wisdom and your understanding in the sight of the nations, which shall hear all these statutes, and say, Surely this great nation is a wise and understanding people."

Plato, de Legibus, lib. iv., confesses that all laws came from God, and that no mortal man was the founder of laws. He says, therefore, that no mortal man ought to institute any law; that is to say, without a divine authority. Hence the most famous legislators of antiquity pretended to have received their laws from some divine oracle, probably in imitation of the manner in which the laws were given to Moses. Numa pretended to have received his laws from the nymph Egeria; Minos from Jupiter; Lycurgus from Apollo; and Zaleucus from Minerva.

So Heraclitus says expressly, that all human laws are nourished by one divine law. But that some divine law must have preceded all human laws, is manifest from this, that in every language the idea of one must precede the idea of many, for the idea of many things presupposes the existence of one thing. So the singular must exist before the plural, and one general law before several special laws. Indeed, the very nature of the term law presupposes the existence of some general rule of universal obligation.

That the laws of Moses are the most ancient of legal institutions, is attested, not only by the Scriptures and by the early Christian writers, but also by many heathen writers, in whom we find occasional references which betray a knowledge of their existence. For instance, Diodorus Siculus, as quoted by Cyril, says, "that according to that ancient institution of life which was in Egypt under the gods and heroes in those fabulous times, it is said that Moses was the first who persuaded the people to use written laws and to abide thereby, and this Moses was commemorated to have been a man of a great soul and well-ordered life."

Mariana, the Jesuit, in his preface to Genesis, thinks that after the invention of letters Moses was the first of all that persuaded the people to use written laws. And, indeed, there is no reference to be found in any book, ancient or modern, to any system of laws anterior to those of Moses.

The earliest authentic records possessed by the Greeks are not prior to the Babylonish captivity. But the probability that the Greeks had access to Hebrew sources for information on many points in their polity rests first of all upon the reluctant and sometimes ambiguous confessions of their own writers, who tell us that many of their institutions, which bore evident traces of Hebrew origin, were derived from barbarians, whom they declined to designate by their proper names, owing to the contempt in which the Jews were held amongst them. Nevertheless it must not be overlooked, that some of their later writers do distinctly mention their obligations to the Jews by name. Plato, in his Cratylus, acknowledges that the philosophers received much of their learning from the barbarians, and the ancients who lived before them, and much nearer to the Gods; which is a very apt allusion to the patriarchs.

Serranus, in his preface to Plato, asserts that this philosopher received his symbolic system from the Jews. Numerius, the Pythagorean, asks in derision of his opponent, What is Plato but Moses atticising? Hermippus, in his life of Pythagoras, as quoted by Josephus (Cont. Apion. lib. i.), says that Pythagoras translated many things out of the Jewish institutions into his own philosophy; and elsewhere he calls his master an imitator of Jewish dogmas. Diogenes Laertius, in his preface to the lives of the philosophers, says that some affirm that philosophy had its origin from the barbarians. Under this title, as will be hereafter shown, the Jews were undoubtedly included in common with all other foreigners. For, owing to their degradation after the Babylonish captivity, the Jews became such objects of contempt, that the Greeks declined to allude to them, except under the names of Syrians, Egyptians, Phœnicians, or generally as barbarians. Of this Herodotus furnishes us with an instance. He speaks of them as Phœnicians, or Syrians, who were circumcised. He says, that the Phœnicians, and those Syrians which dwelt in Palestine, learnt the rite of circumcision from the Egyptians; a rite, as Bochart affirms, unpractised in that country by any people but the Jews; an opinion which is fully confirmed by Josephus. Again, Xenophon reports, that when he came into Babylon he gave commandment that no Syrian should be hurt. And that by Syrians he meant Jews, is explained by Gale, in his Court of the Gentiles, where he observes, that Syria lies upon Judæa, as one shire does upon another, so that all the inhabitants, including Jews, were called Syrians, passing under the name of the country from the neighbourhood of which they had been carried away captive.

So Diodorus, in evident confirmation of earlier allusions to the Jews, tells us that the Syrians first found out letters.

Gale and Bochart both agree that the Greek philosophers owed the choicest parts of their philosophy to the skill and industry with which the Phœnicians had preserved the Hebrew traditions, if not immediately to the Jews.

Aristobulus an Alexandrian Jew who lived about two centuries after Plato, is said to have written a commentary on the books of Moses. This work is now lost, but some fragments of it are preserved by Clemens Alexandrinus and Eusebius. Of Plato this author observes, "he followed the Jewish institutes closely, and diligently examined the several parts thereof." Of Pythagoras he says, "he translated many things out of our discipline into the opinions of his own sect." Josephus likewise affirms that Pythagoras "not only understood the Jewish discipline, but embodied many things therein contained."

Hermippus, according to Josephus, referring to some of the maxims of Pythagoras, says,—"This he did and said in imitation of the doctrines of the Jews and Thracians, which he transferred into his own philosophy." In continuation Josephus adds,—" Nor was our nation unknown of old to several of the Grecian cities, and indeed was thought worthy of imitation by some of them." In support of this, he appeals to Theophrastus, who, in his writings concerning laws, says that "the laws of the Tyrians forbid men to swear foreign oaths;" amongst which he enumerates some others, and particularly that called Corban, an oath which can only be found amongst the Jews. It declares what a man may call a thing devoted to God.

Upon this point the primitive Christians stoutly insisted, in their arguments and apologies for the christian religion.

Clemens Alexandrinus styles Plato the Hebrew philosopher, and frequently asserts that the Greeks stole their chief opinions out of the books of Moses and the prophets.

Justin Martyr affirms that Plato drew many things from the Hebrew fountains, especially his pious conceptions of God and His worship. Tertullian and Augustin speak to the same effect. While Origen suggests that it was the custom of Plato to hide his choicest doctrines under the mask of fables, lest he should displease the people by referring openly to the Jews, who were so infamous amongst them. And Plato himself owns as much by saying, "what the Greeks receive from the barbarians they put into a better shape or garb." Moreover, there can be little doubt that he makes distinct references to the Jews under other names, as Phœnicians, Syrians, Egyptians, and Chaldeans, amongst whom they were dispersed.

Clearchus, a distinguished scholar of Aristotle, in

a book now lost, but cited by Josephus (Cont. Ap.), says that he had heard his master speak of a certain Jew, with whom, when he resided in Asia, he had held frequent conversations. This person Aristotle described as of wonderful learning, wisdom, temperance, and goodness, and said, that he had received more knowledge from him than he was able to impart in return. A wonderful proof of Aristotle's acquaintance with the Jewish law is shown by the conduct of his pupil Alexander the Great, in ordering all his soldiers who had married within the year to return to Macedonia and spend the winter with their wives. It was a military regulation of the Jews, that a soldier should remain at home with his wife during the first year of his marriage. (Deut. xxiv. 5.) Indeed, hardly any historical fact rests upon more solid foundation than that the most celebrated nations and lawgivers of antiquity borrowed many of their wisest institutions from the laws of Moses. Their historical customs furnish abundant proof that these laws were powerfully felt in modifying the religious sentiments and the civil institutions of mankind. But if more direct proof of their traduction were wanting, a strong argument in support of the Hebrew derivation of pagan institutions is supplied by this fact, that the further back you trace them the closer their resemblance appears. While subsequently the purity of their original principles has become partially overgrown by the corruptions of time, and so mixed up with local traditions and customs, as to be in some cases almost lost sight of.

Enough has been already stated to furnish strong presumptive evidence that the ancient Greeks had direct communication with the Jews. But if it fail absolutely to establish such a conclusion, we can resort to the unqualified confessions of the earliest Greek legislators and their biographers, to show that their knowledge was derived from the Hebrews through other channels. The dispersion of the Jews into countries with which the Greeks were familiar, is a fact which will hardly be disputed. By the Ancients themselves it is confessed, that they travelled into Egypt, Phœnicia, and Asia in search of knowledge, and that thence they derived many of their maxims and institutions. Plato tells us of his kinsman Solon's conference with the Egyptian priests, and how they informed him that in ancient wisdom the Greeks were but children compared to the Egyptians. Diodorus Siculus alleges that Lycurgus and Solon, as well as Pythagoras and Plato, gained most of their knowledge and wisdom out of Egypt. Speaking in more general terms, he tells us that all those who were renowned amongst the Greeks for wisdom did in ancient times resort to Egypt, there to participate in learning and laws.

Thales, who is by many supposed to have been of Phœnician extraction, had recourse to Egypt and Phœnicia for his philosophy. Pherecydes was a Syrian by birth, and known to have spent much time in Phœnicia. The travels of his follower Pythagoras into Phœnicia and Chaldea, as well as Egypt, are amply attested. We have also many testimonies that he studied the laws of Minos and Lycurgus. Eusebius asserts that Pythagoras visited Egypt and Babylon at the very time when the Jews abode there in great numbers. Iamblichus says he resided in Babylon for twelve years; and this, too, about the time of the captivity, or soon afterwards, when, although most of the Jews returned to Judæa, great numbers remained behind. However, of the fact that Pythagoras really had converse with the Jews at Babylon, Usher and Stillingfleet have collected ample proofs. After his return to Greece, Porphyry and Iamblichus concur in informing us that he visited Italy. But what can be a stronger evidence of the fact, than the estimation in which he was held by the Romans? This is attested by Pliny, who relates that a statue was erected to him in the horns of the Comitium. Socrates and his scholar Plato pursued their investigations in the same countries; and Plato more than once acknowledges his obligations to "traditional knowledge."

Zeno obtained his morals from Phœnicia; while the systems of Democritus and Epicurus are attributed to Mochus, a Phœnician philosopher, who is reported to have lived before the time of the Trojan war, and whose doctrines agreed so closely with those of Moses, that some learned writers, and amongst them Selden and Gale, think there is good reason for concluding the two names to be identical, as Mochus is sometimes found to be spelt Moschus, and Mosche is the Phœnician form of the Hebrew word Moses.

Zaleucus, the disciple of Pythagoras, from whom he probably received his Institutes, gave laws to the Locrians. He is, indeed, by some authors said to have been the first who committed laws to writing; and this, probably, in imitation of the Mosaic institutes; whence Strabo, speaking of the Locrians, says they were the first to use written laws.

The laws of Minos and Lycurgus were unwritten; but being handed down by oral tradition, were adopted to some extent in the systems of the later Greek legislators, amongst which also are to be distinguished some of the laws of Draco, relating to murder.

But as to the laws which Minos conferred upon his Cretan subjects—which, after those of Moses, are probably the most ancient that deserve the name of a system—the probability of their origin must be determined by the situation of the island, and the fact that Crete was a Phœnician colony, lying at no very great distance from the coasts of Canaan, with which there was carried on such a considerable intercourse by way of trade, as must have revived the knowledge of the Jewish polity.

Plato, in his Minos, in giving an account of the first Greek legislators, mentions three as the most famous, namely, Minos, Lycurgus, and Solon. The chief of these, he says, was Minos, who brought laws out of Crete into Greece. That Lycurgus, the Lacedæmonian legislator, visited Crete, is evident from what is said of him by Plutarch in the beginning of his life, where he relates that Lycurgus travelled into Crete, there to inform himself touching ancient laws. But the most ancient Attic legislator is supposed to have been Triptolemus. Xenocrates relates that there remained in the Eleusine temple three of his laws: that parents are to be honoured; that the gods are to be worshipped with the first fruits of the earth; that flesh is not to be eaten. These bear a striking resemblance to the Mosaic institutes; the last, probably, having reference to the abstinence of the Hebrews from unclean beasts.

The foregoing considerations, therefore, reduce the

Greek sources of information to four nations—the Egyptians, the Phœnicians, the Cretans, and the Chaldeans.

That the Egyptians derived their institutions in a great measure from the Mosaic laws, besides what they had previously received from Joseph, their great lawgiver, has been established by the researches of Gale, Bochart, Selden, and Stillingfleet.

When Joseph, during the famine, bought up the land of Egypt for Pharaoh, it is manifest that in the change of tenure of the land a reconstruction of the legal institutions of the country—at least, so far as the rights of property were concerned—must have been involved. It is, consequently, far from improbable that, from his position, Joseph became the author of a new constitution, framed in accordance with the doctrines held by the Hebrew patriarchs. It is, however, certain that at this conjuncture of Egyptian affairs he took advantage of his influence to establish a college of priests for the instruction of the people; from which it is unreasonable to suppose that the worship of the true God was excluded; and to secure this was the main object of the Jewish laws and institutions.

Elaborate and apparently successful attempts have been made to identify Joseph with the Egyptian Theuth or Hermes, which in their language signifies an interpreter, and is supposed to have reference to Joseph's interpretation of Pharaoh's dream. To Hermes the Egyptians ascribed the institution of their laws. From the excellence of their institutions they became so renowned in the time of Moses, that he is described in Scripture, by way of distinction, as being learned in all the wisdom of the Egyptians.

It was, moreover, the opinion of the Jews themselves, as Josephus informs us, that the Shepherd kings, who for so long a period reigned over Egypt, were their own ancestors, who must have brought with them the doctrine and discipline peculiar to their race. That this dynasty sprang from a successful incursion from Phœnicia, was indeed the Egyptian tradition.

Still there is some doubt whether the Hebrews were, properly speaking, of Phœnician extraction, or the Phœnicians from Hebrew origin, although they were certainly members of the same family. So far as language may be taken as evidence, the Hebrews are generally admitted to have retained the primary tongue, of which the Phœnician is a dialect. Though what chances may have given them the mother language, is still to a great extent a question undecided by conclusive proofs. Referring again to the exodus of the Jews under the guidance of Moses, Josephus quotes Manetho to this effect; he says, "that when they were prepared for revolt, the Jews appointed for themselves a ruler chosen out of the priests of Heliopolis, whose name was Osarsyph, and they took their oaths that they would be obedient to him in all things. He then, in the first place, made this law for them, that they should neither worship the Egyptian gods, nor should abstain from any of those sacred animals which the Egyptians held in the highest esteem, but kill and destroy them all; and when he had made such laws as these, and many more such as were mainly opposite to the customs of the Egyptians, he gave orders that they should prepare themselves for war." This is, at least, a very valuable testimony that the laws of Moses were not made in compliance with Egyptian institutions. But Manetho proceeds to tell us, "it was also reported that the priest who ordained their polity and laws was by birth of Heliopolis, and his name Osarsyph, from Osiris, who was the god of Heliopolis; but that when he was gone over to these people his name was changed, and he was called Moses.' But Josephus questions the accuracy of Manetho's history in this respect; for he says that the "true name of Moses was Moüses, and signifies a person who is preserved out of the water; for the Egyptians call water Mou."

Strabo, Herodotus, and Diodorus, with Homer, Plato, and Plutarch, unite in their admiration for the wisdom of the Egyptians; and this certainly is no mean tribute to its superiority in their days over that of other nations. When, therefore, Solomon's wisdom, which, so far, at least, as related to laws, must have been in a great measure founded on that of Moses, is said to have excelled that of the Egyptians, to what other source can its excellence be traced? We have, moreover, the testimony of many learned writers, showing in how many particulars the sacred rites of the Egyptians were founded upon Hebrew traditions, and to many of the Jewish ceremonies they bore a very close resemblance. Apuleius says that Plato resorted to Egypt, that he might amongst other things learn there the rites of the prophets. Diogenes Laertius moreover tells us that the Egyptian philosophers were styled priests and prophets; and surely such a designation of their sacred functions points to a Hebrew

origin. Josephus, who is in this followed by Ludovicus
Vives, says that the Egyptians derived their philosophy from Abraham and the Chaldeans. Serranus,
in his preface to Plato, rests his argument, that the
Egyptians retained many things from the traditions
of the Patriachs, upon the ancient history of Moses;
and "that they derived many things from the clear fountains of the Scriptures, which yet they contaminated
with their own fables," he tells us, "is no way to be
doubted." Gale gives the testimony of many learned
men, in proof that the deities to whom the Egyptians
attributed the origin of their institutions were all
younger than the patriarchs.

The connection of Moses and Solomon with the
Egyptians is alone sufficient to show the probability
that nations between which there was so much intercourse, should have held many institutions in common.
But even if this supposition is inconclusive, we know
that when the greater part of the Jews were carried
away captive into Babylon, the remainder fled to
Egypt, where it is impossible but that the knowledge
of their laws and doctrines must have been commu-
nicated to a people so proverbially inquisitive as the
Egyptians. Subsequently, multitudes of the Jews,
by the favour of Alexander, settled at Alexandria,
where afterwards, under the direction of Ptolemy
Philadelphus, the Hebrew Scriptures were translated
into Greek, and became a subject of study in the
famous Alexandrian school, to which the learned
resorted from all parts of the world, on account of the
library and antiquities stored up there, even before
the time when Mark Antony added the library of

Pergamos. And by this means many of the Jewish traditions, which had previously been scattered abroad, must have been restored to their original purity.

Let us now pass on to the Phœnician philosophy. Its affinity with, if not its derivation from, that of the Hebrews is to be established by the following considerations. The Phœnicians, who were the ancient inhabitants of Canaan, being expelled by Joshua from their cities and strongholds in the interior of the country, took refuge at Sidon and other places upon the coast of Palestine, where they succeeded in establishing themselves in permanent communities. As they were of a roving disposition, and much addicted to navigation, they soon sent forth numerous colonies to Greece, Africa, and other countries, and peopled some of the islands that are scattered over the Mediterranean Sea; amongst which Crete, so famous for the antiquity of its laws, is supposed to have been one. Its name, indeed, as well as its inhabitants, have been attributed to a Phœnician derivation. It seems to be taken from the Phœnician word Crethi, signifying darters, whence the Cretans became so famous for their expertness in the use of the bow, that it became their national symbol. So the Cherethims, mentioned in Ezekiel, bear the Hebrew form of the same word, having also the same signification. As to the other islands in the Mediterranean, Cicero (De Finibus, lib. 4) tells us that the inhabitants of Citium, a famous city in Cyprus, sprang from Phœnicia. In like manner, Diodorus relates that Malta was a Phœnician colony. But the extent to which they pushed their settlements may be judged of by the Phœnician inscription which Procopius relates was anciently to be seen upon the

pillars of Hercules at Tangiers. It was as follows:—
"We are they which fled from Joshua the robber, the son of Naue," which is the Phœnician form of the word Nun. Their skill in navigation, their aptitude for commerce, their constant intercourse with the Jews and other countries with which they traded, are too well authenticated to need further proof that they must not only have been well acquainted with the Jewish polity, but had abundant opportunities for conveying a knowledge of it to others. If Tibullus is to be believed, they long held the sovereignty of maritime power:

"Prima ratem ventis credere docta Tyrus."

Lucian asserts that there were none more divine merchants than the Phœnicians. The word divine, here used, is an expression of such import as can hardly be explained otherwise than by reference to their Hebrew connection and proverbial acquaintance with Jewish institutions.

In Solomon's time, their friendly relations with the Jews are mentioned in the Old Testament. Gale has furnished us with many arguments by which the learned have concluded that the doctrines of the early Phœnician philosophers Sanchoniathan and Mochus are derived from, and in many respects strictly accorded with, those of the Jews.

Ludovicus Vives says they traversed the world in search of gain, and thence spread the science and philosophy which they had derived from the Jews.

Grotius more explicitly declares that what the philosophers and poets derived from the Phœnicians, they in their turn obtained from Judæa. In confirmation of this may be added the testimony of Bochart.

## ANCIENT JURISPRUDENCE. 45

In his preface to Canaan, he says that sciences and arts flourished amongst the Phœnicians in an age when the Greeks were barbarians, or very little instructed; whence it came to pass, that the most ancient Grecian philosophers had Phœnician masters. Neither, he adds, have a few Phœnician words, both philosophic and mechanic, crept into the Greek tongue.

With respect to their learning, and their regard for it, the very name of their city, mentioned in Joshua, shows it, for the words Kirjath-Sephir, and Kirjath-Sannoth, signify, in the Phœnician tongue, the city of learning, and the city of law. Iamblichus, in the life of Pythagoras, says that that philosopher made a voyage to Sidon, where he conferred with the prophets, the successor of Mochus the physiologist, and with the Phœnician priests, and was initiated into the mysteries of Byblus and Tyre. Casaubon identifies Mochus, otherwise written Moschus, with Moses, to whose doctrines his system in many particulars conforms.

Strabo also mentions Moschus a Sidonian, who lived before the Trojan war, and says that he was the author of certain famous opinions concerning atoms.

As to the influence of Chaldean institutions, Diodorus Siculus tells us that the Egyptians received their philosophy from the Chaldeans; and Cicero (*De Divinatione*) says that the Chaldeans were the most ancient kind of doctors. If we may credit Aristotle, they taught the Babylonians and Assyrians philosophy. Hence also Pythagoras is said by Porphyry to have derived his knowledge of philosophy. Josephus, with Manetho and Berosus, as quoted by him, assert that the Chaldeans derived much of their learning from the patriarch Abraham. Deodale, with Stillingfleet and other writers, suppose that at the time of the Babylonish captivity, the Jews established schools, and settled in certain towns of Chaldea, adjacent to the river Euphrates, by which means the Chaldeans might well have become acquainted with the more developed Hebrew doctrines, besides the traditions they had received from the patriarchs who had in earlier times resided amongst them, and even without the advantages for obtaining a knowledge of the Hebrew system, which the situation of the country and their early association with the Jewish family must have afforded them.

Josephus (Cont. Ap. lib. 1) confesses that the first leaders and ancestors of the Jews were derived from the Chaldeans. He goes on to cite the authority of Manetho the Egyptian historian, who relates that "the gods being averse to the Egyptians, there came, in a surprising manner, out of the eastern parts, men of ignoble birth, who had boldness enough to make an expedition into the country, and with ease subdued it and kept possession of it for 511 years." "This whole nation," he says, "were styled the Hycsos; which in the sacred dialect denotes shepherd kings." But as if to place their identity with the Jews beyond question, in another book the same historian adds, that "this nation thus called shepherds, were also called captives in their sacred books." Manetho also testifies that this nation of shepherds, being at last expelled from Egypt by Tethmosis, went to Jerusalem.

Josephus (Cont. Ap. lib. 2) concludes thus: "We have already demonstrated that our laws have been such as have always inspired admiration and imitation into all other men. Nay, the earliest Grecian philosophers, though in appearance they observed themselves the laws of their own countries, yet did they in their actions and philosophic doctrines follow our legislator, and instructed men to live sparingly and have friendly communication one with another. Nay further, the multitude of mankind have had a great inclination of a long time to follow our religious observances. For there is not any city of the Grecians, nor any of the barbarians, nor any nation whatsoever, whither our custom of resting on the seventh day hath not come, and many of our prohibitions as to food but are not observed."

Having now endeavoured to show the probability, first, that the nations of antiquity recognised the existence of a divine rule of conduct; and secondly, that they had recourse to Hebrew sources for many of the principles upon which their institutions were founded; we shall now proceed to the consideration of their laws, in order to show the resemblance they bore to the Jewish institutions, in which that divine rule of conduct is revealed for the guidance of mankind in their social and political relations.

## CHAPTER III.

#### ON LAWS RELATING TO RELIGION.

The scope of the Mosaic Laws is so extensive as to comprehend, not only the religious, but the moral duties of mankind. The first four commands have for their object the maintenance of the national religion; as if it were the basis upon which the efficiency of the rest depended. If, then, it can be shown that the most polished nations of antiquity were indebted to the Mosaic records for the first rudiments of their mythology and philosophy (and that from these principles the laws of a country take their character) it is not unreasonable to attribute to their laws a similar source. But the truth of such a conclusion is perhaps better supported by illustration than by argument. So many instances of the fact arise, as to render it almost superfluous to produce the reasons for their existence.

All the Mosaic laws, it may be affirmed, are contained in the Ten Commandments. The special laws given to the Jews are no more than commentaries upon the decalogue. To one or the other of its provisions they may all be referred. Indeed, the decalogue, upon examination, will be found to embrace every subject of political legislation. It sets forth both the duty of man to his Maker, and his duty to his countrymen, which latter would naturally include his duty to the state to which he belongs. Beyond this, few statutes affect to reach.

The first commandment enforces the duty of maintaining the worship of God To this, therefore, the Levitical institutions may be ascribed.

The second prohibits the worship of other gods, and therefore comprises all those laws by which the prevention of idolatry was secured. Idolatry, indeed, amounted to treason. It was an offence against the state as well as an insult to religion. For God had appointed himself the king of that peculiar people amongst whom these laws were promulgated. The introduction, therefore, of any strange God, as it diverted their allegiance from that King who was at once the author and the head of their constitution, was so far an invasion of his prerogative.

The third and fourth commands contain all the provisions that were necessary to maintain the solemn observance of the national religion; and to that end the education of the people, and the sanctity of the Sabbath, was repeatedly enforced by special ordinances.

The last six commandments, contained in the other table of the law, will be found to comprise every thing concerning the conduct of men towards each other, both in the private and public relations of life, which can properly become the subject of political regulations. The social duties are clearly prescribed. Public wrongs, both in respect to the person and the property, are vindicated. Private rights, not only in regard to that property which a man can have in his possessions, but even that less tangible interest which he may have in his character and reputation, are protected by simple yet searching statutes. Every species of fraud, however artfully it may be contrived, and however difficult it may be to find for it a definition in the catalogue of crime, is provided against by the prohibition which forbids us to covet anything which belongs to another. Thus, not only the conduct, but the motives of mankind fall within the operation of a code whose grasp it is impossible to evade, and in the terms of which it is impossible to detect a flaw.

These considerations may serve to explain the severity of those denunciations which are directed against the presumption of either adding to or diminishing aught from its provisions. For if the second table includes the subject of all human rights and wrongs, it would be impossible to alter, to add to, or to annul any of its injunctions, without, at the same time, adding a new wrong, and thus impairing an old right. In either case an iniquitous result would follow. In creating a new wrong, liberty of action is unwarrantably restricted. In creating a new right, liberty of conscience is unwarrantably enlarged. But the second table of the Mosaic law rests upon the first. The first relates exclusively to matters of religion. Hence any deviation from the precepts of the first four commandments must necessarily assail and weaken the foundation upon which the obligation of the last six depends. Consequently, as in these ordinances are comprised the whole moral duties of man, the fundamental principles of justice would be disturbed, and thus lose all the authority they derive from their divine institution.

It is obvious that the observance of laws can be

secured by only two means—by the advantage or disadvantage which attends their fulfilment or nonfulfilment. As the one urges to obedience, the other deters from disobedience. Consequently, rewards and punishments are commonly said to be the two great sanctions of all laws; that is to say, the two most obvious methods by which their obligation must be enforced. Some, having regard rather to the reason than to the propensities of man, maintain that virtue is its own reward. Others contend that the observance of a law, as it tends to general convenience, is an actual reward for any temporary inconvenience. While a third class, apparently doubting the value of the two former theories, have attempted to frame systems by which rewards shall be bestowed for the observance, as well as punishments imposed for the breach, of a law. Such a system has, however, never been found capable of being carried into effect; and the others may be said to exist in theory rather than to be maintainable in practice. Yet they all admit this—that a law which rests only on punishment is deprived of half its power.

With the Jews, as the Lawgiver was eternal, so the rewards and punishments were eternal. The temporal punishment of an offence was rather a mark of its guilt than an expiation of the crime. It was as much a warning to the innocent as a punishment to the guilty. As Cicero expresses it, "Pœna ad paucos perveniat metus ad omnes."

The commission of any offence against man constituted an offence against God; not only indirectly, because man is the creature and property of God, but also directly, because such offences are prohibited by

God himself. So the breach of any law imposed primarily for the security of man, was not atoned by submission to a human punishment; because it was equally an offence against God, whose statutes were imposed upon His creatures to maintain His honour as well as to secure their happiness. The penalty was temporal; the punishment eternal.

But the observance of a law consists as much in abstaining from evil as in the actual performance of what is right. Hence it is as much a negative as a positive duty. Yet, as self-restraint is not attended by any visible action, such an exercise of virtue cannot be ascertained by a tribunal which can judge only by outward actions. It is not obvious to the senses of others. It depends entirely upon the power of self-control, and the power of self-control depends, in a great measure, upon the strength of the temptation. The observance of a law may, too, result from various causes. It may arise equally from inclination or self-interest, or it may occur through the absence of temptation, or it may be dictated by obedience to some principle which urges the exercise of self-restraint. Yet it can hardly be maintained, that in each of these cases it is equally deserving of reward. Then, if rewards are to constitute the sanction of laws, they can have reference only to the motives by which their observance is maintained. But before the rewards can be judicially apportioned, it is manifest that the motives of action must be judicially decided. This, however, is a province beyond the reach of human institutions; for it is only the tribunal which searches the heart that can penetrate its secret instigations. We are, therefore, driven to the conclusion, that rewards cannot properly be the sanction of laws whose authority is simply human.

But with regard to the subject of rewards and punishments, the structure of the decalogue demands consideration. If temporal rewards and punishments are the only sanction of laws, how is it that a statute, the invasion of which must precede the breach of many positive laws as between man and man, has no temporal punishment annexed to it? How is it that the only statute in the decalogue which affects the motives of men is the only one for which there is no authority to enforce it by punishment? Yet, to the breach of the tenth commandment, which forbids us to covet, no temporal punishment is annexed. What, then, are its sanctions? A law must rest upon some authority. The author must have the power of enforcing it, or it ceases to be a law. But the power of enforcing a law consists either in punishing disobedience, or in rewarding obedience. Indeed, the very power of rewarding obedience in itself implies the power of punishing, because, to bestow upon one a benefit greater than that enjoyed by another, is, so far, depriving the other of a benefit which it is in the power of the author to bestow. And this deprivation is a punishment. For the deprivation of pleasure is no less a punishment than the infliction of pain. Then, are we to conclude, because no temporal punishment is affixed to the tenth commandment, that it is less obligatory than the other commandments, or, in fact, that it is a mere piece of surplusage, and in truth no law at all? Or, on the other hand, shall we conclude that this law, which affects the motives of most crimes, is the subject of eternal rewards and punishments?

For, as it is the most difficult to keep, so we may not unreasonably believe that its observance deserves the greatest rewards. Yet if it be allowed that the only command to which no temporal rewards or punishments are annexed is the subject of eternal rewards and punishments, how can it be denied that the other commands, which consist in wicked actions which must be preceded by a design, are less liable to future rewards and punishments than the design itself? But St. Paul himself includes this command under the general law. For in the 13th chapter of the Romans, he says:—" For this, Thou shalt not commit adultery, Thou shalt not kill, Thou shalt not steal, Thou shalt not bear false witness, Thou shalt not covet; and if there be any other commandment, it is briefly comprehended in this saying, namely, Thou shalt love thy neighbour as thyself."

The general assertion, then, that "rewards and punishments are the two hinges on which all governments turn," is paradoxical, unless a divine obligation is allowed; because none but a divine power can discern what reward is due. Moreover, as human laws are framed to restrain the bad rather than to encourage the good, reward can, strictly speaking, never be positively conferred by such institutions; but only negatively, in the advantage which their protection affords to such as observe them. If, therefore, rewards are to exist at all, it must inevitably be in a future state. We find this principle recognized in all the ancient systems of legislation. In the resemblance of the statutes themselves, as well as in the principles upon which they were constructed, we may observe how cautiously those who, amongst the ancients, were most famous for the excellence of their institutions, copied the usages of the Jews. This is remarkable not only in the simpler forms of their criminal jurisprudence—which it is possible to conceive may have been the fruit of necessity guided by the light of nature—but is even more apparent in such moral regulations as must have been in some sense the subject of a religious principle. In every state of whose constitution records have been preserved, it will be found that the authority of the laws depended upon the sanctions of religion. As we trace the methods by which the authority of a supreme and overruling power was accommodated to the purposes of political government, it will be seen that they were copied from the principles of obedience upon which the Mosaic institutions were founded. By such a comparison, ample proofs will be furnished that law and religion were derived from the same source. Thus judicial institutions and religious observances lent each other mutual aid, and found a common support in the principle from which they sprang.

From systems so interwoven, it is impossible to exclude the idea of future rewards and punishments. Plato, indeed, in one of his political romances, treating rather of what was excellent than of what was possible, amused himself by constructing a system in which the distribution of temporal rewards was one of the incentives to obedience. But, with the ancients, the qualities and attributes assigned to their gods always corresponded with the nature of their governments and the spirit of their laws. All the laws of the ancients were attributed to a divine origin, and from this pretence to revelation we may gather the sentiments of their lawgivers concerning the use of religion to civil society. Diodorus Siculus truly observes, that they did this, not only to beget a veneration of their laws, but likewise to establish a reverence for the superintendence which the gods exercised over human affairs. But before we institute a comparison with the Mosaic institutions, for the sake of accuracy let us a certain what is meant by the term Law. The works of writers upon jurisprudence abound in such definitions. But as the most exact is perhaps that of Barbeyrac, we adopt his words:—"Law is the will of a superior, sufficiently notified in some manner or other, by which will he directs either all the actions in general of those who depend on him, or at least all those of a certain kind; so that, in regard to such actions, he either imposes on them a necessity of doing, or not doing, certain things; or leaves them at liberty to act, or not act, as they shall judge proper." In the former case, the obligation arises from the necessity of obedience; in the latter, from compact or arrangement. This distinction, according to Grotius, was observed by the Hebrews. They divided laws into precepts and statutes—statutes signifying right instituted or voluntary (*i. e.*, derived from the will of their author). Of these, certainly the first table held the most prominent place.

The consideration, therefore, of the religious institutions of these ancient commonwealths will first occupy our attention.

Of the ancient institutions of the Egyptians our information is far from perfect. What little knowledge we have of their public economy we owe chiefly to the curiosity of Diodorus Siculus, and to the traditions of Herodotus. Fragments, however, have been preserved, sufficient to give us an outline of their system of government. A slight examination will point out the model upon which it was formed, although in some respects the features are obscured by the dust of ages. Their religious ordinances appear to have been at least founded upon the principle of a divine authority, as all such ordinances must be; and that of such authentic antiquity as to preclude the possibility of their being attributed to the invention of deified heroes and to the local deities, which were created just as a political purpose happened to require a new sanction. For the necessity of such an origin Plato acknowledges a sufficient reason. He lays it down as a general concession (De Leg. 6) that all laws and constitutions concerning the worship of God must come from God. His words are—"Laws about divine matters must be fetched from the Delphic oracle." So, again, he says (De Leg. 10) :—" It is not lawful to appoint Gods or sacred rites beyond the laws"—that is, beyond what has been divinely ordained. The functions, therefore, of their priests were defined with great precision. In the regulation of public affairs they were the principal actors. In contrasting their duties with the functions of the Levites, the following peculiarities of their system furnish an ample field for comparison. The preservation of the laws was committed to their care. They were the custodians of the national records. They presided over the national education—the first object of which, it may be observed, was to impart to the people a knowledge of the laws. It was the recognised office of the state to make the people acquainted with their duty to that society by which they were protected, and to implant in them a knowledge of their obligations to the community of which they were members.

But if the Egyptian priests were the guardians of the laws, the colleges, to whose care the preservation of the public records was confided bore a still closer resemblance to the Levitical institutions. With the Jews the tribe of Levi was a permanent institution, where the vacancies were filled up only by hereditary claim. So it was with the Egyptian priests. Their colleges were maintained chiefly for the purpose of imparting a knowledge of the religion and the laws of the state. Beyond these subjects their functions did not extend. We are told by Diodorus Siculus that it was not among their duties to instruct the people either in reading or writing. The object of public instruction was to secure civil obedience, rather than to promote the cultivation of science. Indeed, the trade and occupation of an Egyptian was hereditary, like that of a Chinese. With the Egyptians it was a penal crime for the son to forsake the employment which his father had exercised. Even the practice of medicine was confined by prescriptive usages. The physician was a public officer, to whom was confided the care of the public health. He was paid by the state, and restricted to the use of remedies established by law. If he deviated from these, he was liable to the consequences. By many these cures are supposed to have been discovered by Solomon, having been preserved in books which are said to have been destroyed in the reign of Hezekiah, because the Jews placed undue confidence in their efficacy.

The Jewish priests seem to have exercised the same functions, especially to prevent the contagion, if not to effect the cure, of leprosy.

The great distinction between the Hebrew constitution and the institutions of its imitators, of which the Egyptians were probably the earliest, was this,—that the Hebrew laws sprang from the Hebrew religion, whereas the pagan religions were made subordinate to the pagan laws, and were constructed rather to enforce their application than to regulate their principles. In proof of this, it is enough to mention, that most of their lawgivers were deified after death, not only as models for imitation, but as having the power to confer rewards for obedience. Like the Hebrews, the Egyptians referred their institutions to a divine origin. In cases of doubt they employed the powers of divination, in the same manner as the Hebrews resorted to the oracle of God. The earliest oracle established in Egypt was that of Jupiter Ammon. Its antiquity, though doubtless great, is fixed by Sir Isaac Newton at a date more than four hundred years later than the time of Moses.

Among those nations to whom can be traced the tradition of Jewish institutions in their earliest forms of worship, idols and images seem to have been unknown.

In the early ages of Egyptian civilization, if Lucian may be credited, the temples were without statues. So also the Greeks worshipped their gods without any visible representation till the time of Cecrops, who is supposed to have lived about the age of Moses. This is a remarkable proof of the comparative purity of the earlier religious systems. The practice of paying adoration to the gods under the visible shapes of statues and images, however, seems to have gradually prevailed over a purer creed. Just as the true knowledge of the Deity became obscured, the form of worship became corrupted. Pausanias tells us, that in Achaia there were kept very religiously thirty square stones, on which were engraved the names of as many gods, but "without any picture or effigy." This afterwards, no doubt, led to the consecration of unhewn stones and pillars, and these in their turn were converted into statues, in which, under human shapes, the gods were personified.

With respect to the place which religion held in the Grecian institutions, more positive evidence is available. Their lawgivers, who borrowed as much from Egypt as Egypt did from Canaan, attempted to give to their several codes the authority of a divine origin. They, in imitation of the Hebrews, wherever the provisions of their law were incomplete or dubious, sought for their conduct the guidance of the Delphic and other oracles.

History has preserved to us ample records of the office and duties of their priests. Their functions correspond so closely with the Levitical ordinances, as, in the absence of any other proof of another origin, to leave us no alternative but to attribute them to Jewish traditions. It was their duty to instruct men in the worship of the gods, and to teach them all the ceremonies used in divine worship. On this account the priests were honoured with the next place in dignity to their kings and chief magistrates, and in many places wore the same habit. In many of the Grecian cities, and particularly at Athens, the care of divine worship was committed to the chief magistrates, and these were often consecrated to the priesthood. Thus we find Æneas, in Virgil, king of Delos and priest of Apollo. In Egypt, according to Plato, the kings were all priests; and even if any one who was not of the royal family usurped the kingdom, he was obliged to be consecrated to the priesthood before he was permitted to govern. In some parts of Greece, Plutarch informs us that the dignity of priests was equal to that of kings. At Sparta, the kings immediately after their promotion took upon them the priesthood of Jupiter. This was considered an accession to their honour. All public sacrifices for the safety of the commonwealth were offered by them. In times of national calamity, it was unlawful for any subject (though consecrated to the sacred office) to invade this privilege. The priesthood was sometimes hereditary. At Athens, vacancies were supplied from the sacred families. This, also, according to Herodotus, was the custom in Egypt, where the priests obtained their office and dignity by inheritance. Such was also the practice in many other places. Amongst other regulations, it was required that whoever was admitted to this office should be free from blemish and sound in all his members. Before consecration, the priest was examined to ascertain whether he was free from all bodily defect, or had anything "superfluous." The strictest chastity and temperance was observed by those who were selected to fill such offices. So careful were the ancient Greeks about these matters, that they used to exclude from the priesthood those who had been twice married. In the choice of their wives, the Greek priests were placed under many restrictions. They were generally obliged to marry virgins of their own tribe; but never were allowed to marry slaves or foreigners.

The office of the Greek basileus, or archon, was very similar to that of the Jewish high priest. Demosthenes mentions a law which appointed that the consort of the basileus should be a citizen of Athens, and never before married.

In the same way, as the Levites kept registers of the genealogies of the other tribes, so it was the duty of the Grecian basileus and his officers publicly to enrol the birth of children which were the offspring of citizens. The Jews circumcised their children upon the eighth day. With the Greeks, children were sometimes named with a formal ceremony upon the seventh day, sometimes also upon the tenth day, but generally upon the eighth day, which was observed annually in commemoration of the event. Until this ceremony had taken place, it seems more than probable that they were neither acknowledged as citizens, nor entitled to the privileges of freedom by birth.

With regard to the priesthood, the Jewish laws were remarkably stringent. "They shall not take a wife that is a whore, or profane, neither shall they take a woman that is put away from her husband." The high priest was forbidden to uncover his head, or to rend his clothes. "And he shall take a wife in her virginity. A widow, or a divorced woman, or profane, or an harlot, shall he not take; but he shall take a virgin of his own people to wife... Whosoever he be that hath a blemish, let him not approach to offer the bread of his God," &c.

The accounts we have of the institution of the

priesthood amongst the Romans, are chiefly derived from the writings of Plutarch. The pontifical college, he tells us, was erected by Numa Pompilius. The chief of this brotherhood was the pontifex. His office gave him the authority and dignity of high priest, in which capacity he was the conservator of the pontific law. His office, he adds, was to see " that none break the ancient ceremonies, nor introduce any new thing into religion; but that every one should be taught by him how they should serve the gods." Here we see an order of priests amongst the ancient Romans, whose functions exactly answer to the Levitical system of the Jews. As the Jewish priests were the conservators of the Mosaic law, so were the Romans of the pontific or canon law. In the same manner, the priests were the responsible ministers of public instruction. Cicero informs us that in ancient Rome the very boys were obliged to learn the twelve tables by heart, as a *carmen necessarium*, or indispensable lesson, to imprint in their minds an early knowledge of the laws and constitution of their country. Even the vestments worn by the Roman pontifices were obviously borrowed from those of the Jews. For the mitre and linen ephod of the one, we have the cap or apex and the white garments of the other. The use of the apex, like that of the mitre, was confined to the chief priest alone. Amongst the Greeks, it was ordained by one of the institutes of Pythagoras, that all acts of worship were to be performed in white vestments, and with praises (or a good conscience). According to Diogenes Laertius, Pythagoras taught, "that the gods were to be worshipped with a pure body, and that such purity was to be attained by expurgations, washings, sprinklings, and abstinence from all defilement." In the same way the different orders of the pontific college—the method of their probation, their lustrations, their manner of sacrificing, and their ordinances concerning the mode in which the gods were to be worshipped, and the observances with which their religious rites were to be performed—closely correspond with the Jewish institutions. The Hebrews were forbidden to wear garments dyed with various colours. So we find the Greek law to be thus:—"All who frequent the panathenæa are forbidden the wearing of apparel dyed with colours."

Amongst the Greeks, then, it was provided that a particular tribe should be set apart to preside over and record the national laws. This exactly corresponds to the selection and office of the Levites, whose duty it was to make copies of the law, and to preserve the original statutes, and from time to time to rehearse them publicly. Moreover, their functions answered to those of the Levites in several other particulars, in having the custody of the national records, in presiding over the system of public education, in regulating national solemnities, in performing religious rites, in cultivating literature, and in being the depositaries of the national wisdom. But to trace a more exact resemblance is almost superfluous, when the ordinances themselves are not only manifestly founded upon the same principles, but are in many respects identical. Those who desire more complete illustrations of the fact, can satisfy themselves by referring to Potter's Greek Antiquities, and to Petit " de Legibus Atticis," where authorities upon this point are collected in abundance.

Of the remarkable correspondence between the religious rites of the Egyptians and those of the Jews, Plutarch has furnished us with another instance. At their purifications, the Jews were ordered to sacrifice a red heifer without spot, wherein was no blemish, &c. So strictly was this followed by the Egyptian superstition, that when they sacrificed red bullocks, he tells us, if the animal had but one hair black or white, it was accounted profane. The purity of victims intended for the altar was so superstitiously regarded by the Romans, that sheep without spot or blemish, which were destined for sacrifice, came to be called *eximiæ* (from *eximerentur*), being taken or culled out of the flock. Nor was any man admitted to the more solemn sacrifices, unless for some days before he had preserved his body from all defilement. The circumstances under which purification was required agree so exactly in many particulars with the Levitical ordinances, as to leave little room to doubt but that they were Hebrew traditions. Tibullus warns his Roman countrymen,—

"Discedite ab aris
Queis tulit hesterna gaudia nocte Venus."

So rigid were the Greeks in their observance of this custom, that at some of their solemnities the priests and priestesses were forced to take an oath that they were duly purified. The oath imposed upon the priestess of Bacchus was in this form: "I am pure, undefiled, and free from all sorts of pollutions, (and particularly from certain defilements which are here specified), and do celebrate the festival of Bacchus at the usual time, and according to the received custom of the country." Now here we have a recognition of three ordinances in public worship—a prescribed purification, a prescribed time for worship, and a prescribed form of worship. Each of these regulations are to be found in the religion of the Hebrews, where they were enforced by severe injunctions, and guarded by close restraints. In the Book of Numbers (c. viii.) it is provided, "thus shalt thou do unto them; to cleanse them, sprinkle water of purifying upon them." Every person who attended the solemn sacrifices of the Greeks was first purified with water. For this purpose, a consecrated vessel full of water was placed at the entrance of the temples. It was customary to besprinkle the approaching worshipper with a torch taken from the altar, and dipped into the sacred vessel. Instead of a torch, a branch of laurel was occasionally used for this purpose. So we read, that when Valentinian was about to enter a pagan temple of Jupiter, a priest, holding certain green boughs dropping water, besprinkled them after the Grecian manner. Instead of laurel, Virgil tells us that at the Roman lustrations olive was sometimes made use of:—

"Idem ter socios purâ circumtulit undâ
Spargens rore levi et ramo felicis olivæ."

Hector tells us he was afraid to make so much as a libation to Jupiter, before he had washed:—

Χερσὶ δ' ἀνίπτοισιν Διὶ λάβειν αἴθοπα οἶνον
Ἅζομαι.

Telemachus is said, in the Odyssy, to have washed his hands before he ventured to pray to the gods. The cleanest water, fresh from the spring, was used for this purpose; the water of lakes and ponds was not thought pure enough. Hence *recens aqua*, fresh water, is applied to this use by Virgil:—

"Occupat Æneas aditum corpusque recenti
Spargit aquâ."

The apostle seems to allude to this practice where he says: "Let us draw near, having our hearts sprinkled from an evil conscience, and our bodies washed with pure water." Whoever had committed any notorious crime, as murder, adultery, or incest, was forbidden to be present at the holy rites, until he had been purified. In Deut. xiii. we find this law: "A bastard shall not enter into the congregation of the Lord, even to the tenth generation." At Athens bastards were not permitted to be present at the sacred rites. In other places, servants, captives, and even unmarried women, were placed under the same restrictions. Even those who returned from a victory over lawful enemies were obliged to purify themselves before they were allowed to sacrifice, or pray to the gods. Before the ceremonies were begun, the priest made a solemn proclamation, warning off all those who were profane. Not only those who had touched a dead body (which was likewise a cause of pollution with the Jews) were esteemed to have contracted defilement; but even those who, having been left for dead, suddenly recovered. So also were those who unexpectedly returned, after having from long absence been given up for dead. The garments worn by the priests of ancient Rome were to be pure and spotless, loose, and unconfined by a band. The priests of Ceres wore white robes; others wore purple ones. But the covering of the head with a mitre seems to have been rather a Roman than a Grecian custom (they had it from the Persians, who no doubt copied it from the Jerusalem ritual, with which they were well acquainted); although some of the Roman sacrifices were performed in the same manner as those of the

Greeks, and particularly those of Saturn, mentioned by Plutarch, the rites of which were first brought from Greece.

During the time of child-bed, women were looked upon as polluted. So also any person who had touched a woman under such circumstances required purification before he was allowed to enter a temple.

Women were not permitted to enter the temples until forty days after delivery. A festival was then kept. The woman underwent purification, and returned thanks at some temple; generally at the shrine of Diana, to whom sacrifices were offered. Whence the Athenians enacted a law, that no woman should bring forth in Delos, an island consecrated to Apollo, because the gods were believed to have an aversion to all sorts of pollution.

According to the Hebrew law, the purification prescribed under such circumstances in Leviticus (chap. xii.) was thus defined: " If a woman have conceived seed, and born a man child, then she shall be unclean seven days. On the eighth day the flesh of his foreskin shall be circumcised. And she shall then continue in the blood of her purifying three and thirty days; she shall touch no hallowed thing, nor come into the sanctuary, until the days of her purifying be fulfilled." Thus, it will be observed, the seven days and the thirty-three days of uncleanness make up the exact period of forty days' purification from the time of delivery, after which she was commanded to offer the sacrifice of atonement.

The reverence due to the sanctity of the temple was enforced by many special regulations amongst the Jews. To some of these peculiar ordinances it is not difficult to find a Greek counterpart. Amongst others, we have one couched in almost similar terms in the law of Pisistratus, which enacts that whoever personally defiles Apollo's temple, shall be indicted and sentenced to death. The Jewish temple was divided into the inner and the outer courts. So also many of the Greek temples were divided by a line, beyond which strangers were forbidden to pass. As with the Jews, so with the Greeks, all slaves and foreigners were permitted to come to the temples, either out of curiosity, or for the purposes of devotion. But although slaves and foreigners were permitted to attend the public worship of the Gods, they were forbidden to enter into the holy mysteries. Like the altar of Moses, the most ancient pagan altars were adorned with horns. In reference to the Jewish law, which protected the criminal who took refuge at the altar, we have a very ancient law of Greece to the same effect: "Let no violence be offered to any one who flees to the temples for succour." To this, however, we shall refer hereafter, when we come to consider the laws relating to homicide. In conformity with the immunity provided by the Jewish festivals, the Greeks ordained that no one should be arrested or apprehended during the celebration of their mysteries. So, our own laws declare that civil process is void if executed upon Sunday. And formerly the same privilege was offered in many cases to criminal offenders. With the Greeks, no unclean person who had touched a corpse, or who was otherwise defiled, was, upon any pretence, permitted to approach the altars of their gods.

As the Jewish priests were commanded to keep the fire burning upon the altar; so the Greeks, having probably received some broken traditions of this custom, made a law, under which a continual fire was kept alive upon the altar of Delphi, under penalty of the severest punishment. This fire was called ἑστία, which Gale, in his Court of the Gentiles, derives from *es ja*, signifying in Hebrew, "the fire of Jehovah." Hence, also, he traces the Roman Vesta, in whose honour a perpetual fire was kept up by the Vestal virgins; death being the penalty of any neglect upon their part in the discharge of this duty.

It seems also to have been a very ancient custom with the heathen, to worship with their faces towards the east. The temples, therefore, were so constructed, wherever the situation of the place would permit, that the rays of the rising sun might be admitted through the open windows at the eastern end, where the altars were placed, the entrance being at the opposite end, looking towards the west. Diodorus Siculus testifies that the temple of Memphis in Egypt was so contrived. Herodotus remarks the same peculiarity in the temple of Vulcan, built by another Egyptian king. That such was the universal construction of the most ancient temples, is corroborated by Vitruvius.

One of the oldest Attic laws prescribes that sacrifices be performed with the fruits of the earth. One of Draco's laws was: "Let it be a law among the Athenians for ever, sacred and inviolable, always to pay homage in public towards their gods and native heroes, according to the custom of the country, and with all possible sincerity to offer in private first fruits and anniversary cakes." Now, by the Hebrew laws, public homage to the national religion was enjoined even upon strangers. So likewise personal oblations of the first fruits were prescribed, with which private individuals were invited to propitiate the favour of God.

But if we pass on to consider the severity of the Jewish laws, which made it a capital crime to impeach the sovereignty of their divine ruler by the introduction of strange gods, or even by inciting others to such seductive influences, we find here the counterpart to our own law of treason, which, differing from other criminal laws, brands with equal guilt the offence of the principal and the accessory in any attempt to subvert the sovereign power. We have a prevision similar in its purpose in the Greek law, which under the penalty of capital punishment enacted that no strange god could be worshipped till approved of by the Areopagite senate. This was the highest judicial authority in the state. But as the Jewish laws were dictated by God himself, so He was the highest judicial authority with the Hebrews. Whence it is manifest that both nations recognized the same principle, that it is impossible to invade the prerogative of the governing power, without at the same time subverting the force of those obligations which spring from it.

The Jewish laws provided that no blemished cattle should be offered as sacrifices. The Greek laws enacted that cattle designed for the altar should be culled. They even went so far as to prescribe their weight and quality. One of the most ancient Attic laws provided that "only the best of cattle should be offered to the gods."

We find, also, that the manner of offering propitiatory sacrifices, as prescribed in Leviticus, was very closely imitated. The Levitical law provided that the oblation should be taken as well from bullocks as from sheep and goats. To many heathen gods bullocks, sheep, and goats were offered in common. Achilles, in Homer, offers these three together. Livy more than once describes a bullock as "the greater sacrifice." Then again, Moses enjoins that the bullock must be a male without blemish. Herodotus (lib. 2. c. 41.) tells us that the Egyptians universally sacrificed clean bullocks, and those males and calves which had never been under the yoke. As a confession for sin, the Jewish priest was commanded to put his hand upon the head of the sacrifice. The same custom is related to have prevailed amongst the Egyptians. Herodotus mentions that they were wont to say an execration upon the head of the sacrifice, "that if any evil were impending either over them that sacrificed, or over the whole of Egypt, it might be diverted, and fall upon the head of the victim." Plutarch says, that after they had called down the curse upon the head of the sacrifice, they cut it off.

Again, as secret sacrifices, to prevent idolatry, were prohibited to the Jews; so it was one of Plato's ordinances (De Leg. lib. 10), "that no one have an altar in his private house." The Jewish custom of sprinkling the blood of the victim upon the altar was also followed by the Greeks and Romans. Their poets furnish us with many instances which show that this practice was followed in their sacred rites.

Sacrifices of the fruits of the earth were, like the harvest and vintage feasts of the Jews, specially ordained to be offered at stated seasons, which answered very nearly to the times appointed by the ceremonial laws of the Jews. Indeed, the feast of the new moon was observed almost universally in ancient Greece. This may be gathered, not only from many allusions to be found in the writings of the earliest Greek writers, but from many ancient laws framed specially to maintain such festivals. An ancient Greek law directs, "that sacrifices are required to be offered to the gods at the beginning of every month."

It was commanded by the laws of Athens, that homage should be publicly paid to the national deities, both by strangers and citizens. Amongst other coincidences with the Jewish institutions, we have this Greek enactment,—"That the sacrificer should be allowed to carry home a part of his oblation." The Hebrew worshipper was allowed the same privilege. The remains of the offering were the priests' fees. Such contributions formed the chief means of their support. Indeed, in this manner, by sharing the offerings dedicated to the gods, we read of many instances of their growing rich. Thus their prosperity, nay, almost their existence, was made to depend upon the due fulfilment of their office.

For any profanation or offence to the sanctity of the temple, death was the penalty. As we have seen, the definition of such offences is in terms almost identical with those of the Jewish law.

The institutions of Moses contained very strict injunctions that no sacrifice should be offered without salt. We find this precept in Leviticus (chap. ii): "Every oblation of the meat offering shalt thou season with salt; neither shalt thou suffer the salt of the covenant of thy God to be lacking from thy meat offering : with all thine offerings thou shalt offer salt." This custom was certainly very ancient. The poets furnish many examples of its universal observance. The ceremony of sprinkling the victim with salt was scrupulously observed by the Egyptians, the Greeks, and the Romans. Yet, as it is a custom for which no reason is assigned, we must attribute it to a scriptural tradition.

Pliny tells us that no oblation was thought acceptable to the gods without a mixture of salt:— "Nulla sacra conficiuntur sine mola salsa."

Virgil alludes to it in these words :—

"——— Mihi sacra parari
Et fruges salsæ."

So Ovid, in describing the primitive oblations :—

"Ante deos homini quod conciliare valebat
Far erat et puri lucida mica salis."

Amongst the ancients it was customary to confirm all matters of contract or agreement by an oath. It is remarkable, that the pagan nations of antiquity should seek to strengthen the obligation of their solemn leagues and covenants by the sanction of a religious ceremony.

It seems to be a tacit acknowledgment that no rule of conduct prescribed by arrangement, and arising out of convenience, could be binding, or acquire the force of law, without the sanction of divine authority. With the Greeks, as with most of the eastern nations, public conventions and leagues were usually confirmed with a federal sacrifice. In these salt was generally used as a token of friendship. The Greeks and Romans regarded the eating together of bread and salt as the most solemn form of pledge. In the same way, we find that the covenant of salt, mentioned in Leviticus, was used by the Jews as a token of perpetual adherence to the terms of those conditions and stipulations upon which the favour of the Almighty was vouchsafed to them. But instead of making a direct appeal to the deity, it was sometimes customary with the Greeks and Romans to swear by inanimate things of nature, as trees and rivers, and sometimes by the lesser divinities, who were supposed to preside over them. Pythagoras, and some of the early Greek philosophers, esteemed it profane to swear by the gods, except upon the most important occasions—a regulation which seems to have in view the Mosaic prohibition—"Thou shalt not take the name of the Lord thy God in vain." And it may here be observed, that the Rabbinical writers interpret this command, not in its ordinary acceptation, as a warning against using the name of God with levity upon ordinary occasions, but as an injunction not to swear lightly by the awful name of Jehovah, even upon the most solemn occasions. Yet with the Greeks, to take an oath was sometimes regarded as an act of adoration, being an acknowledgment of the deity invoked. Much in the same sense, those who were true worshippers of God are described by David as swearing by His name. The Jews were commanded to swear only by the name of Jehovah. Thus Solon prescribed the names of appointed gods by which alone the Athenians were to swear in public causes.

But in all solemn leagues and covenants, besides the pledge of an oath, the ancients also sacrificed to the gods by whom they swore; and having invoked their vengeance upon the person who should violate his oath, the ceremony was finished with a solemn libation. Of this rite Homer and Virgil have given many descriptions.

Amongst the Jews, one of the most remarkable appeals to the determination of the Almighty in human affairs was the oath of jealousy, whereby the suspected chastity of a wife was challenged. The terms of this oath are given in the book of Numbers (chap. v.) When a man doubted the fidelity of his wife, and was overcome with the spirit of jealousy, he brought her before the priest, who was commanded to take holy water in an earthen vessel, and mix with it dust from the floor of the tabernacle. With this in his hand, he presented the woman, with her head uncovered, before the Lord, and administered to her the oath of jealousy: "And when he hath made her to drink the water, then it shall come to pass, that, if she be defiled, and have done trespass against her husband, that the water that causeth the curse shall enter into her, and become bitter, and her belly shall swell, and her thigh shall rot; and the woman shall be a curse among her people. And if the woman be not defiled, but be clean; then she shall be free, and shall conceive seed. ... And the priest shall write these curses in a book, and shall blot them out with bitter water."

The purgation oath of the Greeks closely resembles that of the Jews. It is described thus by Achilles Statius: When a woman was accused of incontinency, she was to clear herself upon oath from this charge, which was written upon a tablet, and hung about her neck; then she went into the water up to her mid leg, where, if she was innocent, all things remained in the same state as before; but if guilty, says he, the very water swelled, as it were, with rage, mounted up as high as her neck, and covered the tablet, lest so horrid and detestable a sight as a false oath should be exposed to the sight of the sun and the world.

We have also a relic of the purgation oath in the time of Edward the Confessor, who caused his mother Emma to walk blindfold and barefooted over red hot ploughshares, set at unequal distances apart, to vindicate her honour from the scandal of incontinency with Alwyn, bishop of Winchester. Her innocence was proved by her passing unhurt through this ordeal.

Kunigund, the wife of the emperor Henry II., upon the like imputation, is said to have held a red-hot iron in her hand without receiving harm thereby. The Greeks did the same. We have a case in point in the Antigone.

That the payment of tithes for the maintenance of religious worship was a very ancient custom, can scarcely be questioned. The example of Abraham, who gave tithes of all that he possessed to Melchisedek the king of Salem, and priest of the Most High God, seems to show that the practice of giving tithes to maintain public worship was known in the earliest ages. Diogenes Laërtius relates, that all the Athenians set apart a tenth of their firstfruits for public sacrifices.

The Romans paid tithe to Hercules. So Herodotus (in Clio) mentions that the soldiers of Cyrus were, by the advice of Crœsus, restrained from spoiling the Lydians, that the tithes might first be paid to Jupiter. Xenophon relates that the tenth part of a certain field consecrated to Diana was sacrificed every year. In Pausanias we find that it was the custom of the

Siphnians to present a tenth part of the produce of their gold mines to Apollo.

It was also customary for the kings to receive a tenth portion of the several revenues of their subjects. This probably arose from their frequently uniting in themselves the royal and the priestly office. That, however, this was a very general custom, we may gather from the words of Samuel, where he warns the Jews of some of the inconveniences which would attend the election of a king: "He will take a tenth of your seed, and of your vineyards; he will take a tenth of your sheep."

Amongst the ancient Egyptians, we have the testimony of Scripture, that the priests were maintained at the public expense: "For the priests had a portion assigned them of Pharaoh, and did eat their portion which Pharaoh gave them; wherefore, they sold not their lands." "And Joseph made it a law over the land of Egypt unto this day, that Pharaoh should have the fifth part, except the land of the priests only, which became not Pharaoh's." Here we have the first instance of a church with a national endowment. The Hebrew laws sanctified the seventh day as a day of rest. The Greek laws provided that, "while the festival of the new moon or other festival continues at Athens, it is ordered that no one be defamed or affronted in public or private; and that no business be carried on which is not pertinent to the feast."

But, from the statements of their earlier writers, we have many proofs of the reverence paid to the seventh day by the Greeks and the Romans in ancient times, though it must be admitted that some of their later authors attribute a religious observance of the sabbath peculiarly to the Jews, and treat it, like the Romish church, rather as a holyday, to be dedicated to festivity and ease. Yet at least it must be allowed that any allusion made by them to such an ordinance is sufficient to show their knowledge of a Jewish institution, and this is enough for our purpose. While, upon the other hand, the fact, that the obligation of such an observance was recognized by the most ancient writers, is rather a corroboration of the proposition which we ventured in a previous chapter to advance, that the further back you trace the pagan institutions, the closer is their resemblance to those of the Hebrews.

Selden (de Jure Nat. et Heb.) has collected many instances of the respect paid to the seventh day by the early inhabitants of Greece and Rome; which, indeed, was specially consecrated to many of their festivals, as the Saturnalia and Lupercalia of the one and the hebdomadal rites of the other.

Some unquestionable allusions to the sanctity in which the seventh day was observed, are preserved in a fragment of Hesiod:—

"Πρῶτον ἔνη τετράς, τὰ καὶ ἑβδόμη ἱερὸν ἦμαρ."
"Firstly, the first, fourth, and seventh day is sacred."

Again:—
"Ἑβδομάτη δ' αὖτις λαμπρὸν φάος ἠελίοιο."

From Homer a recognition of the same observance may be gathered:—

"Ἑβδομάτη ἔπειτα κατήλυθεν ἱερὸν ἦμαρ."
"Now shone forth the seventh sacred day."

"Ἕβδομον ἦμαρ ἔην, καὶ τῷ τετελέστο ἅπαντα."
"The seventh day approached, on which all things were perfected."

"Ἑβδομάτη δὴ οἱ λίπομεν ῥόον ἐξ ἀχέροντος.'

So we have a fragment of Linus, as follows:—

"'Εβδομάτη δὴ οἱ τετελέσμενα πάντα τετύκται."

We have, in the foregoing quotations, not only a recognition of the sabbath, but the scriptural reason for it: that all things were finished, and therefore God rested on the seventh day, and hallowed it. And the reason why the seventh day was held sacred by the ancients was, according to their own confessions, because they attributed its origin to a divine institution.

Hesiod says, it was called the ἧμαρ ἱερόν, or sacred day, because it was upon this day that Latona brought forth Apollo. Homer says, that the seventh was a holy day, appointed by Jupiter, the Supreme God:—

"'Αλλ' ὅτ' ἄρ' ἕβδομον ἧμαρ ἐπὶ Ζεὺς θῆκε Κρονίων."

Whence Jupiter is by some supposed to have derived his name Diespater, the father of day.

Aristobulus has preserved a fragment of Linus, which shows that seven was regarded as a sacred number by the ancient Greeks:—

"'Επτὰ δὲ πάντα τέτυκτο ἐν οὐρανῷ ἀστερόεντι
Ἐν κυκλοίσι φάνεντ' ἐπιτελλομένοις ἐνιαυτοῖς."

The seventh day was kept as a holy day with the Romans in honour of Saturn; and there can be little doubt that many of the holydays observed both by the Greeks and Romans were derived from the Jewish festivals. So Porphyry, in his book about the Jews, as quoted by Eusebius, tells us that the Phœnicians consecrated to their principal god Saturn, whom they also called Israel, one day in seven as holy, &c. To the same purpose we have the testimony of Eusebius, that in his days at least it passed for an historical fact, that not only the Hebrews, but the philosophers and poets of pagan Greece, acknowledged the seventh day to be more holy than the rest.

Suetonius alludes to its observance as a well-established custom (In Tiberio, cap. 32):—

"Disputare Sabbatis Rhodi solitus, venientem ut se extra ordinem audiret non admiserat, ac per servulum suum in septimum diem distulerat. Hunc Romæ salutandi sui causa pro foribus adstantem nihil amplius quam ut post septimum annum rediret admonuit."

So Ovid, advising a lover that the best remedy for his passion was separation from the object of it, refers to the Sabbath in these lines:—

"Sed quanto minus ire voles magis ire memento,
Perfer et invitos currere coge pedes.
Nec pluvias opta, nec te *peregrina* morentur
Sabbata, nec damnis alia nota suis."

Again, he refers not only to the observance, but to its Hebrew origin:—

"Quoque die redeunt rebus minus apta gerendis
Culta Palæstino septima festa viro."

Tibullus, complaining of his absence from Rome and his mistress, uses these words:—

"Ipse ego solator quum jam mandata dedissem
Quærebam tardas anxius usque moras—
Aut ego sum caussatus aves, aut omnia dira
Saturni, aut sacram me tenuisse diem."

From this it is manifest, that the day on which the Saturnalia were celebrated was so much reverenced by the ancient Romans, as to be regarded as an impediment to travelling.

Seneca, in like manner, makes this remark:—

"Quomodo sunt dii colendi solet præcipi. Accendere aliquem

lucernam Sabbatis prohibeamus, quoniam nec lumine dii egent, ne homines quidem delectantur fuligine."

This distinction, however, between holy days and working days, which was observed by the Greeks and Romans, is sufficiently obvious, from the foregoing illustrations, to render it unnecessary to prolong the comparison between their religious customs and those of the Jews. We may, therefore, conclude this part of the subject by reverting to the testimony of Josephus. In language which we have before referred to, he asserts that there was no nation amongst the Greeks or the barbarians, in which the Hebrew custom of resting upon the seventh day had not been more or less recognised.

## CHAPTER IV.

### ON THE PRINCIPLES AND CONSTRUCTION OF THE HEBREW LAWS.

THE subject of this chapter is of importance, as to some extent it involves the principles of interpretation which are applicable to the revealed law. Upon these depend the limits within which its provisions may be subjected to that process of reasoning which is commonly called argument by analogy. On questions of morality, this method of induction is frequently adopted upon very insufficient grounds. It must be conceded, in the first instance, that the imposition of moral regulations presupposes the existence of free agency. Liberty of action, then, is limited only by such restrictions as these regulations impose. Hence it follows, that where the rule of conduct is not specially prescribed, in default of a general rule to the contrary, the exercise of this liberty, so far as its temporal relations are concerned, rests with the discretion of the individual. But with respect to the obligations that arise between an individual and the community of which he is a member, it is not here our purpose to inquire how far the implied assent of the individual to extraordinary laws, imposed by the community for the regulation of society, may involve the duty of civil obedience. For such restrictions may be said rather to arise out of compact, or common consent, than to owe their obligation to the supreme authority of law. Hence, in the absence of such municipal restrictions, moral obligations cannot arise unless some higher sanction can be found for such ordinances.

It must be remembered, that the convenience of mankind was not the sole purpose of the moral laws, and therefore convenience or utility is not the standard of their moral obligation. Whatever may have been the special purposes of the Hebrew laws, a general outline of their application is contained in the decalogue. In this code certain duties are commanded, and certain offences are prohibited, in conformity with general principles to which it is subordinate. These offences are afterwards specifically defined. In many instances such actions as are apparently a breach of the general law, become, under certain circumstances, excusable, and even justifiable, and are thus retrieved from the consequences to which they would otherwise be liable. Upon the other hand, also, many actions which primarily are allowable by the general terms of the law of nature (being so far in conformity with the expressed purposes of the Creator) become offences under a special law or regulation subsequently imposed.

Hence arises the distinction between civil liberty and natural liberty. From the principle of law spring two things, obligation upon the one hand, permission or liberty upon the other. Liberty, again, is either absolute or restricted. Cicero thus defines absolute liberty: *Libertati proprium est sic vivere ut lubes.* Restricted liberty is that which is, by the moral force of law, prohibited. In a community only can the latter exist; it is the subject of interdiction, but not of command.

Obligation, upon the other hand, is the subject of command, and is therefore the converse of liberty. The one is imposed by law; the other is conferred by nature. So nature is in some sense superior to law; because the one confers the privilege of doing right, the other restrains the power to do wrong. But nature must be taken in its proper sense, and not in its abuse. By nature is to be understood those properties with which man is endowed, that he may fulfil the purposes of his creation, which are the happiness of man, and the honour of his Maker. Again, it may be observed, that to liberty are referable those actions which become the subject of legislation, while to the laws themselves are referable those obligations by which license is distinguished from liberty. Thus liberty and law are founded upon the same principle, and each has the same object in view. Liberty confers a general right—law prevents the abuse of that right. Hence a moral law can never curtail a natural right. It merely prescribes the mode of its enjoyment. Political liberty (as Paley observes) consists in a man being subject to no restriction that is not counterbalanced by a greater amount of public advantage.

Hence every restriction to natural liberty must be regarded as an evil in itself. In this sentiment archbishop Whately has expressed his concurrence. But to ascertain the extent of a moral obligation, laws must be interpreted by reference to their object and design.

In many cases, what is law for a man under some circumstances, is law for another under the same circumstances. But it does not follow that what is law for one man under certain circumstances, is law for another under all circumstances.

Nor because a thing is lawful for a man under some circumstances, does it follow that the same thing is lawful for a man under all circumstances.

All laws have reference to a pre-existing principle, to the regulation of which they are directed. As all the precepts of Moses manifestly spring from the decalogue, so the commands and the inhibitions of the decalogue have relation to certain principles of right which had previously been bestowed upon mankind. Such ordinances must therefore be regarded in reference to the primary purposes of creation to which they are subservient. Thus the various restrictions contained in the institutions of Moses presuppose the existence of certain privileges. These were, most of them, conferred upon man at the creation, or soon afterwards. For instance, the prohibition against theft, fraud, and violence implies the right of acquisition. That this right was bestowed at the beginning of the world, we have the authority of Scripture for supposing, from the words, "Have dominion over the fish of the sea, over the fowl of the air, and over every living thing that moveth upon the earth. And God said, Behold I have given you every herb bearing seed, which is upon the face of all the earth, and every tree in which is the fruit of a tree yielding seed; to you it shall be for meat." (Gen. i. 28, 29.) Now here is a general right without restriction. The object of laws, which were subsequently imposed to regulate this principle, is manifestly not to abolish the general right, but to secure to each individual the due enjoyment of it.

As the world was made for man, and not man for the world; so if the creation of man was one of the purposes of God, the preservation of his life must necessarily have been intended. So laws against murder imply the sanctity of human life. Thus we find that even before the law was promulgated, the principle of it was implanted in man. Hence the first murderer knew that he had sinned. As the occasions of its infringement multiplied with the growing vice of men, this law was afterwards declared in explicit terms to Noah, (Gen. ix. 5, 6): "And surely your blood of your lives will I require at the hand of man; at the hand of every beast will I require it; at the hand of every man's brother will I require the life of man. Whoso sheddeth man's blood, by man shall his blood be shed."

The object, then, of the laws against murder is to be found in the preservation of life. Thence many acts which indirectly tended to the destruction of life were afterwards included within the operation of those statutes which forbid bloodshed.

But then again, there is another class of laws which has reference to the perpetuation of the human species. The principle upon which they rest is given in the commission to man to be fruitful and multiply. This constituted a general permission under which " men took them wives of all they chose." (Gen. 7.)

To this object, then, as one of the purposes of creation, must be referred those special enactments by which the abuse of this right is restrained; the peace of families being secured in the prohibition of adultery; and the degeneration of the species prevented by the prohibition of incestuous marriages, and such temporary connections as would leave the offspring and the mother without such a provision as the relationship requires, and thus defeat the purpose of the general permission. In the commission to replenish the earth, and to subdue it, is involved the general right of occupancy. Yet this does not authorise one to trespass upon the possessions of another. To restrain such invasions of original right, the subsequent laws against stealing and coveting, and more particularly those relating to boundaries, were imposed. Thus by such restrictions the integrity of the original right is preserved, but not curtailed.

But to treat rather of the permission of the law than of its precepts, is now most apposite to our purpose. First, then, the law of the Hebrews serves to assure us that nothing is enjoined there contrary to the right of nature. Because it must be conceded that the laws of Moses sprang from the same source as the rights of nature, being both dictated by God himself; inasmuch as the Being from whence nature sprang must be the author of the conditions upon which it continues to exist. Nothing could be commanded by the Creator contrary to the principles of the creation, for the principle must have preceded the act of creation. The design must precede the making of the thing, and contemplate the method of its movements. And in the created being, it is the same as with the created thing. The methods of the movements in the one, are the laws of action (or, as some call them, the laws of nature) in the other. Besides, the law of Moses is called, in the Psalms, "pure and right;" and by the apostle Paul, "holy, just, and good."

Now that which is pure and right cannot allow that which is impure and wrong. Consequently, nothing which is absolutely impure and wrong can be permitted by the law of God, either expressly or by implication. So we may safely conclude that what is by the spirit of the New Testament declared to be impure cannot be justified by the letter of the Old.

Permission, when considered with reference to that which has been primarily declared with regard to the express end of our being, consists only in the silence of the law.

It does not however follow, that every action for which no special prohibition can be found is necessarily right in itself; but only that it was not considered by the divine lawgiver as a fit subject for the prohibitions of temporal legislation. Of this the precepts of the New Testament furnish many examples. It must be admitted, then, that silence alone is not an incontestable proof that the legislator approves what he does not forbid. As for example, certain laws concerning divorce were avowedly given by reason of the hardness of men's hearts, rather than by reason of their intrinsic purity, although their ultimate end undoubtedly was to maintain the purity of marriage. Therefore we can only imply from such silence that the lawgiver does not design to employ the means in his power for hindering men from doing such things as he does not specially prohibit. Such, then, being the principles which the Mosaic laws were designed to preserve, we must conclude that whatever was enjoined, so far as concerns the maintenance of virtue and the discouragement of vice, is as much binding upon Christians as upon Jews, if not more so. For a Jew might have justified himself under the law, whilst a Christian can only be justified under the Gospel. Hence arises the right of Christian states to make laws of the same import as those given by Moses, with the exception of such special statutes as have since been abrogated by a change of the circumstances by which they were occasioned. For except where the purpose for which they were ordained has, under divine authority, ceased to require such regulations; or, in other words, where the author of the law has either expressly annulled it, or, by withdrawing from its operation the object for which it was instituted, has by direct implication suffered it to become obsolete; there is no reason why that which the law of Moses established should now be unlawful.

The first rule, therefore, to be observed in the construction of laws, is the consideration of their import and object; for in conformity with this their provisions must be interpreted, in order to ascertain their design.

Secondly, laws are to be reasoned upon by deduction and necessary consequence, but not by comparison or analogy. In other words, while the expressed object of the law is to be regarded, the motives of the lawgiver are not to be questioned. Since under the divine law, in the conduct of men towards each other, that which is lawful is distinguished from that which is unlawful, not by reason of its inconvenience or inconsistence with what imperfect beings assume to be the principles, of justice,—for the principles of justice are the province of, and can only be properly understood by, their author,—but because it is allowed or prohibited by a supreme authority, from which the principles of justice spring. With the acknowledgment of this authority disobedience is incompatible; and without such acknowledgment there can be no obedience. For where a fortuitous accident happens to conform to a principle, it cannot be properly described as an action done in obedience to that principle. For before a man can obey a law which he has by the circumstances of his nature the power of disobeying, he must know what that law is. Hence, in such matters as are the subject of free will, knowledge necessarily precedes obedience. To add, then, to the declared laws, or to give them a new application, (which in effect is the same thing,) by resorting to what appears an analogous principle, is, in the first place, absurd; because, until the reason for a law is ascertained, the analogy cannot be established. And the reason of a law which is of divine institution cannot be ascertained, except so far as its purpose is revealed; and this can only be inferred from its application. Where this occurs, there is no need for the analogy. In the second place, to impose a new obligation is to assume the authority of a divine lawgiver, and to presume an imperfection in such institutions as the innovation affects to improve.

Thirdly. As the whole includes every part, so a restrictive law, imposed upon a class generally, is obviously obligatory upon each member of that class individually; since each member of the class is manifestly within the scope of its operation. So also, where the intention or desire to commit an act is prohibited, the action itself is manifestly unlawful.

In like manner, where an action done without design, by inadvertence or neglect, is declared unlawful, it is *à fortiori* unlawful to do such a thing wilfully. For instance, no express law can be found in the Old Testament which forbids in terms the use of means to procure abortion. Yet if the accidental destruction of an unborn child is declared to be an offence which deserves punishment, how much greater must be the crime when such a thing is done wilfully. "If men strive, and hurt a woman with child, so that her fruit depart from her, and yet no mischief follow, he shall surely be punished, according as the woman's husband will lay upon him, and he shall pay as the judges determine. And if any mischief follow, then thou shalt give life for life." (Exod. xxi. 22, 23.)

The clause with which this statute concludes is sufficient to indicate its purpose, and classes it at once under those laws by which the sanctity of human life is protected.

With some offences the punishment is purely vindictive. This occurs where the injury is not the subject of compensation. It is necessarily the case where the wrong done is incapable of restitution; as for instance, in a case of life lost, for it cannot be restored. Therefore, if punishment be inflicted at all, it must be called a vindictive punishment; being imposed simply to avenge the laws of outraged justice by way of retribution, but not by way of compensation. Yet, it may be here observed, that public wrongs, which admit of no compensation, differ from private obligations, though these in some cases become public wrongs when the compensation fails.

Private obligations are a duty to the subject, and are two fold. In some cases they are satisfied by the discharge of a private right; but in other cases the non-fulfilment of a private obligation becomes a public wrong, being, to the extent of its non-fulfilment, an abridgment of a public right to enjoy the advantages of its fulfilment. Obligation thus arises either out of a contract which requires a return for a benefit received, or the opposite, out of a wrong, which requires a compensation for an injury done. In the first case, both parties ought to be benefitted; in the latter, neither. Because, as soon as the injury ceases to be the subject of compensation, it becomes necessarily the subject of punishment, and falls within the law by which a vindictive penalty is exacted. That which admits of compensation does not necessarily fall within the purposes of a penal law until the power of compensation is lost. Compensation is a matter of arrangement between the parties, preliminary to the last resort for the exaction of justice. In many cases punishment can only be rightly enforced where compensation has failed to satisfy the wrong. For by compensation must be understood, not only the satisfaction of the person seeking it, but the actual restitution of the injury done, which in many cases may affect the public at large as much as the private individual. Under such circumstances, it must be presumed that a vindictive punishment is just and necessary, because it is prescribed by laws whose obligation springs not from convention, but is only to be measured by obedience. In such cases, when the offence itself is pronounced by the law to be a crime, without reference to the motives through which it is committed, it is not allowable to suffer such an offence to escape with impunity. Although the punishment may have been modified in accordance with such conditions, as, under specified circumstances, may have been prescribed by the law which pronounces the crime. Yet it is not lawful to vary these conditions, because, by so doing, a new law is made, involving a new principle of justice. Nor, where the conditions are to be fulfilled by the offender, is it allowable to presume their fulfilment in the face of what the statute has declared to be guilt; any more than it is to abrogate the guilt of the deed done. For it is just as reasonable to declare that evil is good, as to decide that guilt is innocence. Thus, where the same penalty is prescribed to a reasonable and an unreasonable creature, and even to an inanimate thing which is the instrument of the offence, the presumption arises that the guilt of the offence, whereby a general principle of justice is outraged, arises rather by the commission than the motive of the crime. Although, morally speaking, the motive of the offence may add an ingredient to the guilt of the person who perpetrates the crime; yet the absence of the motive cannot atone the guilt which is naturally attached to such an action.

Then, if we find that the crime, although committed without motive or design, is nevertheless visited with the same punishment, it cannot be argued that the want of motive, or the want of reason, from which motive springs, is sufficient to render the offender unaccountable to the temporal punishment prescribed for such an offence, which consists in the act as much as in the action.

Now, the Jewish law prescribed the punishment of death, both to a man and a beast, where either had caused the death of a man. It also prescribed the destruction of the instrument whereby death was occasioned. So that the same law applies to a reasonable and to an unreasonable creature. Whence it is to be inferred, that the want of reason can give no temporal immunity for the offence. To provide an exemption in such cases, arguments founded on humanity are generally resorted to, upon the assumption that the punishment is not deserved by a creature which is not accountable to reason. But this doctrine gives rise to so many difficulties, that it may be well to examine it a little more closely before leaving this part of the subject.

It will be allowed that mercy is a necessary quality of humanity; but mercy is the remission of that which is justly due. Mercy is, then, a comparative action of benevolence, which must be measured by the standard of justice. So, mercy tempered with justice is a virtue; but mercy without justice is a vice. Yet the Mosaic laws, if they be binding at all, are binding because they were dictated by a Being who is supremely good, and the author and exponent of justice itself. Yet, in that which is supremely good, all other virtues or elements of goodness are but the component parts. And with imperfect beings it is impossible to know what goodness itself is. For imperfect beings can only form an approximate idea of that which is supremely good and just, in so far as the elements of that excellence have been partially revealed to them by the author of the thing itself; by whom, also, the faculty of such perception is bestowed, and this more or less perfectly in different individuals. Moreover, every virtue is but relatively good, and, to ascertain its excellence, must be compared to a standard which is perfect in itself. But that which is perfectly good is but imperfectly seen in the distance; and all we know is, that, by obedience to certain rules laid down for our guidance by a perfect Being, we are approaching towards a perfection which it is denied to mortality to attain.

We separate these rules one from another, and are apt to canonize the observance of each as a separate virtue; although, in fact, no virtue can be independent of another or act contrary to it. For virtue, as the very name imports, is not a separate characteristic of excellence, but the very force of goodness from which all excellence springs. Thus mercy and justice are as much a part of goodness as purity or any other virtue. But to constitute perfect goodness, all the elements of good must co-operate evenly together; each independent yet co-ordinate, and tending to the development of the same principle. For of those qualities of excellence which are commonly designated virtues, or the inherent force of that which is in itself intrinsically good, flowing as it were through various channels from one spring, it is manifest that to attribute any regulation wholly to any one of these is to supersede the functions of the rest. Yet these are all but the separate applications of one principle, and it is only when they become separated, and cut off from the fountain-head, that they can do otherwise than act upon the common principle from which they spring. So, then, to take any one of the qualities which constitute goodness, and to attribute to it alone the motive of a regulation which springs from the Author of all goodness, is plainly unreasonable. Therefore it is no more allowable to presume that one of these virtues is to prevail in the application of one law, than it is to presume that one of these virtues prevailed in the construction of another law. Hence to the fountain of justice alone must be attributed the true combination of these qualities. For if the qualities of goodness are to be arbitrarily selected in their application, it will be found that there is hardly a command in the decalogue which cannot, upon one pretence or another, at least in the punishment prescribed to its infringement, be proved unjust, and thence of no obligation.

Similar objections are applicable to that doctrine which makes the obligation of laws to depend upon any of the consequences of goodness, or that which is right in itself. As for instance, to make their obligation to consist in their utility.

The utility of law may properly be said to consist in its recognition of the grand principles of right and justice. Utility is not so much the object, as the consequence, of a good law. It must be regarded either in reference to the interests of individuals, or to the interests of communities. It is a term which may have relation either to private or to public advantage. Then arises the question, in what sense is the word utility to be taken? It is manifest that private interests may be at variance with public advantage. So again, the public interests of one state may be at variance with the general interests of other communities. Therefore, in such a case, what is the public utility of one may very possibly tend to the disadvantage of others. But states and communities make laws for themselves and not for others. A state framing a law in conformity with public utility, has regard only to the advantages of its own community. But it does not necessarily follow that because a law is useful to one state, it would therefore confer benefits upon all whom it might directly or indirectly affect. We may suppose a community to live by the spoil of its neighbours. But can it be said that because the laws by which a society of pirates is regulated are of advantage to that society, and therefore, as regards the purpose and the objects for which it is imposed, of public utility, that thence such laws are founded upon a principle which can impart to them universal validity?

Yet, as men are said to be members one of another, so must states, or societies of men, have relative obligations. Then if it is said that the obligation of a law depends upon its utility, what is meant by this expression? If it refers to a state, is the advantage of the individual to be regarded in preference to that of the majority? If it refer to a number of communities, is the advantage of one to be regarded to the prejudice of the rest? If not, the sense in which the word utility is used is restricted to the objects it tends to benefit, without regard to its effect upon others. But if it is conceded that in a particular society public morality is of greater utility than private advantage, how can it be denied that among many communities the conformity of all to some general principle of right and justice is of greater utility than the private advantage of a single state? But if a state, in framing its laws, is to have regard to the interests of others, it must have reference to considerations external to itself, which do not necessarily fall within the limits of its own advantage. Yet, if this is admitted, to what standard is it to conform, in order to benefit itself without injury to others, unless it has regard to some principle of universal right which is the common inheritance of all?

Now, virtue and vice are relative terms, having reference to that standard of right, by which alone they can be judged. But, inasmuch as this standard of right emanates from the Author of all right, who, we are told, searches the hearts, we must conclude that the vice or virtue of an action depends rather upon its motive than its tendency. For it is not the action, but the agent, which is the subject of a standard of right that judges the motives only; and this with a reference to a future state of rewards and punishments, in the determination of which we have reason to suppose the motives by which agents are actuated, are weighed. But how can we suppose that an inanimate and insensate action—a mere device to express the doings of a man right or wrong, good or bad—can be the subject of a judgment in accordance with principles of right, when it is incapable of being the subject of either reward or punishment? Now we would ask, how can a (so called) virtuous action become vicious, because the design of the agent is vicious? If the action be not virtuous in itself, it cannot be called a virtuous action. Yet if the virtue or vice of an action depend upon the design of the agent, we must conclude that no action in itself is properly either virtuous or vicious; because virtue and vice are not the properties of an action, but are qualities which distinguish the design of him by whom the action is done. Consequently "the virtue or vice of an action," even in its abstract sense, *cannot* "be estimated by its tendency." (See Paley's Moral Phil., Whately's Ed., p. 80.)

If whatever is expedient is right, whatever is right is expedient. Now surely the word expedient must be understood in its general acceptation, as something good for a particular purpose or of advantage upon a particular occasion. If it be good for every purpose and upon all occasions, the thing signified deserves a less restricted term than expedient, which indicates only a particular property. It may then be called good, instead of being confined to such a definition as expedient, which at best is only a good quality, or a quality of goodness, and often the contrary. For to escape the difficulty by saying, you mean by "expedient" that which is universally expedient, is to say you mean to give to the word "expedient" an enlarged sense which its meaning is incapable of embracing. Then, in fact, instead of expedient, you mean what is universally good. But right and goodness spring from the same author, and are themselves the attributes of a perfect being, by whom alone such qualities can be rightly estimated. For no man can pretend to know of himself what is right or good, because he has not in himself the means of ascertaining this. But he may know what has been declared to be right and good; and he knows it to be right and good only because if has been declared so by its author. Hence good and right must be regarded as qualities of divine origin, and not things of convenience, utility, or expedience. But if the secret of their excellence is yet hid from men, how can we declare their purpose, or even their tendency, except from casual experience? If advantage generally attends their observance, it does not therefore follow as a necessary consequence. For it cannot be denied that the author of goodness is the author and director of all things; and therefore it is impossible to prove that the author of goodness may not bestow advantages upon obedience to a rule, which the rule itself could not confer.

But if each seek its own, and if utility is to be measured by its immediate advantages, its standard of right is peculiar to itself. Thus it denies the obligation of that principle of justice which is not only the common source of all rights, but regulates the limits of their enjoyment. Whence we conclude, that obedience to some universal principle of right is followed by utility in its most comprehensive sense; inasmuch as it considers the general advantage of all, and never suffers private interests to usurp the place of public morality. But if utility alone is the principle upon which a law is founded, it is not necessarily framed in accordance with the principles of right and justice, any more than that private advantage is necessarily consistent with public morality.

Utility is a property accommodated to the exigencies of some particular occasion or circumstances, without necessarily implying obedience to that which is right in itself. It affects particular actions, without necessarily being an application of a general principle. Laws bounded by utility establish only an artificial and restricted standard of right. Hence it is that laws founded on the principle of obedience to that which is right in itself, have a great advantage over those which adopt by accident a principle, the obligation of which they do not recognise. The one are rules of morality. The other are but rules of convenience. Thus it is that good laws are so powerful an instrument of public education, teaching not only what acts convenience commands us to abstain from, but what actions are vicious in themselves, and having thus a tendency to evil, detrimental to the public good.

Yet we are told that "it is the utility of any moral rule which constitutes the obligation of it." (Paley's Moral Phil. pp. 80, 81. Whately's Edition.) This we deny. Because utility is the general consequence of a moral rule, it by no means follows that it is the sole object of it. For if utility is alone its object, it is simply a rule of convenience, and not a rule of morality. The morality of a rule consists in its conformity to some principle which is good in itself, without reference to its temporal consequences. The obligation of a moral rule consists in its conformity to the power which imposes it. If no power imposes it, it ceases to be a rule, and becomes a matter of convenience. A man may succeed in breaking a moral rule, and yet benefit by its general utility, because its observance protects him from the injury he has done to another. For instance, in a large community, the breach of a moral rule would only affect its utility in a slight degree. In a smaller community the ill consequences would be more palpable. In a community consisting of only two persons, it is evident that the utility of the moral rule would be at an end as soon as it was broken by either party, and therefore its obligation would cease. We must therefore conclude that the utility of a moral rule depends rather upon its observance than its right. Its obligation must be sought for elsewhere. The obligation of a moral rule depends upon the duty of obedience to the power that imposes it, rather than to the consequences which attend that obedience.

Again, it has been maintained, by Paley and others,

that actions are to be estimated by their tendency; that, in the abstract, actions are right or wrong according to their tendency; but that the agent is virtuous or vicious, according to his design; and that whatever is expedient is right.

But upon the other hand, expedience cannot be said to be of divine origin. It is a term only applicable to human affairs. So likewise it is only of human significance, inasmuch as it has relation only to particular purposes, occasions, or circumstances. Hence it varies with purposes, occasions, and circumstances. Yet right does not. Human reason being clouded and imperfect, men's views differ as to what is expedient. So the same man's view changes from time to time with the occasion. Besides, when men make a law, they make it because they think it expedient for a particular purpose, or perhaps for a general design. It may so happen that, in framing the law, they are guided by principles of right; and in so far, what was designed to be expedient may prove to be right. Nevertheless, if the authors of the expedient are imperfect and liable to error, the expedient itself may be imperfect. Therefore it cannot truly be said that whatever is expedient is right. In short, laws founded simply upon utility or expedience are founded rather upon the rules of convenience than the principles of right. What is truly right must be right in itself, and have reference to a perfect standard. Thence it becomes necessary to consider how far the utility or expedience of a law is to determine its authority. For one man's convenience may be another man's ruin. And who is to determine the obligation of a law, unless its authority depends upon some power superior to all that are the subject of it?

The conclusions by which men have been led to assume that it is the utility or expedience of a rule alone which constitutes the obligation of it, rest probably upon the result of some analogical process of reasoning; as, that good laws are expedient, or are attended by utility, and therefore such as are expedient and attended with utility must be good laws. This amounts to no more than an inference that, because a good law happens to be expedient, therefore a law which happens to be expedient must be founded upon the principle of goodness and right, and thence derive its authority. Such a mode of argument assumes that the object of laws is merely convenience. It therefore assumes that their purpose is only temporary. This amounts to a denial that laws ought to be founded upon a principle of right and justice, which is always the same. But the legitimate use of reasoning upon laws by analogy deserves closer examination, as it is applied not only to explain the authority of laws, but to enforce their application.

An argument by analogy amounts to this: It is a process of reasoning whereby it is shown that, because a law provided for one particular object, having certain characteristics (as for instance, when the object of the prohibition is removed so many degrees in relationship from a common stock), therefore every object having the same peculiarities falls under the same category. This mode of reasoning will lead to a legitimate conclusion where the prohibition is predicated of a class. But where a certain principle is established, as, for instance, the multiplication of the human race, and certain exceptions are made to this general principle, whereby the degrees of relationship or connexion within which marriages may be contracted are regulated in respect to males,—as, that two males in the same degree may not become the husbands of the same female,—it does not follow that two females in the same degree may not become the wives of the same male. For the analogy is imperfect, because it assumes that the degree of relationship of the parties is the only consideration in the mind of the legislator by whom the prohibition was devised, and therefore the only reason for the prohibition. If the law were stated generally, that persons within certain degrees of kindred were disqualified from forming such unions, then the case of a male and female are equivalent, and the analogy is perfect. But where the law is specifically declared, prohibiting marriages between certain persons, it does not follow that, because between these specified persons a certain degree of relationship happens to exist, therefore the prohibition is generally applicable to all between whom the same degree of relationship may be found. Because this assumes that the lawgiver ought to have made a general law where he saw fit to make only a special one. This, moreover, involves a question of his right to make laws at all; upon which principle the obligation of obedience entirely depends. Such a method of interpretation also implies not only a right to infer the motives by which the author of the law was guided in the expression of his will, but also a right to question the accuracy of the terms in which that expression is declared.

Hence, when a general law or license is followed by a special limitation, no inferential prohibition can fairly be added to such limitation. Restrictions of a general principle must be construed strictly.

And where the limitation is not absolute, but conditional, the force of such a caution is the more apparent.

As for example, there is no general law whereby a marriage with two sisters is forbidden, but only a conditional one, in which the period of the limitation, and the reason for it, are both clearly expressed. Levit. xviii. 18: "Neither shalt thou take a wife to her sister, to vex her, to uncover her nakedness, beside the other in her lifetime." So that, where neither the reason for it nor the time of the condition intervenes, the limitation ceases to operate.

So, again: when by the divine law God regulates the manner of a thing, or makes some other regulation with regard to that thing, which necessarily supposes it permitted, although the thing permitted be a modification of a general principle before expressed, yet it cannot be denied that such a modification has the divine sanction to the extent of its terms; such modifications being mercifully accommodated to the infirmities of man. Of this we have an example when we find the legislator directing the manner, the conditions, and the causes of divorces; thus regulating certain cases which suppose such a permission. But still this law is the subject of a conditional limitation. It is the converse of the former case, in which the condition precedes the limitation. Here the limitation depends upon the condition. It is a limitation of the general law under which marriage is an indissoluble bond. But the limitation is to prevail only under certain specified circumstances; and provides a dispensation only for the innocent party; forbidding the marriage of a wife, if guilty of adultery, not only with the adulterer, but with any other person, at least during the lifetime of her husband. Therefore, as divorces are allowed only by way of a conditional limitation to a general law, the conditions of such a limitation are to be construed strictly. The divorce itself is not to be regarded as a general right, but rather as an exception to a general principle.

A general law, then, must be held to prevail, except so far as it is in terms restricted by a subsequent limitation.

The laws of Moses, however, relate only to the outward conduct of men in their social capacity. The permissions, therefore, and the prohibitions, are immediately the subject of temporal punishment. For the purposes of regulating the outward conduct of men, they still prevail; and are the standard by which all human laws are to be measured, except so far as their obligation has been enlarged or abrogated by the declarations of Christ himself in the New Testament. Here the spirit of the law is more clearly developed; yet its terms are no way enlarged. In the New Testament its application is more closely referred to the motive than to the act; so that even a good deed can never justify a bad will. And except so far as the moral laws of the Old Testament are altered and explained by the declarations of the New, their import and obligation remain unimpaired. Indeed, St. Paul enumerates all the moral laws as obligatory upon Christians in the thirteenth chapter of the Romans, as we have shown at page 54.

The foregoing considerations will serve to convince us, not only how strictly the divine laws must be construed in their application, but also how careful we should be so to apply them as not to create a new law, which is not distinctly authorised by the Mosaic code.

The spirit of this injunction was, according to Diodorus Siculus, and Plato in Timæum, strictly followed by the Egyptians, with whom, we are told, a new law was regarded as an unheard-of miracle. Their ancient laws were preserved with the highest veneration. Whatever may have been their origin, their sanctity was so much regarded, that any attempt to introduce a new custom into the country was treated as an act of profanation, and exposed the offender to the penalties of a public crime. "Hence," says Plato, "all things there ran in the old channel;" and consequently no nation ever retained their laws and customs longer than the Egyptians. In the reverence in which the Egyptians held their ancient institutions, the testimony of Herodotus concurs.

With the Greeks, also, the introduction of any new law was guarded with many stringent regulations, to prevent the subversion of the principles of the constitution.

Such was the severity of the Locrians upon this point, that whoever proposed the enactment of a new law, or the abrogation of an old one, was obliged to come into the assembly with a halter about his neck, and in that habit give his reasons for the proposed alterations. If these were judged insufficient, he was immediately hanged. The Athenians, though not quite so rigid, watched any change with great jealousy. Those who preferred any laws contrary to the national institutions were adjudged infamous, which deprived them of their municipal rights, and exposed them to banishment. Hence arose the distinction between the θεσμοι and the νομοι. The θεσμος was the law directing how laws (νομοι) were to be made, and prescribed the principles of legislation. The νομοι were the application of those principles.

## CHAPTER V.

### ON THE INFLUENCE OF THE ROMAN LAWS, THE ANCIENT LAWS OF ENGLAND.

The civil institutions of modern Europe sprang out of the ruins of the Roman Empire. The principles of their laws are borrowed from the Roman laws, and, in many instances, the terms in which they are expressed are identical. This is especially to be remarked amongst such nations as those over which the Romans had sometime established permanent conquests; for it was their invariable policy to assimilate the organization of their foreign settlements as far as possible to their own institutions. By the introduction of their own laws and customs, they taught the usages of barbarism to conform to their superiority.

According to Neibuhr (vol. 2, p. 316), the laws of the Decemviri continued, down to the time of the Emperors, to be the basis of all civil and penal jurisprudence. That the twelve tables were founded upon the Grecian system of jurisprudence, we have elsewhere endeavoured to show. Unfortunately, the peculiar character of these tables is lost, and little information is conveyed by the scanty fragments that have accidentally been preserved. Livy, however, expressly declares that the twelve tables were the fountain head of all law, public and private—fons omnis publici privatique juris. Cicero, to the same effect, repeatedly expresses his veneration for the laws of the twelve tables, as containing the principles of all jurisprudence. Such reverence, indeed, does he profess for their authority, that, fond as he was of philosophy, he does not hesitate to tell us, he prefers them to all the writings of the philosophers. Savigny, in his History of the Roman Laws, confirms Neibuhr's view, that the twelve tables were the materials out of which the codes of the later Emperors were constructed. Yet, although the twelve tables were undoubtedly the foundation of the civil law of Rome, their development was gradual, until at length they were reduced to a regular system of jurisprudence, into which the intermediate edicts and decrees of the Emperors were from time to time embodied. The constitutions of the Emperors thence became, to some extent, a new source of law. During a long period these were, for the most part, rescripts or explanations declaratory of the existing law, given in answer to questions from magistrates or private persons, and resembling in substance the responsa of the jurists, though of greater authority.

Under Constantine, however, legislation assumed a new character. From that time, the edicts or new ordinances became more frequent, and produced often very important changes; while, at the same time, the acknowledgment of Christianity must necessarily have invaded many national characteristics, and superseded many of the corruptions of paganism. Nevertheless, says Savigny, the twelve tables were the basis of the whole, and all later changes may be referred to them, either as additions or modifications. Indeed, he says, "the jurists may be considered as the true guardians and protectors of the strictness and distinguishing features of the old law." Thence, therefore, having shown the sources of the foundations upon which the civil laws of Rome rested, it will only be necessary to recognise such peculiarities as accord with them in the legislative systems of which Rome was the parent, in order to establish their origin. This design perhaps may be properly premised by a cursory glance at the influence of the Roman laws over Europe. For, having ascertained how far this system extended, it will be a task comparatively easy, to bring into comparison such laws of those various nations in which Roman institutions took root, as furnish the best examples of the source from which they were originally derived.

Under the Kings, the laws of Rome were few and simple. After the abolition of the regal power, the commonwealth retained these laws for some time. They were afterwards expressly abolished by the Tribunitian law. From this period, an ill-defined and uncertain sort of right seems to have prevailed until the twelve tables were compiled by the Decemviri. These constitutions were composed chiefly from the laws of Athens. Deputies were sent into the principal cities of Greece, to collect such laws as they should judge the wisest and best adapted to a republican form of government. Although even the subject of the twelve tables in some measure rests rather upon conjecture than absolute proof, yet such of their provisions as have been preserved, are well worth a careful study, because they were the foundation of the great code of laws known in later times by the name of the Roman or Civil Law. This still prevails to a great extent in Italy, Germany, and other parts of Europe.

If, then, the twelve tables be the foundation of the codes promulgated by the later emperors, such of their provisions as bear the marks of a Greek original must be regarded as relics of the twelve tables, and thus furnish another link in our argument, if they be in their turn compared with those of Moses.

The Romans penetrated into Germany under Cæsar and Augustus. The introduction of Roman establishments followed the progress of their arms. Until the close of the fifth century, the influence of Rome continued to prevail. Yet its power fluctuated with the resistance which it encountered. The stubborn spirit of the Germans by turns repelled and yielded to its encroachments, until the final overthrow of the Roman empire. During this period the institutions of those countries which the Romans had subjugated were, without doubt, largely tinctured with the spirit of their laws. Before the time at which they threw off the yoke of their former conquerors, the Germans were brought into constant intercourse with the refinements of Roman civilization. Their condition, their manners, and their laws had already in some degree submitted to its influence. Afterwards the superiority of the Roman laws was voluntarily recognised. In fact, the Roman laws were absorbed into the systems to which they nominally gave place.

Both Savigny and M. Guizot have refuted the erroneous opinion, advanced by many writers of repute, that the Roman law had fallen with the Empire, to be revived, in the twelfth century, by the discovery of a copy of the Pandects at Amalfi. Indeed, the first two volumes of M. de Savigny's History of the Roman Law are devoted to the investigation of this subject. He traces and examines many examples of the Roman law to show, not only that it was preserved, but that it widely prevailed, between the fall of the Empire and the twelfth century. Not only do the barbaric laws everywhere make mention of the Roman laws, but there is scarcely a document of this period which does not, directly or indirectly, attest their observance. A large proportion of their legislative provisions concern facts which could not have arisen until after these nations were established upon Roman soil.

The barbaric laws of the Middle Ages were drawn up soon after the invasion of the Roman empire. They are to be distinguished as the laws of the Visigoths, the laws of the Burgundians, and the Salic laws. The laws of the two former tribes are more Roman than barbarian. The ruder portions of the Salic laws are less so. The most ancient part of the law of the Visigoths belonged to the last half of the fifth century. The Salic law, the elements of which were carried into Gaul by the Franks, when they occupied that country, is by some supposed to have been written under Clovis, but the first digest of it is of a much later date. Into this, and the digests which succeeded it, the Roman law is avowedly imported.

The law of the Burgundians dates from the year 517. The customs of the Goths were first reduced to writing, by king Euric, in the year 506. His successor, Alaric II., caused the laws of his Roman subjects to be collected in a new form. Yet there can be no doubt that the German tribes retained many of their ancient customs. Their laws describe, in many particulars, a social state anterior to the invasion. After this, the Germanic society underwent changes as great as the change between subjugation and dominion.

The preface to one of the manuscripts of Alaric's collection, mentioned by M. Guizot, shows how far the Roman laws were embodied in this system. We give an extract:—

"In this volume are contained the laws and decisions of equity, selected from the Theodosian code and other books, and explained, as has been ordered by king Alaric; the illustrious Count Goiaric presiding at this work. With the aid of God, occupied with the interests of our people, we have corrected, after mature deliberation, all that seemed iniquitous in the laws; in such manner that, by the labour of the priests and other noblemen, all obscurity in the Roman and in our own ancient law is dissipated, and a greater clearness is spread over it, to the end that nothing may remain ambiguous and offer a subject for lengthened controversy.

"It is, therefore, expedient that thou take heed that in thy jurisdiction no other form or law be alleged or admitted. If perchance such a thing should happen, it will be at the peril of thy head or the expense of thy fortune."

This preface contains all we know concerning the history of this code. The collection of Alaric contains,—1. The Theodosian code; 2, the books of the civil law of the emperor Theodosius and others; 3, the institutes of Gaius; 4, five books of Paul the jurisconsult, entitled "Receptæ Sententiæ;" 6, the Hermoginian code; 7, a passage from the work of Papinian, entitled "Liber Responsorum." These formed the text of the law, followed by an interpretation for their application; as for instance "that which was formerly done by the prætor shall now be executed by the judge of the land." (Guiz. vi. p. 453.)

The editions or digests of the Salic law are various. Most of them are designated under titles in accordance with the remoteness of their antiquity. To several of them is appended a kind of preface, in which the history of the Salic law is related. The most comprehensive of these is set forth by M. Guizot. It declares "that the Salic law was dictated by the chiefs of the Franks whilst yet under a barbarous belief, seeking the key of knowledge by the inspiration of God, desiring justice and observing piety according to the nature of its qualities, lately converted to the Catholic faith, and free from heresy." This shows what influence the Christianity of the period exercised over its compilation.

It proceeds:—"Concerning the inventors of laws and their order. Moses was the first who expounded in sacred letters the divine laws to the Hebrew nation; King Phoroneus gave laws to the Greeks; Mercury to the Egyptians; Numa Pompilius to the Romans. Afterwards, because this factious people would not tolerate its magistrates, it created decemvirs to write laws, and these placed upon twelve tables the laws of Solon, translated into Latin.... Little by little the ancient laws fell into disuse through age and neglect; but although they were no longer used, it was *necessary that they should be known*. The new laws began to count from Constantine and his successors.... Afterwards, each nation selected, according to its customs, the laws which were suited to it, for a long custom passes into law. Law is a written constitution. Custom is a usage founded upon antiquity, or unwritten law. . . .

"Theodoric, king of the Franks, when he was at Châlons, selected the wise men of his kingdom, and those who were learned in ancient laws, to write the laws of the Franks, of the Allemanni, of the Boii, and of all nations which were under his power according to the customs of each. He added what was necessary thereto, and took away what was improper, and amended according to the laws of the Christians that which was according to the ancient pagan customs." "And of that which king Theodoric was unable to change on account of the great antiquity of pagan customs, king Childebert began the correction, which was finished by king Chlotaire. The glorious king Dagobert renewed all these things. He caused to be transcribed, with ameliorations, the *ancient laws*, and gave them written to each nation." The Salic law, in many respects, followed exactly the words of the Latin text; as for example, "According to the ancient law, whoever disinterred or stripped a dead and buried body was banished," &c.

M. Wiarda is of opinion that all the barbaric laws were first reduced to writing in the Latin tongue, and that the Salic law was written in the seventh century.

It seems evident, from the character of their law, that it belongs to a period at which the Franks had for a long time lived amidst a Roman population. It constantly mentions the Romans as an important part of the community. We perceive, also, that the influence of Christianity had already marked many of its provisions.

That it was not an original piece of legislation, but an adoption of the Roman law, is evident from its reference to the decisions of the Roman law. Thus: "If any one strips a dead person before he is placed in the earth, let him be condemned to pay 1800 deniers, which make 45 sous; and according to another decision, 2500 deniers, which make $62\frac{1}{2}$ sous." "According to another decision," is exactly the language which would be found in a collection of decrees.

The crimes taken cognizance of by the Salic law are, almost all of them, classed under two heads—robbery, and violence against the person. Of 343 articles in the penal law, 150 have reference to cases of robbery; and of these 74 assign punishment for the stealing of animals: namely,—20 to pig stealing, 16 to horse stealing, 13 to stealing bulls, cows, and oxen, 7 to sheep and goat stealing, 4 to dog stealing, 7 to bird stealing, 7 to bee stealing. The last is a law particularly conspicuous both in the Greek and Roman codes. Under these heads the law enters into the most minute details. The crime and the punishment vary according to the age and sex of the thief, the number of animals stolen, the place and time of the robbery, &c. Cases of violence against the person furnish matter for 113 articles; of which 30 relate to mutilation in every possible shape, 24 to violence against women. The punishments against freedmen are remarkable for their mildness. In all cases, the vengeance of the offended person might be averted by composition. There are but few cases in which the punishment of death was inflicted, and from this the criminal could always redeem himself. There were no corporal punishments except as against slaves, and no imprisonment.

Hence we may perceive, that Christianity had already mitigated the rigour of the old *lex talionis*.

In the same way it will be found that other barbaric institutions of this period betray a combination of Roman laws with German customs. This is the case with the laws of the Ripuarians, the Burgundians, and the Visigoths.

When the German tribes founded kingdoms in countries which were formerly subject to the power of Rome, both races lived together preserving their separate customs and laws. From this state of society arose that condition of civil rights under which, in the middle ages, a distinction arose between personal laws and territorial laws. In modern times, we assume that the law to which an individual owes obedience is that of the country where he is domiciled. In the middle ages, however, it was otherwise. In the same country, and even in the same town, a Lombardian lived under the Lombardic law, and a Roman under the civil law.

The Romans, indeed, had set the example of such indulgence, by permitting conquered races to retain their customs, whilst they themselves observed their own institutions. The same distinction of laws was generally maintained by the different races of Germans when they in their turn became conquerors. The Frank, the Burgundian, and the Goth resided in the same place, each under his own law.

The Ripuarian law much resembled the Salic. In fact, the Ripuarian Franks and the Salic Franks were branches of the same family, deriving their names respectively from the rivers on which they dwelt—the Yssel and the Rhine.

Compurgation, or proof by the oaths of persons who were not, properly speaking, witnesses, held a more prominent place in the Ripuarian than in the Salic system.

So also trial by judicial combat, to decide the guilt or innocence of the accused, was a custom more frequently resorted to under the Ripuarian than under the Salic law.

In the construction of the Ripuarian law, the provisions of the Roman code are openly adopted. Thus, in regulating the formula of enfranchisement, it says,—

"We desire that every Ripuarian Frank or freed-man, who, for the good of his soul, or for a sum, wishes to free his slave, in *the forms indicated by the Roman law,* present himself at the church before the priests, deacons, and all the clergy and people."

Again; it recognizes more fully than the Salic the influence of the Church and the royal authority. This is evident from the following statutes:—

"If any man carry off by violence anything belonging to one of the king's men, or to any one attached to the Church, he shall pay a composition treble what he would have had to pay had the crime been committed against any other Ripuarian.

"If the crime be committed by any one attached to the Church, or to one of the king's domains, he shall pay half the composition which another Frank would have paid. In case of denial, he must appear with thirty-six compurgators.

"A man attached to the domains of the king, Roman or freedman, cannot be the object of a capital accusation.

"Slaves belonging to the king or the Church do not plead by means of defender; but they defend themselves, and are allowed to justify themselves by oath, without being obliged to answer the summonses which may be addressed to them.

"If any one shall attempt to overthrow a royal charter without being able to produce another repealing the first, he shall answer this attempt with his life.

"Whoever shall commit treason towards the king shall forfeit his life, and all his goods shall be confiscated."

The compilation of the law of the Burgundians is attributed to the reign of king Gondebald, between the years 468 and 523, at which period his successor, Sigismond, added a supplement. Although the Burgundian laws contain many relics of barbarism, which are not to be found in the Salic or Ripuarian codes, yet, upon the other hand, the procedure of the Roman law concerning civil rights is introduced with a precision which bespeaks a less rude state of society. Some laws, indeed, concerning dowries and wills, are almost word for word in accordance with the provisions of the Theodosian code.

The laws of the Visigoths, when they were driven into Spain at the commencement of the sixth century, were, properly speaking, composed of two codes; the one comprising their native customs, the other being founded upon the Roman laws. These were, soon afterwards, fused into one law. The character of its provisions are such as to prove it to a great extent to have been the work of the clergy, under whose hands the ruder customs of antiquity were reduced to something like a political system, accommodated to feudal tenures, and regulated by the more humane interpretations of the Roman law.

Thus, undoubtedly, a great part of the law of Europe may be directly traced to the Roman law. But still there remains a considerable proportion for which the source is generally sought in the growth of barbaric customs. For want of a better origin, that portion which is the least artificial is often designated without scruple as the offspring of pure barbarism. But upon a closer examination of the characteristics of these customary obligations, they will be found to preserve a comprehensive simplicity, (though developed in various forms and differently applied, in conformity with local manners,) such as may be easily reconciled to some general principles, which are distinctly enunciated in the Hebrew laws, and were apparently understood by those who copied them. For although customs may vary with the habits of a people, yet the various applications of some general system of justice may be most properly considered, not as the spontaneous growth of the soil on which they are found, but as emanating from some principle of justice, the force of which is universally felt, although the means by which it gained its influence may not be so easily traced.

It is not, therefore, difficult to perceive the influence which the Roman laws must have exercised over a great part of Europe, where many of their leading characteristics may still be discovered. We have already seen how far, during the middle ages, the introduction of Roman institutions retrieved from barbarism the laws of France, of Germany, of Spain, and of Italy. Indeed, the old Roman civil law is to this day the basis of most systems of jurisprudence throughout Europe. As far as local customs could be conformed to institutions which grew up with the prosperity of an empire whose ambition and power had placed it beyond the reach of any influence that did not accord with its national habits, the constitutional systems of European states are conformed to the principles of the Roman laws. The genius of Roman jurisprudence accommodated its use to barbarous manners. Its exquisite construction made all who fell within its reach responsible for its observance.

The civil codes of modern Europe best attest the prevailing genius of Roman civilization. These systems, however, were partly imposed and partly adopted. The Roman laws possessed this peculiar advantage. The principles upon which they were founded, were adapted to the rudest state of society; the methods by which they were applied, were adapted to the highest state of civilization. Hence it is that we find that the milder spirit of southern Europe conformed its local customs to the Roman system; the more stubborn spirit of the North incorporated Roman usages into its national traditions. Thus it is that in England, although the Roman law was never the law of the land, yet the common law has undoubtedly borrowed much from the civil law, and embodied many of its principles and maxims.

The truth of this observation is the more apparent in such maxims of our law as have reference to a state of circumstances which could hardly have existed in a rude state of society. But when the increase of civilization, and the consequent distribution of wealth, gave rise to a variety of contracts and indirect obligations, we find that the maxims of the Roman law are constantly resorted to for their determination. This probably arose from the absence of any other judicial system sufficiently comprehensive to be applicable to such a state of things.

The Romans occupied this country for a period of

between three and four centuries. They brought their laws with them, and did their utmost to cherish their growth in a new soil. Thus the manners of the English must have been more or less influenced by the prevailing institutions of the Roman empire. It is hardly to be doubted that by degrees, and by common use, the spirit of the Roman laws invaded the customs of our ruder forefathers.

Sir John Fortescue, who writes with the utmost jealousy of Roman laws, acknowledges that in many points the laws of England and the civil laws agree. Where they differ, he says, in his advice to the young king, the most worthy are to be preferred. But he takes care to add, by way of qualification, that the customs of England are the best. Amongst these, he justly remarks, that the trial by jury is superior to any method of judicial investigation provided by the Roman laws. He attributes the derivation of our laws to three sources — statutes, customs, and the law of nature. In neither of which, however, does he allow the Roman laws a place.

Upon this point Lord Holt is more candid. Differing in this respect from Blackstone, he assures us that, "Inasmuch as the laws of all nations are doubtless raised out of the ruins of the civil law, as all governments are sprung out of the ruins of the Roman empire, it must be owned that the principles of our law are borrowed from the civil law, and therefore grounded upon the same reason in many things."

Upon the intimate connection between our own laws and the Roman code, Sir J. Mackintosh expresses his concurrence with the sentiments of Lord Holt; "whose name," he says, "can never be pronounced without veneration as long as wisdom and integrity are revered amongst men."

Sir Matthew Hale, who was as great an enemy to the Roman laws as he was to the Romish religion, is forced to admit, in his History of the Common Law, that "The growth of Christianity in this kingdom, and the reception of learned men from other parts, especially from Rome, and the credit that they obtained here, might reasonably induce some new laws, and antiquate or abrogate some old ones that seemed less consistent with Christian doctrines. And by this means not only some of the judicial laws of the Jews, but also some points relating to or bordering upon or derived from the canon or civil laws; as may be seen in the laws of those ancient kings, Alfred, Ina, and Canute."

These laws of the ancient kings, as will be seen from their provisions, were manifestly compiled by the clergy. The method of their construction is remarkable. The first part of these codes consists in the definition of ecclesiastical duties and offences; the second part relates to matters secular. This arrangement distinguishes all the Anglo-Saxon codes. Such were the materials out of which the laws of Edward the Confessor were framed. These are somewhat more full and perfect than the earlier laws, and better accommodated to an improved state of civilization. "So," says Sir Matthew Hale, "they were such whereof the English were always very jealous, as being the great rule and standard of their rights and liberties."

The laws of William the Conqueror consisted, in a great measure, of the repetition of the laws of Edward the Confessor. With the assent of his parliament,

William added some new laws respecting tenures and the preservation of public peace. Some Norman peculiarities are also introduced; but these appear to be rather the Norman definitions of local customs than the introduction of foreign institutions, the laws themselves being written in Norman-French. They will be found substantially to coincide with the provisions of the earlier laws of Alfred, Ethelred, and Canute, enforced only by a new authority.

The important place in the English constitution which was filled by the Anglo-Saxon laws, is sufficiently shown by the circumstances under which they were restored and confirmed at the time of the Conquest.

William the Conqueror solemnly swore upon the Holy Evangelists, at Berkhamstead, that the laws of his predecessors, and especially those of Edward the Confessor, should be inviolably observed. (Hale's History of the Com. Law.) Matthew Paris, in his life of Frederick, abbot of St. Albans, mentions that that prelate administered the oaths to the King upon this occasion :—" Pro bono pacis apud Berkhamstead juravit super animas reliquias sancti Albani tactisque sacro sanctis Evangeliis (ministrante juramento abbate Frederico), ut bonas et approbatas antiquas regni leges quas sancti et pii Angliæ reges ejus antecessores, et maximè rex Edwardus, statuit inviolabiliter observaret."

But other proofs are not wanting. History furnishes abundant evidence that the sanction of parliament was required for the confirmation of any laws introduced at this period. Although, by the oath of Berkhamstead, the ancient laws of England were thus confirmed, yet in this stormy and unsettled period these Anglo-Saxon laws appear to have fallen into some confusion, if not to have lost their authority. For we are told by Hoveden, that, in the fourth year of his reign, William summoned twelve men out of every county to ascertain precisely what were the laws of Edward the Confessor. This circumstance is worthy of remark, because it shows not only an acknowledgment on the part of the Conqueror of the obligations of his oath, but it shows also how jealously its fulfilment was regarded.

Hoveden mentions several of those ancient laws which were then approved and confirmed by the king and the parliament, or *commune concilium*. But the terms in which he describes the re-establishment of the Anglo-Saxon institutions are so explicit, as to set at rest any question upon this point. From his account it appears, that, on the subject of legislation, a constitutional principle of no small importance was recognized by the Conqueror—namely, the obligation of observing the ancient laws of the kingdom, and the necessity of obtaining the sanction of the several estates of the realm convened in parliament, not only for the introduction of new laws, but even for the confirmation of the old ones. Hoveden's words are as follows:—" Willielmus rex anno quarto regni sui consilio baronum suorum fecit summonari per universos consulatos Angliæ, Anglos nobiles et sapientes et suâ lege eruditos, ut eorum jura et consuetudines ab ipsis audiret, electis igitur de singulis totius patriæ comitatibus viri duodecim jurejurando confirmaverunt, ut quoad possint recto tramite, neque ad dextram, neque ad sinistram partem divertentes, legum suarum consuetudinem et sancitam patefacerent, nihil prætermittentes, nihil addentes, nihil prævaricando mutantes."

"By all which it is apparent," says Sir Matthew Hale, "first, that William I. did not pretend, nor indeed could he pretend, notwithstanding his nominal conquest, to alter the laws of this kingdom without consent *in communi concilio regis*, or in parliament. And, secondly, that if there could be any pretence of such right, or if in that turbulent time something of that kind had happened, yet, by all those solemn capitulations, oaths, and concessions, that pretence was wholly avoided, and the ancient laws of the kingdom settled; and were not to be altered or added unto at the pleasure of the Conqueror, without consent in parliament."

Henry I. confirmed these laws, and published a new volume, forming a complete collection or code of laws, which, according to Sir Matthew Hale, is entered in the Red Book of the Exchequer. Then followed the laws of Henry II., called the Constitutions of Clarendon, which were afterwards amended in the reign of Richard I.

Such, then, being the foundation of our English laws, we shall proceed to give some of their provisions in detail; whence it will be perceived that the earliest institutions in this country, of which we have any records, are avowedly founded upon the laws of Moses.

Domesday-book was, in reality, the code of Saxon laws. It is noticed, as such, in the laws of Edward the Elder, and more particularly in those of Athelstane.

From the Mercian laws of Offa, Alfred, in framing

his body of laws, selected such as served his purpose.

The original institutes of the Anglo-Saxons were but scanty, and were probably brought by our forefathers from their German home.

Such portions of the laws of Ethelbert as relate to wounds and other bodily injuries, were common to all the kindred nations of northern Germany. Such injuries, in the first instance, were made the subject of compensation, in default of which the offender became amenable to criminal punishment. It is moreover to be remarked, that the nations nearest of kin to the Angles and Saxons coincide with them the most closely in the form of their laws.

But of all the Anglo-Saxon laws, few are more interesting than those of king Alfred. He succeeded to the crown in the year 871. His "dooms" are prefaced with a Saxon translation of the Hebrew laws. In proof of this, Dr. Thorpe's translations of the Anglo-Saxon laws into English are the best evidence. Their veracity is vouched by the concurrence of an eminent legal antiquary, viz. Charles Purton Cooper, Esq., Q.C., who was associated with Dr. Thorpe in his labours. According to these authorities, king Alfred's "domes" or dooms begin as follows:—

"The Lord spake these words to Moses, and thus said, I am the Lord thy God. I led thee out of the land of the Egyptians and their bondage.

"1. Love thou not other strange gods above me.

"2. Utter thou not my name idly, for thou shalt not be guileless towards me if thou utter my name idly.

"3. Remember that thou hallow the rest-day: work for yourselves six days, and on the seventh rest. For in six days Christ wrought the heavens and the earth, the seas and all creatures that are in them, and rested on the seventh day, and therefore the Lord hallowed it.

"4. Honour thy father and thy mother whom the Lord hath given thee, that thou mayest be the longer living on the earth.

"5. Slay thou not.

"6. Commit thou not adultery.

"7. Steal thou not.

"8. Say thou not false witness.

"9. Covet thou not thy neighbour's goods unjustly.

"10. Make thou not to thyself golden or silver gods.

"11. These are the dooms which thou shall set for them. If any man buy a Christian 'theow,' let him serve six years, the seventh he shall be free without purchase; with such raiment as he went in with such shall he go out. If he have a wife of his own, go she out with him. If however the lord have given him a wife, be she and her child the lord's. But if the 'theow' should say, I will not from my lord, nor from my wife, nor from my child, nor from my goods, let his lord then bring him to the door of the temple and bore his ear through with an awl in token that he shall ever after be a 'theow.'

"12. Though any one sell his daughter to servitude, let her not be altogether such a 'theown' as other female slaves are. He ought not to sell her away among strange folk. But if he who bought her reck not of her, let her go free among a strange folk. If, however, he allow his son to cohabit with her (to do marriage gifts) let him marry her, and let him see that she have raiment, and that which is the worth of her maidhood—that is, the dowry —let him give her that.

"13. Let the man who slayeth another wilfully perish by death. Let him who slayeth another of necessity, or unwillingly, or unwilfully, as God may have sent him into his hands, and for whom he has not lain in wait, be worthy of his life and of lawful 'bot' if he seek an asylum. If, however, any one wilfully and presumptuously slay his neighbour through guile, pluck thou him from my altar, to the end that he may perish by death.

"14. He who smiteth his father or his mother, he shall perish by death.

"15. He who stealeth a freeman and selleth him, and it be proved against him, so that he cannot clear himself, let him perish by death. He who curseth his father or mother, let him perish by death.

"16. If any one smite his neighbour with a stone or with his fist, and he nevertheless can go out with a staff, let him get him a leech and work his work the while that himself may not.

"17. He who smiteth his own 'theow-esne' or his female slave, and he die not on the same day, though he live but two or three nights, he is not altogether so guilty, because it was his own property; but if he die the same day, then let the guilt rest on him.

"18. If any one in strife hurt a breeding woman, let him make 'bot' for the hurt, as the judges shall prescribe to him. If she die, let him give soul for soul.

"19. If any one thrust out another's eye, let him give his own for it; tooth for tooth, hand for hand, foot for foot, burning for burning, wound for wound, stripe for stripe.

"20. If any one smite out the eye of his 'theow,' or of his 'theowen,' and he then make them one-eyed, let him free them on this account. And if he smite out a tooth, let him do the like.

"21. If an ox gore a man or woman so that they die, let it be stoned, and let not its flesh be eaten. The lord shall not be liable if the ox were wont to push with its horns for two or three days before, and the lord knew it not; but if he knew it, and he would not shut it in, and it then shall have slain a man or a woman, let it be stoned, and let the lord be slain, or the man be paid for as the 'witan' decree to be right. If it gore a son or a daughter, let him be subject to the like judgment. But if it gore a 'theow' or a 'theowmennen,' let thirty shillings in silver be given to his lord, and let the ox be stoned.

"22. If any one dig a water pit, or open one that is shut up and close it not again, let him pay for whatever cattle may fall therein, and let him have the dead beasts.

"23. If an ox wound another man's ox, let them sell the live ox and have the worth in common, and also the flesh of the dead ox. But if the lord knew that the ox was wont to push and he would not confine it, let him give him another ox for it, and have all the flesh for himself.

"24. If any one steal another's ox and slay or sell it, let him give two for it, and four sheep for one. If he have not what he may give, be he himself sold for the cattle.

"25. If a thief breaks into a man's house by night, and he be there slain, the slayer shall not be guilty of manslaughter. But if he do this after sunrise, he shall be guilty of manslaughter, and then he himself shall die, unless he were an unwilling agent. If with him living that be found which he had before stolen, let him pay for it twofold.

"26. If any one injure another man's vineyard, or his fields, or aught of his lands, let him make 'bot' as it may be valued.

"27. If fire be kindled to burn 'ryht,' let him who kindled the fire make 'bot' for the mischief.

"28. If any one entrust property to his friend, if he steal it himself, let him pay for it twofold. If he know not who hath stolen it, let him clear himself that he hath therein committed no fraud. If, however, it were live cattle, and he say that the 'here' hath taken it, or that it perished of itself, and he have witness, he needeth not to pay for it. But if he have no witness, and he believe him not, then let him swear.

"29. If any one deceive an unbetrothed woman and sleep with her, let him pay for her and have her afterwards to wife. But if the father of the woman will not give her, let him render money according to her dowry.

"30. The women who are wont to receive enchanters, and workers of phantasms, and witches, suffer thou not to live.

"31. Let him who lieth with cattle perish by death.

"32. Let him who sacrificeth to gods, save unto God alone, perish by death.

"33. Vex not comers from afar.

"34. Injure ye not the widows and the step-children, nor hurt them anywhere.

"35. If thou give money in loan to thy fellow who willeth to dwell with thee, urge thou him not as a 'neidling,' and oppress him not with the increase.

"36. If a man have only a single garment wherewith to cover himself or to wear, and he give it in pledge, let it be returned before sunset.

"37. Revile thou not thy Lord God.

"38. Tithes and first fruits are commanded to be duly rendered to the church.

"40. To the word of a lying man seek thou not to hearken, nor allow thou of his judgments, nor say thou any witness after him.

"42. If the stray cattle of another man come to thy hand, though it be thy foe, make it known to him.

"43. Judge thou evenly; judge thou not one doom to the rich, and another to the poor; nor one to thy friend, another to thy foe, judge thou.

"44. Shun thou ever leasings.

"45. A just and innocent man him slay thou never.

"46. Receive thou never meed-moneys, for they blind oft the minds of wise men and pervert their words.

"47. To the stranger and comer from afar behave thou not unkindly, nor oppress thou him with any wrongs.

"48. Swear ye never by heathen gods, nor cry to them for any cause.

"These are the dooms which the Almighty God himself spake unto Moses, and commanded him to keep; and after the only-begotten Son of the Lord our God, that is our Saviour Jesus Christ, came on earth, he said that he came not to break nor to forbid these commandments, but with all good to increase them.

"I then, Alfred king, gathered these together, and commanded many of these to be written, which our forefathers held, those which seemed to me good; and many of those which seemed to me not good, I rejected them by the counsel of my 'witan,' and in otherwise commanded them to be holden, for I durst not venture to set down in writing much of my own; for it was unknown to me what it would please those who should come after us. But those things which I met with either of the days of Ina my kinsman, or of Offa king of the Mercians, or of Æthelbryht who first among the English race received baptism, those which seemed to me the rightest, those I have here gathered together, and rejected others. I then, Alfred, king of the West Saxons, showed these to my 'witan,' and they then said it seemed good to them all to be holden."

The laws of Ina closely correspond with the code of Alfred, into which many of them were incorporated. We give some examples:—

"If a thief be seized, let him perish by death, or let his life be redeemed according to his 'wer.'

"He who slays a thief must declare on oath that he slew him offending.

"If a far-coming man or a stranger journey through a wood, and neither shout nor blow his horn, he is to be held for a thief, either to be slain or redeemed.

"Let him who takes a thief, or to whom one taken is given, and he then lets him go, pay for the thief according to his 'wer.' If he be an ealderman, let him forfeit his shire.

"He who clandestinely begets a child and conceals it, shall not have the 'wer' for its death, but his lord and the king.

"If a man buy a wife, and the marriage take not place, let him give the money, and compensate and make 'bot' to his 'byrgea,' as his 'borg bryce' may be."

(It may be here observed, that the Longobardic and old Swedish law inflicts a similar penalty for breaking a marriage contract.)

"He who has been in a foray where a man has been slain, let him prove himself innocent of the slaying, and make 'bot' for the foray according to the wer-gild of the slain. If his wer-gild be CC shillings, let him make 'bot' with L shillings, and let the like justice be done with respect to the dearer born.

"He who slays a thief must prove on oath that he slew him fleeing for a thief, and the kinsman of the dead swear to him an uncease oath. But if he conceal it, and it afterwards become known, let him pay for him."

The laws of king Edmund, who reigned from the year 940 to 946, are of similar import, but contain more stringent provisions with regard to matters ecclesiastical. For instance:—

"We have also ordained that every bishop repair the houses of God in his own district; and also remind the king that all God's churches be well conditioned, as is very needful for us.

"A tithe we enjoin to every Christian man by his christendom, and church scot."

King Edgar's statutes provide—

"That God's churches be entitled to every right, and that every tithe be rendered to the old minster to which the district belongs."

The payment of church scot is specially enjoined. So also is the observance of Sunday.

"Let the festivals of every Sunday be kept, from the noontide of the Saturday till the dawn of Monday.

"Let there be, at every bargain, two or three witnesses.

"I will that, with the Danes, such good laws stand as they may best choose."

Ethelred's Mercian laws are founded upon the same principles, and very much in the same terms, but with some few additions. In case of accusation, purgation by the oaths of five thanes is provided.

"Let no man buy or exchange without a witness; if any one do so, let the landlord take possession of the property till the ownership be proved.

"If there be any man who is untrue to all the people, let the king's reeve go and bring him under 'borh' that he may be led to justice to those who accused him; but if he have no 'borh,' let him be slain."

Homicide is made the subject of compensation both between Danes and Englishmen.

It may be here observed, that in these laws Danish and Saxon terms are frequently used in common for the same thing—as bot and lah-slit.

"Let plough alms be paid fifteen days after Easter, and tithes by Allhallows Mass, and Rome-feoh by Peter's Mass; slight scot thrice in the year.

"And let God's laws be henceforth zealously loved by word and deed.

"And if anyone anywhere commit 'forsteal,' or open opposition to the law of Christ or of the king, let him pay either wer, or wite, or lah-slit, always according as the deed may be; and if he resist against right by any violation of the law, and so act that he be slain, let him lie uncompensated to all his friends.

"It is the duty of us all to love and worship one God, and strictly hold one Christianity, and totally cast out every kind of heathenism.

"And it is the ordinance of the witan that Christian men and uncondemned persons be not for altogether too little cause condemned to death; but in general let mild punishment be decreed for the people's need, and let every deed be heedfully distinguished; and doom, according to the deed, be moderated in degree."

The laws of Ethelred differ but little in effect from those we have already alluded to.

"And let every widow who conducts herself lawfully be in God's 'girth' and the king's; and let every one continue twelve months husbandless. Afterwards, let her choose what she herself will."

Hence seems to have sprung the modern observance of twelve months' widowhood.

This code commands that the people—

"Strictly abstain from Sunday marketings and popular meetings and huntings.

"And he who anywhere henceforth shall corrupt just laws, either of God or of men, let him strictly make bôt for it."

Homicides, theft, adultery, fornication, perjury, false witness, plundering, gluttony, drunkenness, false weights and measures, and all breaches of the law, are made the subject of bot, fine, or compensation. Fighting or stealing in the king's "burh" is declared to be a capital offence.

"And respecting tithes, the king and his witan have chosen and decreed, as is just, that one-third part of the tithe which belongs to the church go to the reparation of the church, one-third part to the servants of God, and a third part to God's poor and the needy ones in thraldom."

Canute, king of Denmark, became monarch of all England on the death of Edmund Ironside, A.D. 1017. He imported into the earlier laws some provisions of Danish origin. His code also contains the earliest enactment I have been able to find in the laws of this country concerning the degrees of affinity.

"And we instruct and beseech, and in God's name command—

"That no Christian man marry in his own family within the relationship of six persons.

"Nor with the relict of his kinsman who was so near of kin.

"Nor with the relative of the wife whom he had previously had.

"Nor with his godmother.

"Nor with a hallowed nun.

"Nor with one divorced let any Christian man ever marry, nor any fornication anywhere commit.

"Nor have more wives than one, and let that be his wedded wife; but let him be with her alone as long as she may live, whoever will rightly keep God's law, and secure his soul against the burning of hell.

"And Sunday marketings we also strictly forbid, and every folkmote unless it be for great necessity; and let huntings and all other worldly works be strictly abstained from on that holy day."

After a repetition of many of the previous laws, almost verbatim as to tithes and good behaviour, these provisions follow:—

"And we earnestly instruct all Christian men, that they ever love God with inward heart, and diligently hold orthodox Christianity, and diligently obey the divine teachers, and meditate on and enquire into God's doctrines and laws oft and frequently for their own behoof.

"And we instruct that every Christian man learn so that he may at least be able to understand a right orthodox faith; and to learn the Paternoster and Creed, for Christ himself first sung Paternoster and taught that prayer to his disciples."

It may here be observed that fornication, adultery, and incest, although they were, under most of the other Anglo-Saxon laws, ecclesiastical offences to be punished in the first instance with "bot" to the church and clergy, are treated in this code simply as civil crimes. The following ordinances are, among others, remarkable:—

"Henceforth let every man, both poor and rich, be deemed worthy of folk right, and let just dooms be doomed to him.

"Let manslayers, perjurers, and adulterers make bot, or retire from the country."

Cheats, liars, and robbers are also subjected to "bot" or fine.

"He who after this shall make counterfeit money, let him forfeit the hands with which he wrought that false, and not redeem them with anything.

"Every man shall be in a tithing, or shall not be entitled to 'wer' in case any one slay him after he is twelve years of age.

"Let no one buy anything above the value of four-pence, unless he have the true witness of four men.

"Let no man be entitled to any vouching to warranty, unless he have true witness whence that came to him which is attached with him.

"If any man find a thief and voluntarily let him escape without hue and cry, let him make 'bot,' or clear himself with a full oath that he knew no guile in him."

Incest entailed the forfeiture of all a man's possessions.

Adultery was also punished with severity.

"If any man commit adultery, let him make 'bot' for it as the deed may be. It is a wicked adultery when a married man lies with a single woman, and much worse with another's wife or one in holy orders."

The ravishing of a widow or a maid was likewise the subject of fine or "bot."

If a married woman committed adultery, she forfeited to her husband all she possessed.

This law seems to imply that in those days the wife's property did not vest in the husband by virtue of their marriage.

In the laws of Canute, the king expressly reserves his rights under the Danish laws and the laws of Wessex and Mercia, which thence became so far a part of his code.

His laws proceed as follows:—

"Let no one apply to the king unless he may not be entitled to any justice within his hundred.

"Let no man take any distress, either in the shire or out of the shire, before he has thrice demanded his right in the hundred. If at the third time he have no justice, then let him go at the fourth time to the shire-gemote, and let the shire appoint him a fourth term. If that then fail, let him take either from hence or thence that he may seize his own.

"Let weights and measures be carefully rectified. Whoever does a deed of outlawry forfeits his lands to the king."

It may be mentioned, that certain heinous crimes were "bôtless," or not the subject of compensation; as, for instance, housebreaking, open theft, arson, and treason. Such deeds entailed outlawry upon the criminal. The consequence of this was, the loss of all municipal privileges. If any outlaw was slain upon any occasion, his death needed no compensation: such an one, having thus suffered civil death, might be killed with impunity.

Such remained the law of the land until a comparatively recent period. Indeed, the principle of outlawry still survives, although the rigour of its consequences has been mitigated by the humanity of modern legislation.

With regard to the much vexed question of church rates, it is curious to observe that in Anglo-Saxon times the repairs of the church were provided for out of the tithes. By the laws of Ethelred, as we have just seen, the tithes are divided into three parts: one-third for the minister, one-third for the poor, and one-third to go for the reparation of the church. The laws of Edgar direct that the "tithes shall be rendered to the old minster to which the district belongs." The laws of Edmund impose upon the bishop the duty of repairing the churches in his own district; as, no doubt, through the minster he received a third part of the tithes for that purpose. Indeed, for any neglect of the bishop to repair the church some of the Anglo-Saxon laws gave a penal remedy. Thus it appears that in early times church-rates formed no part of the endowments by which the national church was maintained. Church rates must not be mistaken for a tradition of "church scot," which is frequently mentioned in the Anglo-Saxon laws. Church scot was quite a different thing, and payable for a different purpose. By degrees, probably, the clergy appropriated to their own use that part of the tithes which was set apart for the repair of the church, and under various pretences imposed upon the people contributions to supply this deficiency. This device was one which the minsters and other religious societies were not slow to enforce, both by example and precept. They by degrees appropriated the whole of the tithes; and having thus got possession of the emoluments of their parishes, they put in vicars or substitutes, at small stipends, to serve the churches in their stead. So what the national bounty had provided for parochial charity and the maintenance of the parish church was by degrees withdrawn; until at length church rates and other oblations acquired the force of custom, and came to be recognised by the very laws which they had defrauded. This is a matter of history. But now that so much of the tithes and church property has passed into the hands of the laity, it is no argument against the validity of such customs as have acquired the force of law at the expense of the church. It merely serves to show that the avarice of the clergy defeated its own object, and that the laity have reaped the benefit of ecclesiastical encroachments; which have thus distributed amongst them a large proportion of the endowments of the national church. How it was that the clergy were enabled to divert the revenues of the church from their original purpose may be easily conceived from the power which they acquired under the Anglo-Saxon system. Before the Conquest, and even afterwards, a large proportion of crimes and offences were punished by a "bot" or fine to the bishops and clergy. Although from the terms of the Anglo-Saxon laws it appears evident that at first the temporal power exercised a concurrent jurisdiction in punishing such offences; yet the influence of the clergy was such, and the administration of this kind of justice so profitable, that by degrees they managed to secure for themselves the sole jurisdiction over some crimes, which thus escaped the grasp of the common law, and have since passed under the name of "spiritual" offences, simply because the offenders were accountable only to the spiritual powers.

## CHAPTER VI.

### ON THE LAWS OF RETRIBUTION.—HOMICIDE.—VIOLENCE.—FALSE WITNESS.

The functions of justice in its simplest form may be divided into two classes. The first embraces the laws of retribution; the second the laws of restitution. From these, however, spring a third sort of laws, affecting matters which may be occasionally either the subject of retributive justice or of restitution, as circumstances aggravate the guilt of the offender or palliate the consequences of the offence. This class of laws, therefore, chiefly concerns personal offences; which may thus become, according to circumstances, the subject either of a civil remedy or a criminal punishment.

The laws of restitution chiefly apply to trespass upon property, and to the invasion of personal rights, in cases where the character of the offence is such as to admit of amends for the injury. Hence civil wrongs are for the most part the subject of restitution. The nature of this class of laws will be considered more fully hereafter.

The laws of retribution have reference to criminal offences. Of these, the most prominent are wrongs accompanied with personal violence. Some offences, the nature of which will not allow of restitution, such as false witness, are also the subject of this class of laws. To these, however, in their turn, we shall refer. But of such offences as are the subject of retributive justice, those which are accompanied with personal violence will first engage our attention.

In all communities, the first efforts of political government are directed to the restraint of personal outrages. Such enactments necessarily take the form of criminal laws. In the rudest forms of society personal violence is an offence most prevalent. Men had felt the impulse of passion before they had learnt to acquire possessions. So communities grew up at a time when the rights of property were few and ill defined. Families congregated together in situations whose abundant pasturage and remote situation invited their choice and secured them from intrusion. Here they assembled for mutual protection, long before they formed themselves into associations for the preservation of rights in property. These had yet to be acquired. Hence we find that in all societies laws for the protection of the person existed before any occasion arose for laws to secure property.

Of criminal laws many spring so obviously from the dictates of natural justice, that it may seem almost superfluous to assign to them the sanction of an express revelation. They are found to exist, in a more or less perfect degree, amongst nations in which it is now impossible to trace any more distinct evidence of their origin than what may be supposed to arise from necessity and the dictates of nature.

But upon the other hand, the systems of jurisprudence which prevailed in many ancient nations renowned for their civilization and their laws, display a purpose and a method which, for want of any evidence of progressive jurisprudence, we are compelled to attribute to some model of more perfect construction than the general principles of natural justice. Where we find that the intention is dealt with as much as the action, we must conceive a state of things which involves not merely the origin of social regulations, but the development of the principles from which such institutions spring. Hence we must concede to such constitutions an acquaintance with some more perfect system of justice than the uncontrolled impulse of necessity or revenge.

Such distinctions with reference to the motive of men's actions will be found to pervade the earlier laws of the Greeks, the Romans, and to some extent those of the Egyptians. In determining the guilt of those who were accused of the most malignant crimes, these considerations formed an important element in their jurisprudence.

In another Chapter, we have endeavoured to show the possibility that, in the construction of their most celebrated laws, these nations had access to the judicial system of the Hebrews. But the probability that their legislators adopted the Mosaic laws as their model, will best be shown by a comparison of their judicial codes.

We have already seen how far the laws, by which Europe was governed after the introduction of Christianity, owe their principles to the Mosaic laws. We shall now, therefore, confine ourselves chiefly to the consideration of those peculiarities in the ancient systems which present the most striking resemblance to the Jewish constitution.

Among crimes involving personal violence, murder is the most prominent.

In the Hebrew jurisprudence, the various degrees of guilt assigned to homicide are defined with remarkable precision. The sanctity of human life was guarded with stringent precautions, the infringement of which was jealously vindicated in the punishment of the offender. His guilt was presumed: his innocence was to be proved. Wilful murder is punished capitally. Accidental death is punished with banishment. Where death was occasioned by negligence of precautions which are prescribed by the Mosaic laws, the offender rendered himself liable to capital punishment. For instance, where a man built a house and neglected to put a battlement to the roof. Upon the other hand, under certain circumstances, bloodshed is excused by the Jewish laws. But both in the degrees of guilt to which punishment was awarded, and in the circumstances under which the punishment was remitted, it will be perceived that the Hebrew laws have been closely imitated by the earliest constitutions of antiquity. Most of the judicial systems of Europe have avowedly adopted them. Amongst others, our own institutions furnish many examples. These may, perhaps, be described as the illustrations of a remote and unsettled age, though their character was doubtless influenced by the introduction of Christianity. Nevertheless, such examples furnish evidence of the foundation of the system. And it is remarkable how many of its provisions, though of more recent growth, may be accommodated to the principles from which it originally sprang.

It is not, however, within the scope of our purpose to discuss the canons or the ecclesiastical laws of this period. Yet it is a remarkable proof, at once of the superior refinement of the Normans at the time of the Conquest, and of the influence which the Mosaic institutions exerted upon them, that after the Great Battle, as it is termed—the battle of Hastings, a penitential code was issued, in which penances are enjoined for those who had taken a share in that great contest. The Norman who had killed a man in the Great Battle was enjoined an annual fast and penance, of great severity, through life; he who had wounded a man had a shorter discipline; nay, he who had struck at an opponent and missed him, but with intention to hurt or kill, had, likewise, a penance enjoined. Such a discipline, imposed by the victors on themselves in a dark and barbarous age, is surely to be noticed as one of the great triumphs of Christianity, however corrupted by superstition.—But to return to our secular institutions:

The English law divides homicide into three kinds: justifiable, excusable, and felonious. Homicide is held to be justifiable, first, where it arises by some unavoidable necessity, and by permission or command of the law; as in the case of a public execution of a criminal duly condemned, or for the advancement of justice, as if a felon be killed in the attempt to take him. This is similar to the old Gothic constitution, which permitted a thief to be slain if he offered resistance to his apprehension.

So, until trial by battle was abolished in the reign

of George III., if one of the champions was killed, such homicide was deemed justifiable, and was imputed to the judgment of God.

By the law of England, it is justifiable to kill another in the attempt to commit murder, or in the attempt to break open a house in the night-time. So the Jewish law, which punishes no theft with death, makes homicide justifiable in case of nocturnal housebreaking. At Athens, if any theft was committed by night, it was lawful to kill the criminal if taken in the fact. And by the Roman law of the twelve tables, a thief by night might be slain with impunity; or even by day, if he were armed with any dangerous weapon. The Roman law also justifies homicide when committed in defence of the chastity of one's-self or relations.

Thus, according to Selden, the Jewish law was understood. The English law, Blackstone says, justifies a woman in killing one who attempts to ravish her. According to the same authority, the husband or father may be justified in killing a man in the attempt to commit a rape upon his wife or daughter.

According to our law, homicide is excusable, as distinguished from justifiable, when it is committed either by misadventure or for self-preservation. In the first case, to render the offence excusable, the person committing it, according to Blackstone, must not have been engaged in an unlawful act at the time. This doctrine, however, has been somewhat qualified by later English jurists, who incline to attribute the offence rather to the design than the action. Yet, at the same time, to the consequences of a felonious action the law attributes a felonious design. Hence arises a distinction to which the severity of some statutes has given rise, where they exceeded the just bounds of punishment. Those acts which are crimes by the laws of God, under our earliest laws amounted to felonies. These are denominated *mala in se*. Those which have been by statutes made felonious, for the better prevention of some prevalent offences, are designated as *mala prohibita*. They generally entailed only such special consequences as the peculiar law by which they were interdicted happened to provide. They did not, from being made felonies by statute, involve necessarily the same consequences as those crimes which were felonies by the common law.

Felony, in its original sense, was a feudal term used to denote all such criminal acts as occasioned a forfeiture of lands and goods. Conviction of this offence was followed by the disqualifications of outlawry. These, by at once depriving the offender of his social privileges and his municipal rights, thrust him beyond the pale of humanity. The Saxon word felon signified the price of a fee or feud. Formerly all felonies were the subject of capital punishment. It will be found that most crimes which amounted to felonies, and were by the ancient laws of England followed by capital punishment, were dealt with as severely by the Jewish laws. In cases of homicide by misadventure, the laws of Moses banished the offender to his city of refuge. Amongst the Greeks, homicide by misadventure was expiated by voluntary banishment for a year. In Saxony, a fine was paid to the kindred of the slain. Amongst the Western Goths, in such cases, the punishment of death might be averted by compensation.

Felonious homicide is the killing of a person without either excuse or justification. It applies also to self-murder: in this case, the Greeks cut off the hand by which the deed was done. But when the offence consists in killing another man, our law draws a distinction between manslaughter and wilful murder.

Manslaughter is defined to be the killing of another upon an unlawful occasion, without malice expressed or implied. This distinction was also recognised in the Gothic constitutions. It is either voluntary or involuntary. It is said to be voluntary where one kills another in a quarrel. It is called involuntary where one kills another upon an unlawful occasion. In this particular it is distinguished from excusable homicide, which occurs where one kills another involuntarily upon a lawful instead of an unlawful occasion. Manslaughter, though involuntary, is a crime which amounts to felony, but is not punished with death.

Murder is the wilfully killing of another upon an unlawful occasion; and not only by our own laws, but almost universally, is punished with death.

The Mosaic laws emphatically prohibit the pardon of the murderer. In imitation of this, by our ancient laws the king himself is excluded the power of pardoning murder. The prerogative of pardon, however, was enlarged in the reign of George III.

According to our law, it is not murder to procure abortion, unless the child be actually born alive, and afterwards die of the injuries it received before its birth. But Josephus (Cont. Ap.) tells us, that in his time the Jewish law was understood to punish such offences capitally. He says:—" The law, moreover, enjoins us to bring up all our offspring, and forbids women to cause abortion of what is begotten, or to destroy it afterwards; and if any woman appears to have so done, she will be a murderer of her child, by destroying a living creature and diminishing humankind. If any one, therefore, proceeds to such fornication or murder, he cannot be clean."

Our law of deodands is obviously borrowed from the Jews. By our old laws (see Blackstone's Com.), "if a horse, or ox, or other animal, of his own motion kill an infant or an adult, or if a cart ran over him, in either case they were forfeited as deodands." A like punishment was, in such cases, inflicted by the Mosaic law. If an ox gore a man that he die, the ox shall be stoned, and his flesh shall not be eaten. Among the Athenians, whatever was the cause of a man's death by falling upon him, was exterminated, or cast out of the dominions of the republic.

Thus, too, by our ancient law, a well in which a man was drowned was ordered to be filled up, under the inspection of the coroner. But our law somewhat refined upon the original principle; for where a thing not in motion was the occasion of a man's death, that part only which was the immediate cause was forfeited; as, if a man climbing up the wheel of a cart were killed by falling from it, the wheel alone was a deodand. But wherever the thing was in motion, not only that part which gave the immediate wound (as the wheel which ran over his body), but all things which moved with it, and helped to make the wound more dangerous, as the cart and loading which increase the pressure of the wheel, were forfeited. It mattered not, says Blackstone, whether the owner were concerned in the killing or not. "For if a man kills another with my sword, the sword is forfeited as an accursed thing." A similar rule obtained among the Goths. In all indictments for homicide, the instrument of death, and the value, were formerly presented and found by the grand jury; as, that the stroke was given with a certain penknife, value 6*d*.

The Roman laws, in regard to damage done by wild beasts or furious cattle, contain many provisions which resemble the Hebrew laws.

The law of the Twelve Tables, and the *lex Pesulania, De cane*, forbade any one to keep a savage beast near to a public road. And the beast, if it did damage to the passers-by, was forfeited by way of indemnity. The Ædilitian edict of later date assigned damages to double the value of the mischief against the owner of the beast.

The first declaration of the divine law relating to bloodshed was that given to Noah. "And surely your blood of your lives will I require; at the hand of every beast will I require it, and at the hand of man; at the hand of every man's brother will I require the life of man. Whoso sheddeth man's blood, by man shall his blood be shed: for in the image of God made he man."

Although the rigour of the punishment is subsequently modified, according to the various degrees of guilt under which the offence was perpetrated, yet the principles of this law are nowhere abrogated.

For bloodshed, death is the punishment both to man and beast.

The same penalty is exacted from a reasonable and an unreasonable creature. No exception is to be discovered in favour of want of reason, or any aberration of mind, from whatever cause it may arise, either in the case of men or women; unless what may be inferred from the absence of malice or wilful intention, for there is often as much malignity and design in the insane as in the sane.

The next exposition of this law is to be found in Exodus. Here a means of escaping capital punishment is provided for accidental manslaughter. "And if a man lie not in wait, but God deliver him into his hand; then I will appoint thee a place whither he shall flee. But if a man come presumptuously upon his neighbour, to slay him with guile; thou shalt take him from mine altar, that he may die." Thus it appears that the altar afforded only a temporary shelter to secure the offender from the vengeance of the deceased's relations until his guilt could be judicially determined. After this had been decided, if the crime was proved to have been wilfully committed, death was inflicted. But if the deed was the result of accident, without enmity, guile, or design, the offender was restored to the city of his refuge, where he must remain until the death of the high priest. If before this he ventured beyond its bounds, the avenger of blood, who was one of the nearest relations of the slain, was allowed to take his life with impunity.

It is also provided by the Jewish laws, that no murderer shall be condemned to death by the testimony of less than two witnesses, and that the hands of the witnesses shall be the first to execute the punishment. This precaution has been adopted by many of the most ancient laws. It was the law of this country at the Conquest, and long afterwards.

The next allusion to this crime (Numb. xxxv.) appoints cities of refuge, and regulates their use—"That the slayer may flee thither, which killeth any person at unawares. And they shall be unto you cities for refuge from the avenger; that the manslayer die not, until he stand before the congregation in judgment."

Cities of refuge, therefore, were temporary asylums until the manslayer could be judicially tried. They only provided security for those who had caused death accidentally.

No satisfaction was allowed to be taken, either for a murderer or one guilty of manslaughter. The appointed punishment could, under no circumstances, be remitted.

In case a person guilty of wilful murder fled to a city of refuge, the elders of his city were commanded to deliver him up, to expiate his guilt by death at the hands of the revenger of blood.

Where a man was found slain, and the murderer was unknown, the city next to the place where the body was found was commanded to make expiation for his blood, with a solemn declaration of innocence on the part of the elders. This institution answers very closely to our coroner's inquest. Indeed, the resemblance was still more remarkable under our ancient system, when the hundred was held responsible for all crimes committed within its jurisdiction.

It will be seen, too, that the severity with which the Jewish laws punished the crime of parricide was strictly followed by the Egyptians, the Greeks, and the Romans.

Diodorus Siculus, in giving an account of such laws

of the Egyptians as were most remarkable for their antiquity, amongst others mentions several concerning bloodshed, whose peculiarities bear an extraordinary resemblance to those of the Jews.

"1. He that wilfully killed a freeman, nay a very bond-slave, was by law to die.

"2. If any upon the road saw a man likely to be killed, or to be violently assaulted, and did not rescue him if he were able, he was to die for it; and if in truth he were not able to defend him, yet he was bound to discover the thieves and to prosecute them in due course of law. If he neglected this, he was, according to the law, to be scourged with a certain number of stripes, and to be kept without food for three days together."

Xenophon and Cicero mention two laws of the Greeks which agree with the Egyptian statutes. It was a law of the Greeks that "no stranger should be wronged or injured." Another was in these words: "Put the bewildered traveller in his way, and be hospitable to strangers." The words of the Jewish law (Exod. xxii. 21) are: "Thou shalt neither vex a stranger, nor oppress him: for ye were strangers in the land of Egypt." A still stronger analogy is furnished by the following (Exod. xxiii. 4, 5): "If thou meet thine enemy's ox or his ass going astray, thou shalt surely bring it back to him again. If thou see the ass of him that hateth thee lying under his burden, and wouldest forbear to help him, thou shalt surely help with him."

But with regard to the murder of children, the Egyptian laws were not so severe as those of the Jews. In this immunity, as far as the parents were concerned, the Egyptian laws were more closely followed by the Romans than by the Greeks.

With the Egyptians, "Parents who killed their children were not to die, but were forced for three days and nights together to embrace the dead bodies of their children in their arms, under a guard which was placed over them all the while to see that they did it. For they thought it not fit that they should die who gave life to their children, but rather that men should be deterred from such actions by a punishment that seemed to be attended with sorrow and repentance."

"But for parricides," says Diodorus, "they provided a most severe kind of punishment; for those that were convicted of this crime were laid upon thorns and burnt alive, after they had first mangled the members of their bodies piecemeal with sharp canes about the bigness of a man's thumb. For they counted it the most wicked act that a man could be guilty of to take away the lives of them from whom they had their own."

Wilful murder was punished with death, whatever might be the condition of the murdered person, whether he was freeborn or otherwise. In this the humanity and equity of the Egyptian law was superior to that of the Romans, whose constitution at one time gave the master an absolute power of life and death over his slave. The severity of this law was, however, subsequently mitigated by the emperor Adrian.

So also the Egyptians had a law which in effect agrees with the English usage in such cases, and one which Josephus relates to have been practised by the Jews. Diodorus Siculus says: "Those that were with child were not to be executed till they were delivered; which law was received by many of the Grecians, judging it very unjust for the innocent to suffer with the guilty, and two to die for the offence of one only. Besides, inasmuch as the crime was maliciously and advisedly committed, it was unreasonable that the child, that understood not what was done, should undergo the same punishment. And that which is of the greatest consideration is, that it was altogether unjust (seeing the mother only was accused and condemned as guilty,) that the child, common both to father and mother, should lose its life. For that judge is as unjust who destroys the innocent, as he that spares him that is guilty of murder." "These," he says, "are the capital laws of the Egyptians which are chiefly worthy of praise and commendation."

The laws of Athens forbade the assassin's counsel to make any preliminary apology, to use any motives for the gaining of compassion, or to speak anything foreign to the cause.

Another Athenian law enacts, that the thesmothetæ shall punish murderers with death.

"The assassin shall suffer death in the murdered person's county, and being dragged away to the thesmothetæ, according to the appointment of the law, he shall be liable to no other violence or ill-usage besides what his capital punishment includes. Nobody shall take money for his pardon. He that doth, shall pay double the money he received of the criminal; his name likewise, by anybody, shall be carried in to the archons."

The terms of this law exactly coincide with the Jewish statute which forbids compensation to be taken for bloodshed, except where the death was accidental. Again, the principle by which, under the Jewish law, an uncondemned murderer was entitled to the security of his city of refuge, is recognized in the following Greek enactment—" If any one kills or assists in killing a murderer that abstains from the forum, consecrated places, public sports, and the Amphictyonic festivals, he shall undergo the severity of the law as much as if he had killed a citizen of Athens. The epithetæ are to take cognizance of this matter." This law relates to a murderer uncondemned.

By this it appears that if an uncondemned murderer presented himself on public occasions, he forfeited the security of retirement, and exposed himself to the consequences of his temerity. It was the same with the Hebrews, as appears sufficiently from the statutes relating to the cities of refuge, to which we have already referred.

Another Athenian law directs, that "one accused of murder shall be debarred the privileges of the city." The same consequences followed such an accusation under the Mosaic law. The offender, by voluntary banishment, abandoned his municipal rights. But as the protection which the cities of refuge were designed to afford was well defined, so the Greek law enacted,—"He that puts him in trouble who was forced to make flight out of Attica for chance-medley, shall undergo the same with him who doth the like to any citizen of Athens." Then again, by the Jewish law, the conditions of banishment for accidental homicide are relaxed where the kindred of the slain could be induced to accept compensation.

The terms of the Athenian law are precisely to the same effect :—" He who commits chance-medley shall flee his country for a year, till satisfaction be made to the dead person's kindred; then he shall return, sacrifice, and be purified." This is a very ancient law, and existed before the time of Solon.

" He shall not have an action of murder brought against him who binds him over to his appearance before the magistrate that returned from banishment before his limited time is completed." One of Draco's laws.

The following Greek laws furnish sufficient evidence of their origin.

" If any one hath unadvisedly given his antagonist in the exercises his death, or killed by chance a man lying in ambuscade, or being in the brunt of an engagement of war, or one debauching his wife, mother, sister, daughter, mistress, or the nurse of his legitimate children, let not such a one be banished."

" It shall be lawful to kill that person who shall make an assault on the innocent."

" If any one, being banished for chance-medley, shall have an indictment of wilful murder laid to his charge before *he hath made up the difference* with those who banished him, he shall make his defence before the court in a small vessel, which shall not be permitted to come to shore; but his judges shall give sentence on the land. If he is cast, he shall answer justice for wilful murder; but if absolved, shall undergo the former sentence of banishment for chance-medley."

"If any archon, or man in private capacity, is instrumental in the depravation or repeal of these statutes, let him and his children be infamous, and his goods be sold."

"It shall be lawful to drag a murderer, if found in any religious place or the forum, to jail; and if he prove guilty, to put him to death; but if the committer of him to jail do not procure the fifth part of the votes, he shall be fined a thousand drachmas."

"If any one comes to an untimely end, his nearest relations may bring the action of Ανδροληψια against those people they suspect either to be abettors of the murder or protectors of the felon; and till such time as these make satisfaction, or surrender the delinquent, the murdered man's relations are privileged to seize three men of their body."

With the Jews the avenger of blood was the nearest relation. Under the Greek law—

"The right of the prosecution of murderers belongs to the kindred of the murdered—kinsfolks, children, their sons-in-law, fathers-in-law, sisters' children, and those of the same φρατρια (or borough). The murderers have liberty granted of imploring the father of the murdered to be mild and favourable; but if he is not alive, then his brother or sons all together shall be entreated; for without the joint consent of them all, nothing shall prevail. If these fore-mentioned persons are all dead, and the death of the person came by chance-medley, according to the determination of the fifty ephetæ, ten of the same φρατρια may, if they think fit, convene and delegate one-and-fifty out of the nobility to the ephetæ." "All they who were murderers before the making of this law shall be subject to its obligation." "If any one has been murdered in any of the boroughs and nobody removes him, the demarchus shall give orders to his friends to take him away, bury him, and perform the duty of lustration toward the borough that very day on which he was killed. When a slave is murdered, he shall inform the master; when a freeman, the succeeding heirs. But if the person murdered was not a moneyed man, or had no possessions, the demarchus shall acquaint the relatives; and supposing they give no heed, and neglect to take him away, the demarchus himself shall see him taken away and buried, and take care the borough be lustrated. But all this with as little charges as may be; which if he neglect, he shall be fined a thousand drachmas, to be paid to the public exchequer. He shall take of the murdered person's debtors double the money he expended for the funeral; which if he neglect, he shall pay it himself to those of his borough."

"He who is a self-murderer shall have the hand cut off that did the murder, which shall be buried in a place separate from the body."

"No murder shall be permitted to be within the city."

In the following is recognised the principle from which the English law of deodands also sprang:—

"Inanimate things which have been instrumental to people's deaths shall be cast out of Attica." One of Draco's laws.

"He who strikes the first blow in a quarrel, shall be liable to the action termed αικιας δικη."

"He who hath maliciously hurt another's head,

face, hands, or feet, shall be proscribed the city of that man to whom he offered the detriment, and his goods be confiscated; if he return, he shall suffer death."

In our translation of the Mosaic laws, murder by poisoning does not appear to have been specially provided against. Josephus, in his Jewish Antiquities, includes the following in his account of the Hebrew laws:—"Let no one of the Israelites keep any poison that may cause death or any other harm. But if he be caught with it, let him be put to death, and suffer the very same mischief that he would have brought upon them for whom the poison was prepared." In Whiston's note to the above passage, he says, "What we render *witch*, according to our modern notion of witchcraft, Philo and Josephus understood of a poisoner, or one who attempted by secret and unlawful drugs, or philtra, to take away the senses or the lives of men."

The conformity of the Roman laws relating to homicide with those of the Hebrews is hardly less remarkable than the resemblance of the Greek statutes which we have mentioned.

The Lex Cornelia inflicted the punishment of banishment "upon him who killed a man either for the sake of killing him, or for the purpose of theft; as well he who did it with a weapon, as he who, for the purpose of killing a man, either had poison in his possession, or sold or prepared it, or gave false testimony whereby life was lost or placed in jeopardy."

" All which evil deeds in the better sort of folks (honestiores) are to be vindicated with capital punishment; whilst the lower sort (humiliores) are either to be crucified or thrown to wild beasts."

Ulpian says that the first chapter of the Cornelian law concerning cut-throats declares—"That the prætor or the judge of the question before whom, by lot, the trial of murder has come respecting a deed done within a mile of the city of Rome, should, with the assistance of judges chosen by lot, try capitally him who had waylaid a man with a weapon, either for the purpose of slaying or simply of robbing him, whether the man were slain or whether the deed was done with the malicious design of slaying him." Ulpian comments thus upon this law:—"It does not," he says, "punish all who have waylaid or compassed the death (ambulaverunt) of a man with a weapon; but it includes him only who carried a weapon for the purpose of killing or robbing a man. Also it is enforced upon him who slays a man; and, as it does not specify the condition of the man, it applies as much to a stranger as to a sojourner."

Paulus defines homicide thus:—"A homicide is he who, with any kind of weapon, has killed a man or been the cause of his death."

According to Ulpian, the distinction between casual and wilful homicide was observed by the emperor Hadrian in these words, which are a translation of his rescript; and, as we have in another chapter endeavoured to show, the rescripts of the emperors were not the enunciation of a new law, but were merely declaratory of the ancient laws which previously prevailed at Rome:—

"And he who kills a man ought to be absolved if he did it without the design of killing him; and he who did not kill, but wished to do so, ought to be condemned for homicide.

"Wherefore it was determined with what weapon Epaphroditus struck; for if he drew a sword, or smote with a dart, how can it be doubted but that he must have struck with the intention of slaying? If he struck with a nail, or a brazen vessel, by chance in a quarrel, he certainly struck with a weapon, but not necessarily with the intention of slaying.

"Therefore these circumstances are to be inquired into; and if the murder was voluntary, the punishment of crucifixion is to be inflicted even upon the murderer of slaves."

Paulus, in his comment upon the Roman laws of homicide, adds that he who kills a man may sometimes be acquitted, and he who does not take life may be sometimes condemned as a homicide. "For it is the design, not the deed, which is to be punished." "And, in the same way, if any one wishes to slay, and by some accident was unable to accomplish his purpose, he is to be punished as a murderer; whilst he who without design should carelessly thrust a man with a dart, is acquitted. So, if a man struck in a quarrel dies, since the blows must be deemed to have been directed against each one singly, on that account the poorer sort are condemned to make sport at the public spectacles, or to work in the mines, and the better class are released under a fine of half their goods."

This doctrine is affirmed by a rescript of the emperor Antonine; which is followed by others of similar import, promulgated by Diocletian, where wilful murder is distinguished from accidental homicide, the punishment being proportioned to the degree of guilt; "because," says the rescript, "things which happen by accident instead of by design, are to be ascribed to fate rather than mischief."

The laws of Moses (Exod. xxi. 18, 19) make an injury by personal violence the subject of compensation when accidentally inflicted. Under the law of the Twelve Tables, personal violence was punished with a fine, whether the injured person was a freeman or a slave. Under the Aquilian law, damages were to be paid for wounds; and in case of slaves the compensation was determined by the degree of mischief which the slave had suffered. This law also gave compensation for defamatory reproaches. The Mosaic laws provide that if a man beat his servant to death, he should be punished; but if the servant survived a day or two, no punishment was to be inflicted.

With reference to the Cornelian law, Paulus says— "That if a slave died from the effects of chastisement, his master was not liable to punishment unless he had maliciously beaten the slave with the intention of causing his death, and not for the purpose of correcting his fault."

Ulpian, On the office of Proconsul, cites a rescript of one of the emperors to the same effect. It states that the power of masters over their slaves ought to be unlimited, but that protection against intolerable brutality must not be denied the slaves.

So Hadrian severely punished a woman for ill-using her female slave. Another edict commands that slaves be treated with justice and moderation. A rescript of Diocletian forbade the immoderate chastisement of slaves.

We may notice also a species of murder in which the Gothic, the Roman, and the English laws agree with those of Moses, in punishing the offender with death. It is where the innocent person is condemned upon false witness. Here the Cornelian law followed the Mosaic, and treated the perjurer as an assassin.

In Deut. xix. the punishment is thus prescribed for false witness:—"Then shall ye do unto him as he had thought to have done unto his brother."

Plutarch, In Solone, mentions a Greek law, that "a discoverer who alleges truth shall be secure; but if falsehood, shall suffer death." The Greek laws provided two special forms of action against false witness, and against those who suborned false witnesses; conviction upon such indictments rendered the delinquent liable to capital punishment, outlawry, banishment, fine, confiscation, or imprisonment, at the discretion of the judges. Diodorus Siculus mentions as one of the primary laws of the Egyptians a remarkable ordinance in these words:—"And, in the first place, those were to die who were guilty of perjury, being such as committed the two greatest crimes,—that is, impiety towards the gods and violation of faith and truth, the strongest bond of human society." Again, he proceeds:—"False accusers were to suffer the same punishment as those whom they falsely accused were to have undergone if they had afterwards been convicted of the offence." But this author gives a still more extraordinary instance of the Egyptian application of retributive justice: "They that coined false and adulterated money, or contrived false weights, or counterfeited seals, or scribes or clerks that forged deeds, or erased public records, or produced any forged contracts, were to have their hands cut off, that every one might suffer in that part wherewith he had offended, in such manner as not to be repaired during their life; and that others, warned by so severe a punishment, might be deterred from the commission of the like offences."

With the Romans, the Cornelian law inflicted banishment upon those who had given false testimony upon any matter whereby the accused had either suffered death or stood in jeopardy of capital punishment.

In other cases, the false witness was either crucified or thrown to wild beasts.

Paulus, in the fifth book of his Commentaries upon the Cornelian laws, relating to witnesses, with regard to the suborning of perjury, says:—"That any one who shall have either given or received a bribe to obtain false testimony, or for the corruption of a judge, or the perversion of justice, shall, if of the lower class, suffer capital punishment; if of the upper class, forfeit his goods and suffer banishment."

## CHAPTER VII.

LAWS OF RESTITUTION.—THEFT; TRESPASS; PLEDGES; REDEMPTION.

THE laws of restitution are nearly akin to those of retribution. But they apply to civil injuries, not to criminal offences. It is, however, a remarkable feature in the Hebrew laws, that many personal wrongs are treated as civil offences, where justice could be satisfied by reparation; and yet where reparation was not made, such injuries are punished as public crimes.

The law of compensation, indeed, appears to be so conformable to the first principles of natural justice, that among the most civilized systems of antiquity the process of the *lex talionis* is freely resorted to where its principles are forgotten. Because traces of its adoption have been discovered in the most barbarous as well as in the most polished forms of society, many writers have endeavoured to show that it is one of the first principles of right revealed by the wisdom of the ancients. It is frequently described as the foundation of their civil jurisprudence; while, in fact, it is an element imported from other sources, and stripped of many qualifications which tempered its application, and restrained the vindictive impulse of passion.

Both the spirit and the letter of the Jewish law make it manifest that retaliation was never meant to be exercised as an arbitrary right. Now, the enactments of the Mosaic law, concerning such injuries as are made the subject of restitution, in point of order come after, and appear to some extent to be a consequence of, the law of retaliation. This consideration may furnish some explanation of the principle upon which this law is founded. The vigorous maxims by which such statutes are illustrated express rather the measure than the method of justice. If the mode in which, under the Mosaic code, justice was administered be considered, it will be apparent that such judicial penalties as eye for eye, and tooth for tooth, are not to be understood as examples which justify the gratification of revenge. Such penalties will be found simply to indicate the degree of guilt by which the amount of compensation was to be estimated, and the measure of punishment to be judicially awarded where due compensation for an injury was not promptly given by the offender. But that the license for revenge was never intended to be conferred upon the individual injured, without the intervention of a judicial determination of the crime, is not only clear from the functions exercised by the tribunal of the elders, who decided upon the crime and adjudged its punishment, but it is placed beyond question by an express law in Leviticus, xix. 18:—
" Thou shalt not *avenge*, nor bear any grudge against the children of thy people, but thou shalt love thy neighbour as thyself." And if such an observation

be not here out of place, it is not unreasonable to suppose that, in conformity with the principle which appealed to the motive as well as to the act, thus making the law the vehicle of public instruction, provisions of this character had regard to the moral effect upon an offender that would result from an acknowledgment of his fault, and a voluntary effort to make amends for the wrong he had done. The Anglo-Saxon laws, which were for the most part avowedly based upon the Mosaic code, certainly adopted many wholesome restraints upon retaliation. In the laws of King Ina we find the following statute:—"If any one take revenge before he demand justice, let him give up what he has taken to himself, and pay the damage done, and make 'bòt' with xxx. shillings."

As we have already seen, the laws of retribution are chiefly directed towards offences against the person. Injuries to the property are the subject of the laws of restitution.

Such injuries consist of four classes.

First. The wrongfully taking what belongs to another.

Second. The wrongfully withholding what belongs to another.

Thirdly. Wilful damage or trespass to the property of another.

Fourthly. Injury to the property of another by carelessness or negligence, although the act by which the mischief was caused be neither wilful nor wrongful.

Of these, the laws relating to theft, or the wrongful taking of what belongs to another, will first engage our consideration. But the difference between withholding what belongs to another and taking what belongs to another is so slight, that debt may not be improperly considered as a subject nearly akin to theft. For in many respects the same consequences are common to both. Both consist in a wrongful possession, in the one case acquired by consent, in the other without consent. The one being wrongful in its inception; the other becoming wrongful as soon as the borrower refuses to restore what is lent.

Under the same head, also, pledges may be treated of; inasmuch as the security for a debt becomes properly the subject of restitution as soon as the obligation of the borrower is either fulfilled by repayment, or is satisfied by the claims of humanity. The duty of lending what a man can spare, is imposed by many scriptural injunctions. At the same time the obligation of returning what is borrowed is enforced by many ordinances of great severity. Yet, upon the other hand, where a man has undergone a certain probation sufficient to show that to the best of his power he is unable to redeem or to restore that which necessity compelled him to borrow, the Hebrew laws seem to have regarded it as a greater hardship to condemn him to further thraldom, than to oblige the lender to forego the return of what he could afford to lend.

Now, with respect to injuries to property, whether they arise from wilful malice or from carelessness, and a negligent regard to the interests of others, such offences become the subject of compensation. For such injuries the Mosaic laws compelled restitution, sometimes twofold, sometimes fourfold, according to the malignity of the offender.

The earliest laws of which we have any records treat theft, when not accompanied by violence, as a subject of compensation in the first instance. In illustration of this principle, the Hebrew laws furnish many examples by which its purpose and its limits are defined. Under the Mosaic institutions, the wrongful taking of what belonged to another did not render the aggressor amenable to criminal punishment until after an opportunity of making restitution and amends had been allowed him.

The primary law is succinctly stated in the words —"Thou shalt not steal." As the same authority forbids also to covet, we need not now concern ourselves with any technical definitions of what constitutes stealing; because it is manifest that the intention and the act are equally prohibited. But not only does the Mosaic law condemn positive acts of fraud; it also punishes the wrongful act or negligence whereby another is undesignedly injured, or deprived of what belongs to him. Consequently many acts, which cannot be described as theft, became the subject of restitution or compensation. Lest the purpose of the general law contained in the Decalogue should be evaded, such occurrences are specially provided against. Exod. xxi. 33—36: "And if a man shall open a pit, or if a man shall dig a pit, and not cover it, and an ox or an ass fall therein; the owner of the pit shall make it good, and give money unto the owner of them; and the dead beast shall be his. And if one man's ox hurt another's, that he die; then they shall sell the live ox, and divide the money of it; and the dead ox also shall they divide. Or if it be known that the ox hath used to push in time past, and his owner hath not kept him in, he shall surely pay ox for ox; and the dead ox shall be his own."

These statutes provide the most equitable adjustment of accidental damage. Where there was no proof of negligence upon the part of the owner, neither party could profit by the misfortune of the other. But where the accident might have been prevented, the owner was bound to make good the loss at his own expense.

But even with respect to such offences as tended wilfully to deprive another of his property, the nice distinctions of the Hebrew laws bear out the supposition that they were primarily regarded as the subject of civil remedy rather than of criminal punishment. It is remarkable to observe that in such offences the various degrees of guilt depend rather upon the amount of injury actually inflicted, than upon the wilfulness of the attempt. For it appears that the accomplishment of a design to steal was attended with a greater penalty than an intention which was only imperfectly carried out. Where the deliberate intention of stealing is accomplished, the law runs thus:—Exod. xxii. 1: "If a man shall steal an ox, or a sheep, and *kill* it, or *sell* it; he shall restore *five* oxen for an ox, and *four* sheep for a sheep." But where the thing stolen has not been so completely converted to the use of the thief, the penalty is modified. Ver. 4: "If the theft be certainly found in his hand alive, whether it be ox, or ass, or sheep, he shall restore double." Ver. 5: "If a man shall cause a field or a vineyard to be eaten, and shall put in his beast, and shall feed in another man's field; of the best of his own field, and of the best of his own vineyard, shall he make restitution."

In illustration of this part of this subject, the Roman laws may be mentioned. By the law of the Twelve Tables, it was a capital offence for a person who was of age to drive cattle at night on to the land of another. A fine was imposed for driving cattle upon a public pasture in the day-time. If the pasture were enclosed, a remedy for the offence was provided by the Aquilian law.

Where the injury was accidental, it was redressed by simple restitution, instead of by the penalty imposed where the trespass was wilful.

Ver. 6—8: " If fire break out, and catch in thorns, so that the stacks of corn, or the standing corn, or the field, be consumed therewith; he that kindled the fire shall surely make restitution. If a man shall deliver unto his neighbour money or stuff to keep, and it be stolen out of the man's house; if the thief be found, let him pay double. If the thief be not found, then the master of the house shall be brought unto the judges, to see whether he have put his hands unto his neighbour's goods."

The general law of theft is thus summed up:— Ver. 9—15. " For all manner of trespass, whether it be for ox, for ass, for sheep, for raiment, or for any manner of lost thing, which another challengeth to be his, the cause of both parties shall come before the judges; and whom the judges shall condemn, he shall pay *double* unto his neighbour. If a man deliver unto his neighbour an ass, or an ox, or a sheep, or any beast, to keep; and it die, or be hurt, or driven away, no man seeing it: Then shall an oath of the Lord be between them both, that he hath not put his hand unto his neighbour's goods; and the owner of it shall accept thereof, and he shall not make it good. And if it be stolen from him, he shall make restitution unto the owner thereof. If it be torn in pieces, then let him bring it for witness, and he shall not make good that which was torn. And if a man borrow *aught* of his neighbour, and it be hurt or die, the owner thereof *being not with it*, he shall surely make it good. But if the owner thereof *be* with it, he shall not make it good: if it be a hired thing, it came for his hire."

This seems to imply the doctrine that a bailee or borrower is *primâ facie* liable for what was committed to him. To derive any advantage from the possession or hire of a thing, with the Jews involved the liability to make it good in case of accidents. But where the person to whose charge the thing was committed derived no advantage from its possession or use, he was liable only for wilful damage or negligence.

But the law of restitution seems not only to have been applicable where a person had obtained the wrongful possession of what belonged to his neighbour, but even where, being perfectly innocent of the loss, he nevertheless had the means of restoring it. To enforce restitution, where other means failed, the Hebrew laws, as a last resort, suffered the person injured to work out the debt by the personal services of the thief or the debtor. Thus slavery for debt became a recognized institution. But to the harshness of such exactions limits were imposed by various statutes, the terms of which are very explicit, and have reference to the various circumstances under which such obligations might arise. The consideration, therefore, of this subject leads us to the statutes relating to the redemption both of personal service and of things pledged, as well as to those relating to the restoration of lands sold. For to maintain the influence of the several tribes, and to distinguish the families which composed them, the right of hereditary possession was so interwoven with the Hebrew polity, and so jealously regarded by the Mosaic laws, that it seems to have been presumed that nothing but the most abject necessity would compel a man to part with his birthright. To this end various statutes were imposed, which certainly imply a state of bondage such as that to which we have referred.

Of such limitations the following are among the most prominent.

Deut. xv. 1.—"At the end of every seven years thou shalt make a release.

"And this is the manner of the release: Every creditor that lendeth aught unto his neighbour shall release it; he shall not exact it of his neighbour, or of his brother; because it is called the Lord's release.

"If a foreigner, thou mayest exact it again: but that which is thine with thy brother's thine hand shall release."

Verse 12.—"And if thy brother, an Hebrew man, or an Hebrew woman, be sold unto thee, and serve thee *six* years; then in the seventh year thou shalt let him go free from thee."

Verse 18.—"It shall not seem hard unto thee when thou sendest him away free from thee; for he hath been worth double a hired servant unto thee, in serving thee six years."

These laws probably are the origin of our modern statutes of limitation, by which a debt is recoverable only within a certain time, since which the debtor has either incurred or acknowledged his obligation. After this period has elapsed, the debt is barred.

For this purpose the limit fixed by our laws is six years, which is precisely the time prescribed by the Hebrew laws.

The laws of the Anglo-Saxons nowhere more closely conform to the Mosaic laws than upon this subject. Such institutions, therefore, will furnish the best illustrations of the influence of the Mosaic laws upon English jurisprudence. The Anglo-Saxon laws clearly demonstrate that the ancient laws of this country adopted three very prominent features in the Jewish laws.

In the first instance, they treat theft as the subject of restitution. Secondly, in default of restitution, they give the power of selling the thief, or allowing him to redeem himself by his personal services, unless any one else would come forward to redeem him. And thirdly, in cases of suspicion, the accused was allowed an opportunity of clearing himself on oath.

In support of this, many examples occur. The laws of Æthelbright declare,—"If a man steal from the king, let him pay ninefold."—"If a freeman steal from a freeman, let him make threefold 'bot.'"—"If any one take property from a dwelling, let him pay threefold 'bot.'"—"If a 'theow' steal, let him make twofold 'bot.'"

The laws of Hlothhœre and Eadric, who were

kings of the Kentish men from the year 673 to the year 685, contain the following provisions, which prevailed in the kingdom of Kent:—"If one man steal property from another, and the owner afterwards lay claim to it, let him vouch to warranty at the king's hall, if he can, and let him bring thither the person who sold it to him. If he cannot do this, let him give it up, and let the owner take possession of it."

The laws of Withrœd will also be found to conform to the Mosaic laws:—"If any one slay a layman while thieving, let him be without 'wergild.' If a man seize a freeman with stolen goods upon him, let the king have power of one of three things: either that he be slain, or sold beyond sea, or redeemed with his 'wergild.' Whoever shall seize and secure him, let him have half of him. If any one slay him, let him be paid LXX. shillings." "If a 'theow' steal, and he be redeemed, LXX. shillings, as the king may choose: if any one slay him, let half his value be paid to the owner."

The laws of Athelstan are quite as explicit with regard to theft, as will be apparent from the following examples:—"First, that no thief be spared who may be taken 'hand-hœbbende' above twelve years and above eight pence. And if any one do so, let him pay for the thief according to his 'wer,' and let it not be the more settled for the thief, or that he clear himself thereby. But if he will defend himself, then let him not be spared. If a thief be brought into prison, that he be forty days in prison, and then let him be released thereout with CXX. shillings, and let the kindred enter into 'borh' for him, that he evermore desist. And if after that he steal, let him pay for him according to his 'wer,' or bring him again therein; and if any one stand up for him, let him pay for him according to his 'wer,' as well to the king as to him to whom it lawfully belongs, and let every man of those who there stand by him pay to the king cxx. shillings as 'wite.'"

The laws of Ina contain the following declarations:—"If a thief be seized, let him perish by death, or let his life be redeemed according to his 'wer.'" "A ceorlish man, if he have often been accused, if he at last be seized let his hand or foot be cut off."

Even suspected theft was punishable. The circumstances under which suspicion might be imputed, are more than once defined in the Anglo-Saxon laws. "If a far-coming man, or a stranger, journey through a wood out of the highway, and neither shout nor blow his horn, he is to be held for a thief, either to be slain or redeemed."

In King Alfred's dooms the following laws respecting theft are framed upon the same principle as the preceding illustrations:—"He who steals on Sunday, or at Yule, or at Easter, or on Holy Thursday, and on Rogation-days, for each of these we will that the 'bot' be twofold, as during Lent fast."

The same law refers to the various amounts of compensation for a gold thief, a mare thief, a bee thief, and a man thief.

It may be observed, that under the laws of Alfred, in case compensation was not rendered, the thief was liable to capital punishment.

The laws of Ina contain this statute:—"If any one steal, so that his wife and children know it not, let him pay LX. shillings as 'wite.' But if he steal with the knowledge of all his household, let them all go into slavery." A boy of ten years may be privy to a theft. "If a 'ceorl' steal a chattel and bear it into his dwelling, and it be attached therein, then shall he be guilty for his part without his wife, for she must obey her lord. If she dare to declare by oath that she tasted not of the stolen property, let her take her third part" This third part probably refers to the wife's right to dower or thirds in her husband's estate, which was thus relieved from the forfeiture that generally followed such offences.

The laws given by king Æthelstan to the city of London contain various provisions concerning theft, from which it is manifest that such offences were in the first instance made the subject of compensation. And the fact that the payment of such compensation might be made by the lord, is sufficient to show that the person to whom the compensation was due had the option of commuting the penalty for the personal services of the offender; or in other words, reducing him to the condition of slavery until he was released by payment of the statutable penalty. For it must be borne in mind, that, under the Anglo-Saxon form of government, society was composed of various subordinate ranks, whose relative condition is distinctly specified in the laws of our Anglo-Saxon kings—each rank being distinguished by its possessions, acquirements, or services. Thus we find that "if a ceorl thrived so that he had fully five hides of his own land, church and kitchen, bell-house and 'burh'-gate, seat and special duty in the king's hall, then was he thenceforth of thane-right worthy." "And if a thane thrived so that he served the king, and rode among his household, if he then had a thane who him followed, who to the king's 'ut-ware' five hides had, and in the king's hall served his lord, and thrice with his errand went to the king, he might thenceforth with his 'fore-oath' his lord represent at various needs, and his plaint lawfully conduct wheresoever he ought. And if a thane thrived so that he became an 'eorl,' then was he thenceforth 'eorl'-right worthy. And if a merchant thrived so that he fared thrice over the wide sea by his own means, then was he thenceforth of thane-right worthy."

But to return to the laws concerning theft. In the *Judicia Civitatis Lundoniæ* we have the following statute, which will be found to be in strict accordance with the principles and, indeed, almost the language, of the other Anglo-Saxon laws to which we have already referred. "And he who oft before has been convicted openly of theft, and shall go to the ordeal, and is there found guilty, that he be slain unless the kindred or the lord be willing to release him by his 'wer,' and by the full 'ceop-gild,' and also have him in 'borh,' that he thenceforth desist from every kind of evil. If after that he again steal, then let his kinsmen give him up to the reeve to whom it may appertain, in such custody as they before took him out of, from the ordeal, and let him be slain in retribution of the theft. But if any one defend him, and will take him, although he was convicted at the ordeal, so that he might not be slain; that he should be liable in his life, unless he should flee to the king, and he should give him his life; all as it was before ordained at 'Greatanlea,' and at Exeter, and at 'Thunresfield.'" "And whoever will avenge a thief, and commits an assault or makes an attack on the highway, let him be liable in cxx. shillings to the king. But if he slay any one in his revenge, let him be liable in his life and in all that he has, unless the king is willing to be merciful to him."

The laws of Canute provide the following ordinance:—"And we will that every man above twelve years make oath that he will neither be a thief nor cognizant of theft."

But the statute which follows this reflects the spirit, and almost the language, of a Jewish law of similar import.

From this it will be manifest that the ancient usage of vouching to warranty was derived from the Jewish custom, under which a suspected person was bound to clear himself by oath and witness:—"And let no man be entitled to any vouching to warranty unless he have true witness whence that come to him which is attached with him, and let the witness declare, by the favour of God and his Lord, that he is a true witness for him, as he saw with his eyes and heard with his ears that he rightly obtained it."

As additional safeguards against theft, as well as to prevent the unlawful possession of stolen goods, the Anglo-Saxon laws provided stringent regulations as to the manner in which bargains were to be made. To render such transactions valid, witnesses were required. Similar formalities appear to have been requisite under the Jewish law, before civil questions of this kind were recognised as the subject of judicial determination.

The Anglo-Saxon laws, however, not only insisted upon having bargains properly witnessed, but in many cases prescribed the class of persons who were competent to fulfil the office of witnesses.

The 25th doom of king Ina runs thus:—"If stolen property be attached with a chapman, and he have not bought it before good witnesses, let him prove according to the 'wite,' that he was neither privy to the theft nor thief, or pay as 'wite' xxxvi. shillings."

To the same effect are the laws of Æthelstan:— "And let no man exchange any property without the witness of the reeve, or of the mass priest, or of the landlord, or of the 'hordere,' or of other unlying man. If any one so do, let him give xxx. shillings, and let the landlord take possession of the exchange." "And we have ordained that no man buy any property out of port over xx. pence, but let him buy therewithin on the witness of the port reeve, or of another unlying man, or further on the witness of the reeves of the folk-mote."

The laws of Edward contain the following statute:—"And I will that every man have his warrantor, and that no man buy out of port, but have the port reeve's witness, or that of other unlying man." The term "port" seems here to have obtained the extended sense given to the word *portus* by the Roman law, signifying an enclosed place for the sale of merchandise, or market-place, and doubtless gave rise to that distinction between private bargains and sales in market overt, which is to this day the source of so many nice distinctions in the law of contracts.

The laws of Edgar, upon this point, are equally precise:—"And let every man, with their witness, buy and sell every of the chattels that he may buy and sell, either in a 'burh,' or in a wapentake."

The laws of Ethelred repeat the same precaution:—"And let no man either buy or exchange, unless he have 'borh' and witness; but if any one do so, let the landlord take possession of and hold the property till that it be known who rightfully owns it."

The laws of Canute enact as follows:—"And let no one buy any thing above the value of four pence, either living or lying, unless he have the true witness of four men, be it within a 'burh,' or be it up in the country."

In hand to hand dealings, the same securities against dishonesty were imposed by the laws of the ancient Greeks. This is apparent from the following regulations, which, in common with most of the other Greek laws to which we have had occasion to refer, have been extracted from Potter's "Greek Antiquities" and Petit "De Legibus Atticis." "All private bargains that are struck up between parties before witnesses, shall stand good in law." "Do not make any covenant or bargain contrary to the laws." "There shall no after wranglings be raised concerning those things which have been once agreed."

But to return to the immediate subject of this chapter. Amongst the laws of Canute the following statute occurs:—"If any one find a thief, and voluntarily let him escape without hue and cry, let him make 'bot' with the thief's 'wer,' or clear himself with a full oath that he knew of no guile in him. And if any one hear the hue and cry and disregard it, let him pay the king's 'ofer-hyrnes,' or fully clear himself."

Housebreaking, and arson, and open theft, and open 'morth,' and treason against a lord, are by the secular law "botless." That is to say, such offences cannot be redeemed by compensation.

The laws of William the Conqueror, incorporating many of the earlier laws of the Anglo-Saxons, contain an enactment concerning theft, as follows:—"Si quis appellatur de furto et sit liber homo, si bone fame hujusque fuit et testimonium bonum habuerit, purgabit se per juramentum suum. Quod si ante culpatus fuit, purgabit se duodecimo manu, et eligentur XIIII legales homines ex nomine qui juramentum hoc faciant. Quod si defecerit, et jurare cum eo noluerint, defendet se per judicium aque vel ignis; et appellator per VII legales homines ex nomine jurabit, quod nec ex odio nec alia aliqua causa hoc ei imponit nisi tamen ut jus suum adipiscatur."

Our laws, however, concerning theft appear to have increased in severity in proportion to their remoteness from their original source. Thus we discover, in the laws attributed to Henry the First, a more reluctant disposition to treat theft as the subject of restitution than is justified by the spirit of the earlier laws. These, indeed, they seem in some degree to have superseded, rather than to have developed. Under the tenth head, De Jure Regis, we have the following enactment:—"Hæc sunt jura quæ Rex Angliæ solus et super omnes homines habet in terra sua commoda pacis et securitatis institucione retenta—furtum morte impunitum." Again, under head XII.,—"Que placita emendari debeant,"—§ 3, "Hæc emendantur wera si ad emendacionem veniat: persolucio furti vel robarie; qui furem plegiatum amiserit; qui ei obviaverit et gratis sine vociferatione dimiserit; qui ei consenciet in aliquo." XXVI. "De furti placito.—Defensor aut dominus de furto pulsatorum, si semel aut amplius respectaverit erga vicinum diem, vicinaliter et absque justicie majoris auctoritate condictum curiam suam perdet; pulsator autem quos pulsaverit ad majorem audienciam protrahendi potestatem accipiet." XLIII. "Ne quis inplacitatus a rege alieni respondeat. Qui furtum fecerit, qui proditor domini sui fuerit, quicumque ab eo obviacione hostili vel bello campali fugerit, vel victus erit, vel feloniam fecerit, terram suam forisfecerit." XLIX. "Omne autem furtum, mobile vel immobile, simplex aut multiplex, redimendum non est. Redimendorum alia membris, alia pecunia." § 22. "In omnibus vero furtis, aut solus compellans est aut plures, servi aut liberi, divisim vel permixtim, fugitivi vel non fugitivi, unum dominum habentes vel non." § 23. "Si servus in redimendis immobilibus intra VIII denarr estimatis furetur, reddat dominus ejus repetenti capitale suum semel, et verberetur et signetur ab eodem repetente prima vice. Si in mortificantibus haud habbenda sit, sicut liber moriatur." § 24. "Si liber cum servo furetur, liber solus paciatur. Quicquid evenerit dampnacionis vel redempcionis servus domino suo reddatur, jure castigandus." § 25. "Si plures servi furentur, unus pro omnibus paciatur, et is sit quem sors obtulerit. Si furtum redimendum sit capitale repetentis simul conjectent. Si plures furentur unam ovem aut porcum, aut deinceps aliquid majus, aut morte puniendum simul omnes paciantur, sive furtum simplex sit aut multiplex."

The Greek laws respecting theft are scarcely less remarkable for their simplicity than for their adherence to the principles embodied in the Hebrew laws:—

"He who steals, shall pay double the value of the thing he stole to the owner, and as much to the public exchequer." (Solon's law.) "If anybody hath had any thing stolen from him, and has it restored, the thief, with the abettor, shall pay double the value; but in case the thief doth not make restitution, ten-fold, and be set in the stocks five days and as many nights, if the heliasts so order it—this order shall then be made when they consider what punishment to inflict upon him." (Solon's law.)

"If any one have filched away by day any thing worth above fifty drachms, let the action called απαγωγη be put in execution against him before the Eleven. But if in the night, any one hath liberty to kill him, or upon his making away, to wound him, and to issue the same action against him; by which, if he be cast, he shall die without any concession for sureties to put in bail for the restitution of the stolen goods."—"He that shall pilfer out of the Lyceum, Academia, Cynosarges, or any of the gymnasia, any thing of the least value, as a garment, oil, vial, &c., or above ten drachms out of the baths or ports, shall suffer death."—"All cut-purses, burglars, and kidnappers, if convicted, shall suffer death."—"He who takes away any thing which is not his own, shall be liable to die for it." (One of Draco's laws.)

It is a capital crime to break into a man's orchard and steal his figs. This law, however, was abrogated by the following one:—"They who steal figs shall be fined. They who steal dung shall be punished corporeally."—"He that puts a man in prison for theft and cannot prove it, shall be fined a thousand drachms."—"He who makes search after thieves in another's house, must have only a thin garment hanging loose about him."

This last law seems to be founded on the same principle as the Jewish law respecting pledges, which it very much resembles. "When thou dost lend thy brother any thing, thou shalt not go into his house to fetch his pledge. Thou shalt stand abroad, and the man to whom thou dost lend shall bring out the pledge abroad unto thee." (Deut. xxiv.) "He who wilfully does damage, shall refund twice as much; he who does it involuntarily, an equivalent." This exactly agrees with the distinction observed by the Hebrew law. "His eyes shall be both plucked out who hath blinded any one-eyed person." (One of Solon's laws.) This statute answers closely to the Mosaic law of retaliation:—"That dog shall be tied up with a chain four cubits long who hath bit anybody." (One of Solon's laws.)

The different punishments for theft in use at Rome were borrowed from the Athenians. As we have already seen, by the laws of the Twelve Tables a thief in the night-time might be put to death; as, indeed, he might in the day-time, if he defended himself with a weapon. But no one was justified in his death, without having first called out for assistance. The punishment of slaves was more severe than the punishment of freemen. Slaves were scourged and thrown from the Tarpeian rock.

Amongst the fragments of the Twelve Tables which have been preserved, there occurs the following instance of the extent to which the principle of retaliation was adopted by the Romans:—" Si membrum rupsit, ni cum eo pacit talio esto." This corroborates the opinion we have ventured to advance, that the vengeance of retaliation was originally resorted to only when compensation had failed to redress the injury.

But as an illustration of how far, in this respect, the Roman laws followed those of the Greeks, we may mention one which both Plato and Aristophanes refer to as a maxim at Athens. Whence we infer that it was borrowed from the Athenians. The Æbutian law of the Romans is said to have abolished many of the precautions with which the exercise of rights conferred by the Twelve Tables were guarded. Amongst other curious customs which were thus abrogated by the Lex Æbutia, was that "of searching for stolen goods without any clothes on but a girdle round the waist and a mask on the face."

The punishments for theft seem to have increased in severity with the growing love of acquisition fostered by prosperity. Such penalties, however, were afterwards mitigated by various laws, until at length they were restored by the edicts of the prætors to the simple principle of restitution. These edicts, as has been shown elsewhere, were for the most part declaratory of the ancient law, and thence may be taken to sanction the earliest principles of jurisprudence. A man caught in manifest theft was obliged to restore fourfold besides the things stolen. For the recovery of such penalties, a particular form of action was provided. If, say the Roman jurists, a person was not caught in the act, but was so evidently guilty that he could not deny it, he was called *fur nec manifestus*. This degree of guilt was punished by the compulsory restoration of double the value of the theft.

If any one hindered a person to search for stolen goods, or did not produce them when sought for, actions were granted by the prætor against him; in the latter case, for double their value. What the penalty was in the other case is uncertain. But in whatever manner theft was punished, conviction was always attended with infamy.

The Romans made a distinction between theft and robbery. According to their definition of such offences, robbery took place only in movable things; immovable things were said to be invaded. The possession of them was recovered by the interdict of the prætor.

Robbery was punished less severely than theft. An action was granted by the prætor against the robber for fourfold, including what he had robbed. There was no difference whether the robber was a freeman or a slave. But the proprietor of a slave was obliged either to give him up or to pay the damage. If any one slew the slave or beast of another, he was obliged, by the Aquilian law, to repair the damage. By the same law also, the injured person could recover double value for any injury done to his property or his slaves.

The principle upon which these distinctions are founded, in many particulars agrees with the provisions of the Mosaic law, to which we have been already referred, if indeed their very terms are not borrowed from that source. When a thing stolen was found, after "much search," in the possession of any one, the offence was, by the law of the Twelve

Tables, punished as "manifest theft," but afterwards as *furtum nec manifestum*. If a thief, to avoid detection, offered things stolen to any one to keep and they were found in his possession, he had an action against the person who gave him the things, whether it was the thief or another, for triple their value.

Personal injuries or affronts were variously punished. By the Twelve Tables, a fine of twenty five asses, or pounds of brass, was imposed for trivial injuries to the person or reputation. But where the injury was more atrocious, as if a person was deprived of the use of a limb, the offence was punishable by retaliation, in case the person injured would not accept of any other satisfaction. An action also might be had against a person for an injury done by those under his power. This means of redress was called *actio noxalis*. If, for instance, a slave committed theft, or did any damage, although without his master's knowledge, he was nevertheless to be given up to the injured person. And so, if a beast did any damage, the owner was obliged to offer a compensation or give up the beast.

The spirit in which the Roman laws were interpreted under the later emperors best illustrate the principles upon which they are based. Of this the comments of the Roman lawyers afford sufficient examples. Thus Paulus declares, "If anyone shall kill a thief, either in the day or night time, who defended himself with a weapon, this is not taken account of by the law; but he would have done better if, having taken him and conveyed him to a safe place, he had brought him before the magistrates."

So Ulpian comments upon the slaying of robbers:—"The wilful killing of a man is necessary to be referred to, for the killing alone is not sufficient; the thing must be done wilfully. Wherefore if a slave should kill a robber, the Aquilian law does not apply, because he did not kill him wilfully."

"So if anyone should kill another who was seeking him with a weapon, he will not appear to have killed him wrongfully. Thence, if the law of the Twelve Tables allowed one to kill a thief in the night-time in every case, and equally allowed it in the day-time; but in that case if he defended himself with a weapon, we shall see whether the Aquilian law applied; for Pomponius doubts whether this law was in use. But when anyone killed a thief in the night, we have no doubt but that the Aquilian law did not apply, except that when it was possible to apprehend him, and it was preferred to kill him, it evidently appears to have been done wilfully; therefore, even the Cornelian law will apply. We must understand this wilfulness not as that from an effect of hurt from a former affront, but that which is done illegally, that is, contrary to right; the other is, if any one should kill unwittingly."

But of all laws concerning theft, those which relate to cattle-stealing are the ones which the interpretations of the Roman lawyers seem to have reconciled most closely to the principles laid down by the Mosaic laws.

The commentaries of Paulus exhibit this inclination of the Roman lawyers in a striking light. A few extracts from his comments will show the tendency of Roman law, when it reached its highest state of perfection, to revert to the simplest rules of jurisprudence. In the writings of this commentator the following passages occur. In these, many distinctions peculiar to the Hebrew laws will be met with in respect to a class of offences for which the Hebrew laws contain special statutes:—

"The heinous drivers away of cattle are for the most part condemned either to death or to work in the mines; but some are condemned to public labour. Those are infamous who drive horses and flocks of sheep away from the stable or pastures, especially if they do it often, or while armed.

"Cattle-lifters are those who drive away one or two horses and the same number of oxen, or ten goats or five hogs; whoever might be within that number suffered punishment as a thief, according to his condition. It is either agreed to return double or treble the number, to be beaten with rods, to be condemned for one year to the public works, or that it be made good under the punishment of slavery. If one drives away the cattle as to which another is sueing him, he is to be sent before a judge and convicted in that way, and condemned as a thief to return either double as much or three times as much.

"Whoever leads away with him a stray horse, ox, or other cattle, it would be preferable to treat him as a thief rather than as a cattle-lifter.

"Whoever drives away cattle about which there is a dispute, is tried before the judge, and if convicted, he is compelled to repay double or treble the amount."

Concerning the punishment of cattle-lifters, Ulpian's comments accord with those of Paulus. He cites the rescripts of Hadrian. He repeats, for instance, Hadrian's instruction to the council of Bœtica, in the following terms:—

"Where cattle-stealers are punished most severely, it is usual to condemn them to death; but they are not punished so severely everywhere—only where this species of crime is very common: they are otherwise condemned to labour, and sometimes for a term of years. Wherefore I think that amongst you the kind of punishment is to be chosen which can be most easily imposed for this crime, namely, that cattle-stealers may be condemned to death; or, if there was any one so known and skilled in cattle-stealing who might be first deterred from this crime by some punishment, it would be well to send him to work in the mines."

"The rescript of Hadrian thus speaks as if the severer penalty was to work in the mines; unless by chance he supposed, that speaking of the penalty of death was a condemning to the public games."

"But there is a difference between those who are condemned to death and those who are condemned to public games; for the condemned to death are immediately destroyed, or else ought certainly to be destroyed within a year. This is contained in the warrant of those who are condemned to the public games. Not every one is destroyed."

The Egyptian laws punished theft with great severity. Where the crime was aggravated by violence, the offender rendered himself liable to capital punishment. In other cases, stealing seems to have been regarded as the subject of restitution or compensation. This appears from the allusions of various ancient authors, to which Sir Gardner Wilkinson refers in his Egyptian Researches; but, as far as I can learn, no evidence has yet been discovered of the precise terms in which the laws of Egypt were expressed beyond what we may gather from the traditions of Diodorus Siculus and Strabo.

But a very strange custom is mentioned by Diodorus Siculus in his book on Egypt. He says:—"There is a very remarkable law among the Egyptians concerning theft. Those who enter into the list of thieves are to give in their names to one who is their chief and head, and whatever they steal they engage to bring to him. They that have lost anything are to set down in writing every particular and bring it to him, and set forth the day, hour, and place when and where they lost their goods. Everything being thus readily found out, after the things are valued, the true owner is to pay a fourth of the value, and so receive his goods again. For seeing it was not possible to restrain all from thieving, the law-maker found out a way that all might be restored, except a small proportion for redemption."

From the subject of theft we pass on to the laws relating to borrowing and lending. And as by the earliest usages of society both lands and goods were employed as securities, we may without confusion treat of the laws relating to the redemption of possessions under the same head as those concerning usury. Upon this subject there is one very remarkable characteristic of the Jewish law. In conformity with the jealousy with which the Hebrew polity regarded the hereditary rights of families, it placed such limits to the power of borrowing, as defeated any attempt on the part of the most extravagant person to deprive himself or his family of their possessions beyond a certain limited period.

The wisdom of such restrictions was appreciated by subsequent legislators; and many of the restraints upon alienation which distinguished the Hebrew polity have been imitated by other ancient systems of jurisprudence; yet in none of them are the limitations so stringent and so comprehensive as those imposed upon the Jews.

Selden, in his treatise De Successionibus apud Hebræos, has gathered from the comments of the Rabbins some interesting particulars concerning the Jewish laws of inheritance, which are not so obvious from the text of the Mosaic law.

" 1. It appears that the inheritance was divisible amongst all the sons, but the eldest son took a portion double that of any of his brothers. Thus, if there were three sons, the estate was divided into four parts. The eldest son took two-fourths, his younger brothers took one-fourth each.

" 2. If the son died in the father's lifetime, his children represented him, and in the same proportions succeeded to their father's share.

" 3. The daughters did not succeed to the inheritance of the father as long as there were sons or any descendants of the sons in being. But if any of the sons died in the lifetime of his father, leaving daughters, but without sons, the daughters succeeded to his part as if he had been himself possessed.

" 4. In case the father left daughters but no sons,

the daughters succeeded in equal shares to their father's estate, without any preference in favour of the eldest daughter.

"5. If the son had purchased an inheritance and died without issue, leaving a father and brothers, the inheritance reverted to the father, without any exception in favour of the brothers, except in the case where the next brother had married the widow of the deceased to raise up children to his brother's name.

"6. But if in this case the father was dead, the inheritance passed to the brothers as heirs to the father; with this exception, that the eldest son did not take a double portion. But in case the father died without leaving sons or any descendants from them, then the estate descended to all the sisters of the deceased brother.

"7. But if the father was dead without issue, then the estate passed to the grandfather. But if he was dead, then it went to his sons and their descendants, and for want of them then to his daughters or their descendants, as if the grandfather himself had been actually possessed and had died.

"8. But the inheritance of the son never reverted to the mother or any of her ancestors. Both she and they were totally excluded from the succession to the inheritance."

The Greek laws concerning inheritances in some respects resembled the Jewish laws. The terms, however, in which they are couched are not free from obscurity. From what may be gathered from Petit's Comments on his Leges Atticæ, the substance of them appears to be this:—

First, that all the sons equally inherited to the father. If he had no sons, then the husbands of his daughters were the next in succession to the inheritance. If the deceased had no children, then his brothers and their children were his heirs. If he had no brothers, then his next of kindred on the part of his father, the males being preferred before females. In failure of the father's line, then the estate descended to the mother's line, *ad sobrinorum usque filios.*

Such is the interpretation which Sir Matthew Hale places upon the meaning of Petit's compilation of the general laws of the Greeks regulating descents. But some of their special laws bear a more obvious resemblance to those of the Jews.

An ancient Greek law, which was subsequently abrogated by Solon, contains the following statute, which bears a remarkable resemblance to the Jewish laws of inheritance:—"The right of inheritance shall remain in the same family."

To this rule the Jewish law made an exception in the case of daughters; amongst whom the property of the father became equally divisible, for the first time, amongst the daughters of Zelopehad. It will be found that the Greeks not only observed the Jewish rule with regard to inheritance, but they also adopted the Jewish exception. An ancient Greek law has been preserved in terms which correspond with those of the Jews:—"Anyone, though he hath daughters alive, may give his estate to another body, on this proviso, that the persons enjoying it shall marry the daughters."

One of Solon's laws provided that "all legitimate

sons should have an equal portion of their father's inheritance."

Another Greek law, mentioned by Demosthenes in Macart, is to the following effect:—"The estate of him that dies intestate and leaves daughters, shall come to those who marry them; but if there are no daughters, these shall enjoy it, viz., his brothers by his father's side and their sons; if he hath neither brothers nor nephews, then males descended from them, though very far distant in kindred; but if none of the grandchildren remain down to the second cousins by the man's side, the wife's relations shall put in for the inheritance: admit there are none living of either side, they who have the nearest pretence to kindred shall enjoy it. As for bastards, from Euclides' archonship, they shall pretend no right of kindred; if there is a lawfully begotten daughter and an illegitimate son, the daughter shall have preference in right to the inheritance, both in respect of divine and civil affairs."

The Greek laws regulating the period within which inheritances might be recovered, seem to agree in some respects with the Jewish laws of redemption, although the period was different. The following limitation is to be found in the Greek laws:—"Five years being expired after the death of the immediate successor, the estate is to remain secure to the deceased person's heirs, without being liable to lawsuits."

Among the Romans, the laws of succession varied at different times. The laws of the Twelve Tables excluded females from the inheritance. But many alterations in the laws of inheritance were afterwards introduced by the emperors. It is not our purpose to trace the successive changes of the Roman laws in this respect. The distribution of estates was ultimately governed by the following rules. These remedied many hardships which had previously thwarted the wants of society. Three channels were opened for descents and successions. Estates passed first, in the most natural course, to the children in the descending line; in default of this, the heir was to be sought in the parents or the ascending line.

This stock being exhausted, the property devolved upon the collateral line; either in *agnatos a parte patris*, or in *cognatos a parte matris*.

The descending line was the first in which the right of inheritance accrued. In this the rights of the children were determined by the following rules:—

"1. In remote descents the children represented the parent, and succeeded in that right which the parent should have had.

"2. This descent or succession was equal amongst all the sons and daughters, without preference in favour of either sex; so that if the common ancestor had three sons and three daughters, each of them took a sixth part of the estate. If one of them had died in the lifetime of the common ancestor having three sons and three daughters, these children took the sixth part to which their parent would have inherited. This sixth thence became again divisible into six equal shares."

In the ascending line these two rules were observed:—

"1. If the son died without descendants, having a father and mother living, the father and mother succeeded equally to his estate; if only a father or only a mother, he or she succeeded alone to the exclusion of the collateral line—except brothers and sisters, in whose favour the Roman law provided,

"2. That if the deceased left a father and a mother, with a brother and a sister by the same parents, they all four took equal parts of the estate."

In respect to the collateral line, whose claims could only be asserted where the person died without father or mother, son or daughter, or any descendants in the right line, the rules were these:—

"1. Brothers and sisters by the same parents succeeded equally. Their children represented them, and in their turn took their parents' shares in equal portions.

"2. If there were no brothers and sisters of the whole blood, then the brethren and the sisters of the half-blood succeeded to the deceased, with a right of representation in favour of their descendants, similar to that enjoyed of the whole blood.

"3. In failure of brethren, both of the whole and the half-blood, the inheritance passed to the next kindred.

"4. If the next kindred stood in the same degree of relationship to the deceased, whether on the part of the father as *agnati*, or on the part of the mother as *cognati*, they succeeded to the inheritance in equal shares."

In England, under the most ancient laws, earldoms and baronies were the inheritance of the eldest son, to the exclusion of younger children. These were then principalities, with large jurisdictions annexed to them, the power and use of which would have been destroyed had they been divisible. They were small kingdoms. The very purpose for which they were created, therefore, rendered it necessary for their preservation that they should, like the crown of the realm, pass from one hand to another unimpaired by diminution or curtailment. But ordinary freeholds descended to all the children. This custom also prevailed in Wales.

Sir Matthew Hale mentions a statute relating to the rights of succession enacted in the reign of Edward the First. From the terms of this law it appears, first, that the succession of the eldest sons was then known to be the common and usual law of England.

Secondly, that the succession of all the sons was the ancient and customary law among the Britons in Wales; for by this statute the custom was confirmed.

Thirdly. This law abrogates a custom under which bastards had anciently been admitted to inherit in Wales, as well as the legitimate children. The rule, therefore, thus abrogated, must have existed long before it acquired the force of a custom. Its abrogation implies its previous establishment.

The Anglo-Saxon laws contain few provisions concerning the course of descents. But Sir Matthew Hale expresses his opinion that although baronies and royal inheritances devolved upon the eldest son, yet in the times of the Saxons and Danes ordinary lands descended amongst all the sons alike. Sir Matthew Hale mentions, on the authority of Lambard, a law of Canute's (though I must confess that I have been unable to find it in Dr. Thorpe's collection of the Anglo-Saxon laws) from which it appears, that until the Conquest the descent of lands was to all the sons alike, and for anything that appears to the contrary, to all the daughters also. It may be gathered also that at this period there was no difference in the hereditary transmission of lands and goods, at least in reference to the children. His view is corroborated by the laws of Edward the Confessor, as confirmed by William the First. In the time of Henry the First, the eldest son took the principal fee of his father's land, but did not succeed to the whole estate. In default of children, the father or mother inherited before the brother or sister; failing these, the land descended to uncles and aunts. It appears, also, the father's line was preferred before the mother's, unless the land descended from the mother, and then the mother's line had the preference.

The laws of Henry II. introduced further restrictions, in conformity with the system of feudal tenures. If the lands were held by knight's service, they generally went to the eldest son; and in case of no sons, then to all the daughters; but in case there were no children at all, then to the eldest brother.

Lands held in socage tenure were equally divided among the sons, though the chief house went to the eldest; for this the rest were entitled to compensation. Under these laws a bastard could not inherit. In case the purchaser died without issue, the land descended to the brothers; and for want of brothers, to the sisters; and for want of them, to the children of the brothers or sisters; and for want of them, to the uncles. But the father or mother did not inherit to the son.

It was not till the time of Henry III. that the

laws of inheritance made the eldest son of common right the heir not only of lands held by knight's service, but also of socage lands, unless there were a special custom to the contrary, as is still the case in Kent and in some other places. Yet such exceptional rules as now exist may be more properly regarded as remnants of the ancient law that once generally prevailed, than as local customs sprung from peculiar circumstances.

In respect to the redemption of debts and possessions, the chief characteristics of the Hebrew laws may be gathered from the following provisions:—

Lev. xxv. 10. "And ye shall hallow the fiftieth year, and proclaim liberty throughout all the land unto all the inhabitants thereof: it shall be a jubilee unto you; and ye shall return every man unto his possession, and ye shall return every man unto his family." Ver. 14. "And if thou sell aught unto thy neighbour, or buyest aught of thy neighbour's hand, ye shall not oppress one another." Ver. 15, 16. "According to the number of years after the jubilee thou shalt buy of thy neighbour, and according unto the number of years of the fruits he shall sell unto thee: according to the multitude of years thou shalt increase the price thereof, and according to the fewness of years thou shalt diminish the price of it; for according to the number of the years of the fruits doth he sell unto thee." Ver. 23. "The land shall not be sold for ever; for the land is mine; for ye are strangers and sojourners with me." Ver. 24. "And in all the land of your possession ye shall grant a redemption for the land." Ver. 25—27. "If thy brother be waxen poor, and hath sold away some of his possession, and if any of his kin come to redeem it, then shall ye redeem that which his brother sold. And if the man have none to redeem it, and himself be able to redeem it, then let him count the years of the sale thereof, and restore the overplus unto the man to whom he sold it, that he may return unto his possession." Ver. 28. "But if he be not able to restore it to him, then that which is sold shall remain in the hand of him that hath bought it until the year of jubilee; and in the jubilee it shall go out, and he shall return unto his possession."

The manner in which the redemption of lands was observed by the Jews is illustrated by the account which Josephus gives of the Hebrew laws in his Jewish Antiquities:—

"When the Jubilee is come, which name denotes *liberty*, he that sold the land, and he that bought it, meet together, and make an estimate, on the one hand, of the fruits gathered, and on the other hand, of the expenses laid out upon it. If the fruits gathered come to more than the expenses laid out, he that sold it takes the land again; but if the expenses prove more than the fruits, the present possessor receives of the former owner the difference that was wanting, and leaves the land to him; and if the fruits received and the expenses laid out, prove equal to one another, the present possessor relinquishes it to the former owners. Moses would have the same law obtain as to those houses also which were sold in villages, but he made a different law for such as were sold in a city; for if he that sold it tendered the purchaser his money again within a year, he was forced to restore it; but in case a whole year had intervened, the purchaser was to enjoy what he had bought."

The Mosaic laws forbade the Jews to take usury amongst themselves. But they were allowed to take usury from strangers, subject to certain restrictions imposed to prevent extortionate oppression. The merciful spirit in which the Hebrew laws concerning pledges was conceived, seems to have commended them to the admiration of the ancient legislators.

Among other prohibitions in the Hebrew statutes, these provisions are remarkable:—

Deut. xxiv. 6, 12, 13: "No man shall take the nether or upper millstone to pledge; for he taketh a man's life to pledge." "And if a man be poor, thou shalt not sleep with his pledge: In any case thou shalt deliver him the pledge again when the sun goeth down, that he may sleep in his own raiment and bless thee."

The Egyptian laws respecting loans and usury are recorded in the following paragraph, which we have extracted from the account given by Diodorus Siculus of the Egyptian customs:—

"They say that Bocchoris made the laws concerning merchandize. As to these, it was a law that if a man borrowed money and the lender had no writing to show for it, and the other denied upon his oath, he should be quit of the debt. To that end, therefore, in the first place, they were to sacrifice to the gods, as men making conscience and tender and scrupulous in taking of an oath; for it being clear and evident that he that swears often again and again, at last loses his credit, every man to prevent that mischief will be very cautious of being brought to an oath. Moreover, the lawgiver had this design, that by grounding a man's credit and reputation wholly upon the integrity of his life and conversation, every one would be induced to honest and virtuous actions, lest he should be despised as a man of no credit or worth. Besides, it was judged a most unjust thing not to believe him upon his oath in that matter relating to his contract, to whom credit was given in the self-same thing without an oath before.

"For those who lent money by contract in writing, it was not lawful to take usury above what would double the stock, and that payment should be made only out of the debtor's goods, but his body was not to be liable in anywise to imprisonment; and those were counted the debtor's goods which he had either earned by his labour, or had been bestowed upon him by the just proprietors. But as for their bodies, they belonged to the cities where they inhabited, who had an interest in them for the public service both in times of peace and war, for that it was an absurd thing for him who was to venture his life for his country to be carried to gaol for a debt by his creditors (if it should so happen), and that the public safety should be hazarded to gratify the covetousness of some private men. This law seems to have been established in Athens by Solon, which he called *sisactithy*, freeing all the citizens from being imprisoned by their creditors for debt. And some do justly blame the law-makers of Greece that they forbade arms, ploughs, and other things absolutely necessary for labour, to be taken in pawn, and yet permitted them that should use them to be taken to prison."

The Greek laws concerning loans and usury are very explicit. The terms in which they are expressed are the best evidence of their origin. We adduce the following laws:—

"A banker shall demand no more interest than what he agreed to at first.

"Let usurers' interest money be moderate.

"Nobody who hath put in surety for any thing may sue for it, he or his heirs.

"Pledges and sureties shall stand but for one year.

"No one, to clear his debt, shall make himself a slave."

Although the two last-mentioned laws somewhat mitigate the rigour of the application of the Hebrew laws, they manifestly proceed from the principle of the Mosaic code, in which, however, the limit was more extended. The period of redemption for goods and chattels was limited by the Jewish laws to seven years. The power of redeeming a debt by personal servitude was recognized. But the period of such servitude was limited by the return of the next recurring year of jubilee, or fiftieth year, whatever might have been the period of commencement. Thus the recurrence of this period established a standard by which the value of property was calculated. In accordance with this the price of land, as well as the value of personal service and the use of money, was regulated. In this respect the polity of the Jews possessed an advantage, which hitherto the faculty of no civilized nation has succeeded in attaining. For it is manifest from this, that neither the value of money, or of personal service, was made to depend upon the prosperity of the country, or upon the value of land; but that the value of both depended entirely upon their proximity to a certain recognized period, at the expiry of which all engagements were freed. But, of course, where hereditary possession was the law of the state, the circumstances and the conditions of enjoyment were very different from those which are essential to a state of society whose prosperity depends upon the right of acquisition, and whose wealth is not only distributed, but enhanced, by a constant change of property and the means of improvement which the continual circulation of wealth confers. With the Romans, it was not lawful for free-born citizens to sell themselves for slaves. Nor was it allowed any other person to sell freemen. In this respect their laws agreed with those of the Jews. But to this law there were two exceptions. Fathers were permitted to sell their children for slaves, although the children reduced to slavery under such circumstances were not entirely deprived of their municipal rights, which, upon the expiry of their servitude, they were suffered in some measure to resume. Another exception prevailed in the case of insolvent debtors who were given up as slaves to their creditors.

The laws of the Romans contain many enactments with regard to usury. The interest permitted by the Twelve Tables was only one per cent. But by various devices usurers increased the rate of interest to an exorbitant amount. To check their avarice various laws were from time to time enacted. Amongst others, the *Lex Licinia Sextia* provided that what had been paid for interest should be deducted from the capital, and the remainder paid in three years by equal portions.

By the *Lex Lætoria*, which was intended to protect minors from fraud, no one under twenty-five years of age was capable of making a legal bargain.

If a man was indebted to several persons, his goods were divided among his creditors.

To check the cruelty of usurers, a law was subsequently made, by which it was provided that no debtors should be kept in irons or in bonds; and that the goods of the debtor, but not his person, should be given up to his creditors.

## CHAPTER VIII.

### ON ADULTERIES.

Upon offences of this nature the provisions of the Mosaic laws are very explicit.

"If a man entice a maid, and lie with her, he shall surely endow her to be his wife. If her father utterly refuse to give her unto him, he shall pay money according to the dowry of virgins." (Exod. xxii. 16, 17.)

"And whosoever lieth carnally with a woman, that is a bondmaid, betrothed to an husband, and not at all redeemed, nor freedom given her; she shall be scourged; they shall not be put to death, because she was not free." (Levit. xix. 20.)

"And the man that committeth adultery with another man's wife, even he that committeth adultery with his neighbour's wife, the adulterer and the adulteress shall surely be put to death." (Levit. xx. 10.)

Again. "If a man be found lying with a woman married to an husband, then they shall both of them die." (Deut. xxii. 22.) "If a damsel that is a virgin be betrothed unto an husband, and a man find her in the city, and lie with her; then ye shall bring them both out unto the gate of that city, and ye shall stone them with stones that they die; the damsel, because she cried not, being in the city; and the man, because he hath humbled his neighbour's wife." (Deut. xxii. 23, 24.)

Here the betrothal, or consent to marry, is expressly treated as the foundation of marital rights. It is a remarkable illustration of the principle adopted by the Roman law: *Consensus non concubitus facit nuptias.* From this it seems probable, that under the Mosaic law the obligations of the matrimonial contract were founded rather upon the consent of the parties than by virtue of any formal ceremony.

"But if a man find a betrothed damsel in the field, and the man force her, and lie with her; then the man only that lay with her shall die: but unto the damsel thou shalt do nothing; there is in the damsel no sin worthy of death." (Deut. xxii. 25, 26.) "If a man find a damsel that is a virgin, which is not betrothed, and lay hold on her, and lie with her, and they be found; then the man that lay with her shall give unto the damsel's father fifty shekels of silver, and she shall be his wife; because he hath humbled her, he may not put her away all his days." (Deut. xxii. 28, 29.)

Thus it appears that a criminal connection between a man and a married woman, or a woman betrothed, was in either case punishable with the death of both parties, unless there was a reasonable presumption that the woman was not a consenting party, or was incapable of resistance. Under such circumstances the man alone suffered capitally.

Rape was a crime punished with death.

The seduction of an unmarried girl is made the subject of compensation to the woman's father; the seducer being at the same time compelled to endow her to be his wife.

In the latter case, the Jewish law agreed with our own laws so far as that the compensation was to be given to the father.

By our law, where the woman is living with her father, in case of her seduction the father is entitled to compensation for the injury occasioned by the loss of her services. Where she is in the service of another, her master is the person to sue for damages; but in no case can the woman herself recover compensation for the injury. By the Saxon laws before the Conquest, the amount of compensation was fixed according to the social condition of the woman, as it appears to have been by the Jewish laws. Formerly, also, rape was a felony punishable with death.

It is remarkable that, by the present laws of this country, adultery with the wife of another is not punished as a crime, but is treated as a civil injury for which the husband is entitled to recover a compensation from his wife's seducer. In this respect our laws differ from those of the Hebrews, and also from the institutions of many civilized states. Over the greater part of Europe such offences are the subject of a penal code, and are treated with becoming severity. There is, however, reason to believe that, by the laws which prevailed here at the time of the Conquest, adultery was punished with a rigour more in conformity with the Mosaic model, upon which such laws were avowedly framed. This is a part of the Hebrew laws which has been the subject of much learned comment by their Rabbins and historians. The Jews strictly observed an ancient superstition which forbade any one but the appointed officers to quote their law in its exact words. They therefore contented themselves, when referring to such matters, with giving a general outline of their laws, studiously avoiding a repetition of the terms in which they were expressed. This, however, renders their accounts the more interesting, as it shows the more clearly how they understood the text. We give, therefore, an extract from the Jewish Antiquities of Josephus, in which that historian gives the substance of the Mosaic laws concerning adulteries, in the following terms:—

"If any one has been espoused to a woman as to a virgin, and does not afterwards find her so to be, let him bring his action and accuse her, and let her make use of such indications to prove his accusation as he is furnished withal; and let the father or the brother of the damsel, or some one that is after them nearest of kin to her, defend her. If the damsel obtain a sentence in her favour that she had not been guilty, let her live with her husband that accused her, and let him not have any further power at all to put her away, unless she give him very great occasion of suspicion, and such as can in no way be contradicted. But for him that brings an accusation and calumny against his wife in an impudent and rash manner, let him be punished by receiving forty stripes save one, and let him pay fifty shekels to her father; but if the damsel be convicted as having been corrupted, and is one of the common people, let her be stoned, because she did not observe her virginity till she were lawfully married; but if she be the daughter of a priest, let her be burnt alive. If any one has two wives, and if he greatly respect and be kind to one of them, either out of his affection to her, or for her beauty, or for some other reason, while the other is of less esteem with him; and if the son of her that is beloved be the younger by birth than another born of the other wife, but endeavours to obtain the right of primogeniture from his father's kindness to his mother, and would thereby obtain a double portion of his father's substance, for that double portion is what I have allotted him in the laws—let not this be permitted, for it is unjust that he who is the elder by birth should be deprived of what is due to him on the father's disposition of his estate, because his mother was not equally regarded by him. He that hath corrupted a damsel espoused to another man, in case he had her consent, let both him and her be put to death, for they are both equally guilty—the man because he persuaded the woman willingly to submit to a most impure action, and to prefer it to lawful wedlock; the woman because she was persuaded to yield herself to be corrupted, either for pleasure or for gain. However, if a man light on a woman when she is alone, and force her, where nobody was present to come to her assistance, let him only be put to death. Let him that hath corrupted a virgin not yet espoused marry her; but if the father of the damsel be not willing that she should be his wife, let him pay fifty shekels as the price of her prostitution. He that desires to be divorced from his wife for any cause whatsoever (and many such causes happen among men), let him in writing give assurance that he will never use her as his wife any more; for by this means she may be at liberty to marry another husband, although before this bill of divorce be given she is not to be permitted so to do, but if she be misused by him also, or if, when he is dead, her first husband would marry her again, it shall not be lawful for her to return to him."

As we have seen, by the Jewish law rape upon a woman, married or betrothed, was punished with death. Where the woman was not betrothed, by a heavy fine, without that power of divorce, which was generally permitted under the Jewish law.

The Roman law punished this crime with death and confiscation of goods. The offence of forcible abduction, or taking a woman from her friends, was punished with the same severity as that of forcibly dishonouring them. Either offence is, by the civil law, sufficient to constitute a capital crime. The Roman law, by restraining and making highly penal the solicitations of the seducer, attempted to secure effectually the chastity of women:—"Si enim ipsi raptores metu, vel atrocitate pœnæ, ab hujusmodi facinore se temperaverint, nulli mulieri sive volenti sive nolenti peccandi locus relinquitur; quia hoc ipsum velle mulierum ab insidiis nequissimi hominis, qui meditatur rapinam, inducitur. Nisi etenim eam solicitaverit, nisi odiosis artibus circumvenerit, non faciet eam velle in tantum dedecus sese prodere." But, as Blackstone observes, our English law does not entertain quite such sublime ideas of the honour of either sex as to lay the blame of a mutual fault wholly upon one of the transgressors.

Rape was punished by the Saxon laws with death. In this particular, the laws of Athelstan are the most severe. The same punishment was also inflicted by the old Gothic and Scandinavian constitutions.

The laws of William the Conqueror reduced the severity of capital punishment for such crimes to castration and loss of the eyes. This continued down to the reign of Henry the Third. But in order to prevent malicious accusations of this kind, so easily asserted and yet so hard to disprove, it was very wisely provided that the woman should, immediately after the alleged insult, go to the next town and there make discovery to some credible persons of the injury she had suffered; and afterwards should acquaint the high constable of the hundred, the coroners, and the sheriff, with the outrage. This, as Blackstone observes, agrees in some respects with the laws of Scotland and Arragon. These constitutions required the complaint to be made within twenty-four hours, in order to sustain a prosecution. The civil law supposes a prostitute or common harlot incapable of sustaining such injuries, and consequently denies her any remedy for such outrages. But in this respect our law is more considerate, and holds it felony to force even a concubine or a harlot.

"In relation to women," says Diodorus Siculus, "the Egyptian laws were very severe; for he that committed a rape upon a free woman was to have his privy members cut off, for they judged that three most heinous offences were included in that one vile act, namely, wrong, defilement and bastardy."—"In case of adultery, the man was to have a thousand lashes with rods, and the woman her nose cut off." For he quaintly observes, "It was looked upon as very fit that the adulteress that tricked up herself to allure men to wantonness, should be punished in that part where her charms chiefly lay."

As to marriages he says:—"The Egyptian priests only marry one wife; all others may have as many wives as they please." A regulation which agrees entirely with the Jewish usage. "And all are bound to bring up as many children as they can for the further increase of the inhabitants, which tends much to the well-being either of a city or a country." "None of the sons," he relates, "are ever reputed bastards, though they be begotten of a bondmaid; for the Egyptians conceive that the father begets the child, and that the mother contributes nothing but place and nourishment."

Upon matters of adultery the laws of the Greeks were very severe, not only in punishing the offence when committed, but also in punishing those who in any way by neglect of duty might be regarded as its abettors, and also such as did not take the precautions in their power to prevent such scandals. In many particulars the enactments of the Athenians will be found to agree with the peculiarities of the Hebrew institutions.

We find it provided by one of Solon's laws, in order to preserve the distinction between the free-born and slaves, that "No slave shall caress or be enamoured with a free-born youth. She who is shall receive publicly fifty stripes. If any one, whether father, brother, uncle, or guardian, or any other who hath jurisdiction over a boy, take hire for him to be effeminately embraced, the catamited boy shall have no action issued out against him, but the chapman and pander only, who are both to be punished after the same manner. The child, when grown up to maturity of age, shall not be obliged to keep his father so offending; only, when dead, he shall bury him with decency suitable to a parent's obsequies."

The Jewish law forbids a man to prostitute his daughter. (Exod. 19.)

The Greek law runs thus:—"If any one prostitute a boy or woman, he shall be prosecuted with an action called γραφη, and if convicted, punished with death. Any Athenian empowered so to do may bring an action against him who hath vitiated a boy, woman, or man, free-born or in service, for the determination of which the Thesmothetæ are to create judges to sit in the Heliæa, within thirty days after the complaint hath been brought before them; or suppose any public concern hinders, as soon as occasion will permit. If the offender is cast, he shall immediately undergo the punishment, whether corporal or pecuniary, annexed to his offence. If he be sentenced to die, let him be delivered to the Ενδεκα, and suffer death the same day. If the vitiated servant or woman belong to the prosecutor, and he let the action fall, or doth not get the fifth part of the suffrages, he shall be fined a thousand drachms. If the criminal be only fined, let him pay within eleven days at the farthest, after sentence is passed. If it be a free-born person he hath vitiated, let him be kept in bonds till payment thereof."

Here we find the crimes of rape and seduction are made capital offences, and treated with as much severity as they were by the Mosaic laws.

So, again, another law of Athens fixes the penalty of rape, and protects the chastity of young females under still heavier penalties. "He that deflowers a free woman by force, shall be fined an hundred drachms." This was one of Solon's laws:—"He who in the same manner violates a young maiden's chastity, shall be fined a thousand drachms."

The following enactment corresponds entirely, not only with the spirit, but even with the letter of the Hebrew laws:—"He that catches an adulterer in the fact, may impose *any arbitrary punishment.*" This law was enacted by Draco, and afterwards confirmed by Solon.

"If any one is injuriously clapped up on suspicion of adultery, he shall make his complaint by appeal to the Thesmothetæ, which if they find justifiable, he shall be acquitted, and his sureties discharged from their bail; and in case he be brought in guilty, the judges shall lay on him (death only excepted) whatever punishments they will, and he shall be forced to get friends to pass their word for his future chastity."

Another of the Greek laws runs thus:—" If any one commit a rape on a woman, he shall be amerced twice as much as is usual otherwise." (That is, when the woman was a consenting party.)

"No husband shall have to do with his wife any more after she hath defiled his bed, and her gallant convicted; and if he does not put her away, he shall be esteemed infamous. Hereupon she is prohibited coming to public temples, where if she does but enter, any man may inflict any penalty except death."

"No adulteress shall be permitted to adorn herself. She that doth shall have her garments cut or torn off her back by any that meets her, and likewise be beaten, though so as not to be killed or disabled."

Λιθοβολια, or stoning, was a common punishment, and was usually inflicted by the primitive Greeks upon such as were taken in adultery. There is an instance of this in the Iliad, where Hector tells Paris he deserves to die this death.

The laws of Rome punished such offences with great severity. The first chapter of the Julian law on adulteries repeats several earlier laws on this subject. The second chapter enumerates the persons which it is lawful to kill under such circumstances. It allows a father who in his own house shall find a daughter living under his care in the arms of a man, to compel the seducer to marry her. But the law also allowed him the alternative of inflicting death upon the adulterer.

Paulus, in his commentary upon the Julian laws, writes:—" If an adulterer is seized with an unmarried girl, both he and the daughter shall suffer death for their unchastity." This, he adds, is allowed as of right to be done. In support of this proposition, Marcellus, in the thirty-first book of his Digest, is cited.

According to Marcellus, under the authority of the Roman law, a father may kill a man, even if he be qualified for the consulship, or be his patron, if he take him in the act of adultery with his daughter. But in this case the law compelled the father to kill both his daughter and her paramour as soon as he discovered them. If he delayed his vengeance, or spared the life of either, the death of the other exposed him to the charge of homicide. The early Roman laws permitted the husband to kill a man taken in adultery with his wife. But the laws of the later emperors do not justify the death of the wife under such circumstances. Where the wife's adulterer is slain by the husband, the Roman laws are remarkable for the recognition of three principles which distinguished the Hebrew statutes. First, the right to slay the adulterer; second, the necessity of abandoning the wife; and thirdly, that institution to which we have already referred, whose duty it was to account for the death of any body within its jurisdiction.

Paulus states the law thus :—" But it ought to be clearly declared before the person who has jurisdiction over the place, both where and under what circumstances the adulterer was killed, and also that the husband has put away his wife in consequence. If this should not be done, the adulterer's death cannot be passed over with impunity to the husband."

But the decrees of Antoninus Magnus spared the

lives of those who, urged on by unpremeditated fury, killed adulterers.

By the Julian law of adulteries, a Roman citizen who cohabited with a mistress cannot exercise the right of a husband in punishing the paramour of his mistress.

Even the right of killing the adulterer appears to have been restricted, to some extent, by Imperial edicts. For the Julian law mentions particular persons whom it is allowable to kill under such provocation. The infliction of such summary vengeance was latterly confined to slaves and freedmen. Paulus observes, that though condemned by public opinion, it is lawful to kill the son of a freedman either belonging to oneself or one's father, and whether a citizen of Rome or a Latin, if taken in adultery. It appears by various other laws, that those who illegally killed adulterers were punished only with moderate penalties. The infamy of the adulterer's conduct was regarded as such, that he was punished, in case he were a freedman, with a heavy fine of 30,000 sesterces.

The Rescripts of Severus and Antonine declare that the adultery of a wife may be avenged by the husband, by virtue of his marital right, but that such marital right shall not be held to extend to the offences of a woman betrothed. In this particular the Roman laws recognise a distinction made by the Hebrew laws, although they do not adopt it.

By the Cornelian law concerning cutthroats, if a father killed the adulterer of his daughter, but spared his daughter's life, he rendered himself liable to the penalties of homicide. But if the father endeavoured to kill his daughter, and she escaped him by an accident, he was no longer exposed to any such penalty.

"The husband, however, who kills his wife taken in adultery ought to be punished with lenience, because he was unable to restrain the outbreak of justifiable anger." "The adulterer having been slain, the husband is bound at once to dismiss his wife, and within three days at latest to declare publicly with what adulterer, and in what place, he discovered his wife." "An husband finding one in adultery with his wife may kill him if he take him in his own house." "He who shall not immediately dismiss his wife taken in adultery may be accused of bawdiness." "Slaves, as well of the husband as of the wife, may be tortured in case of an adultery. Nor does it avail if they are freed under the hope of eluding punishment."

Under the second chapter of the Julian law the following provisions occur:—"If a father shall take an adopted son in adultery with his daughter, the words of the law, strictly construed, cannot justify the father in killing him, nevertheless it is permitted him to do so." This rescript obviously has reference to the earlier laws of Rome.

"A husband may kill none taken in adultery with his wife but those who are infamous, and those who make a trade of their bodies, whether slaves or free, the wife being excepted, for her he may not kill."

Papian comments thus on the foregoing passage:—
"If a father who kills an adulterer has spared his daughter, I enquire what is enacted against him? It

is answered without doubt, that father is a murderer; therefore he will be bound by the Cornelian law as to assassins. But it is clear that if the daughter, without the father's will, is saved by accident, the father will not the less have a defence that the daughter fled by chance. For the law so punishes homicide, in case the act is an evil deceit; but in this case the father did not preserve his daughter because he wished it, but because he could not kill her."

" If a husband kills his wife caught in adultery, I enquire whether it is under the law as to assassins. It is answered, in no part does the law allow a husband to kill his wife; whence it is clear, that his having acted contrary to the law is not to be doubted. But if brought up for punishment, something is not unjustly allowed for his honourable anger; so that he is not punished capitally as a homicide, but sentence is passed of deportation, or even exile."

The second chapter of the Julian law as to adulterers allows a father, as well adopted, as natural, to kill an adulterer taken by his own hands with his daughter, for the sake of the honour of his house or family.

Several Anglo-Saxon laws have been already mentioned in Chapter V., which show that adultery was severely punished by the secular power. Offences of this nature were moreover the subject of ecclesiastical mulcts and penances. The severity, however, with which such sins were restrained was not peculiar to any one of the earlier codes. It appears to have pervaded all the Anglo-Saxon constitutions down to the time of the Conquest. Adultery was a crime which occupied a prominent place in the laws of the Conqueror, and thence found its way into the institutions attributed to Henry I. The manner in which it was punished by the secular power sheds a strange light upon the social customs of the age.

The first law we find is one of Æthelbirht's:—"If a freeman lie with a freeman's wife, let him pay for it with his 'wer-geld,' and provide another wife with his own money, and bring her to the other."

The laws of Withrœd command, "That foreigners, if they will not correct their fornication, depart from the land with their goods and with their sins." "If it happen that a 'gesithcund' man, after this 'gemot,' take to illicit intercourse, contrary to the king's command and the bishops and the book's doom, let him make a 'bot' for it to his lord of c. shillings according to *ancient usage*. If it be a 'ceorlish' man, let him make a 'bot' of l. shillings; and let either with penitence desist from his fornication."

By one of the statutes of Alfred, to some of which we have already referred in a previous chapter, a recompense is provided for the husband of a woman with whom adultery had been committed, apparently without the infliction of any public fine. "If a man lie with the wife of a twelve-'hynde' man, let him make 'bot' to the husband with cxx. shillings. To a six-'hynde' let him make 'bot' with c. shillings. To a 'ceorlish' man let him make 'bot' with forty shillings.

Under this code, assaults and rapes appear to have been punished with a fine. Thus, "If a man seize hold of the breast, let him make 'bot' to her with v. shillings. If he throw her down and do not lie with her, let him make 'bot' with x. shillings. If he lie with her, let him make 'bot' with lx. shillings. If another man had before lain with her, then let the 'bot' be half that. If she be charged therewith, let her clear herself with sixty hides, or forfeit half the 'bot.' If this befall a woman more nobly born, let the 'bot' increase according to the 'wer.'"

The assault of a nun, however, under this code, was punished with greater severity. "If any one with libidinous intent seize a nun, either by her raiment or by her breast without her leave, let the 'bot' be twofold, as we have before ordained concerning a laywoman." "If a betrothed woman commit adultery, if she be of 'ceorlish' degree, let 'bot' be made to the 'byrgea' with lx. shillings, and let it be in live stock, cattle, goods, and in that let no human being be given: if she be of six-'hynde' degree, let him pay c. shillings to the 'byrgea.' If she be of twelve-'hynde' degree, let him make 'bot' to the 'byrgea' with cxx. shillings."

"If a man commit a rape on a 'ceorl's' female slave slave, let him make 'bot' to the 'ceorl' with v. shillings, and let the 'wite' be lx. shillings."

If a male "theow" committed a rape upon a female "theow," he was punished in a barbarous manner with mutilation. "If a man commit a rape upon a woman under age, let the 'bot' be as that of a full aged person."

The severity of these "bots," or fines, may be estimated by the value of money in those days. A law of Ina's declares that a ewe with her lamb shall be worth a shilling. The laws of Edmund in the same manner punish this offence with 'bot.' Thus, "he who commits fornication with a nun, let him not be worthy of a consecrated place of burial (unless he make bot) any more than a manslayer. We have ordained the same respecting adultery."

The terms in which these laws are expressed furnish abundant proof that such immoralities were punished by the secular laws. The law of Withræd, to which we have just referred, upon the face of it had the sanction of the "gemot" — the word "gemot" signifying a moot, meeting, or public assembly. In this, and in the other Anglo-Saxon laws, "bots" and "wite" are imposed. The distinction between a "bot" and "wite" was this: "bot" signified simply amends, atonement, compensation, or indemnity; "wite" was a penalty, which fell to the king or the state, for a violation of the law. Some of these penalties were payable to the byrgea, or surety. These penalties, it will be observed, were apportioned according to the degree of the offender. A twelvehind man was one whose wer-gild was twelve hundred shillings. This was the highest class of Anglo-Saxon aristocracy. The "wer-gild," it is necessary to explain, was the price at which every man was valued according to his degree. In the event of his being slain, it was to be paid to his relatives, or to his "gild brethren," by the homicide or his friends. If a man was himself proved guilty of certain offences specified in the laws, his "wer-gild" was the sum which he was condemned to pay by way of fine. "Wer" or "were" is merely an abbreviated form for wer-gild.

A "twy-hinde" man was one whose "wer-gild" was two hundred shillings. This was the lowest class of freemen, who are otherwise called "ceorls," or churls, as the word is afterwards expressed. A "theow" was a slave. This was generally understood of a slave by birth; but it also signified one who had been condemned to slavery for a crime, or from inability to pay the fines incurred for violation of the law. This may perhaps account for the increased severity of the punishment for adultery with which persons of this degree were visited.

The laws of Edward and Guthrum are in these words:—"If foul, defiled, notorious adulteresses be found anywhere within the land, let them be driven from the country, and the people cleansed; or let them totally perish within the country, unless they desist, and the more deeply make "bot."

Many other Anglo-Saxon laws contain provisions of similar import. But it is needless to multiply examples. Sufficient proof has been already adduced to show beyond question that the earliest laws of England punished such offences with severity, and at this period had not assigned the delinquents over to the jurisdiction of the spiritual authorities. Yet many offences which were the subject of secular punishment were at the same time visited by the clergy with spiritual penances. Thus the Liber Penitentialis of Theodore archbishop of Canterbury contains several clerical ordinances concerning such matters. Under head xvi., De Fornicatione laicorum, many interdictions occur, in which the penance for fornication varies from one to fifteen years, according to the circumstances under which the offence was committed; the penance to which a married man was liable being heavier than that to which a single man exposed himself. Of this the following extracts are instances:—

"Si laicus fornicaverit cum viduâ aut cum puellâ, iii. annos pœniteat, reddet tamen humiliationis ejus precium parentibus ejus. Si uxorem non habet, et voluntas illorum et parentum est, ipsam accipiat in uxorem ita ut annos v. pœniteant simul. Si quis virgo virgini conjunctus fuerit, si voluerint parentes ejus, sit uxor illius ; tantum i. annum pœniteant et sint conjugales ; si vero noluerint, ii. annos pœniteant. Si quis laicus cum multis laicis, id est, cum vacantibus fœminis, unaque cum propinquis fornicationem imitatur simulque latrocinio serviens, xii. annos pœniteat, iii. in pane et aquâ. Vidua stuprum faciens annos iii. pœniteat."

The penances for adultery are in the same manner regulated by circumstances :—" Si quis laicus propriam uxorem dimiserit uxoremque alterius duxerit, viii. annos pœniteat. Si quis vacuus uxorem alterius polluit, v. annos pœniteat. Si uxoratus virginem polluit, similiter pœniteat. Si mulier suaserit alterius mulieris maritum ut cum illa dormiat, et ille ei consentit in tali peccato, illa sit excommunicata a Christianis, ille vero vii. annos pœniteat, i. in pane et aquâ. Si cujus uxor adulterata fuerit, vel si ipsa adulterium commiserit, vii. annos pœniteat. Mulier si adultera est et vir ejus non vult habitare cum ea, dimittere eam potest juxta sententiam Domini et aliam ducere, illa si vult monasterium intrare iiii$^{tam}$ partem suæ hæreditatis obtineat."

The Pœnitentiale of Ecgbert archbishop of York (lib. ii. § 7) imposes fasting on bread and water three days a week for seven years by way of penance :— " Si vir adulteret, vii. annos jejunet, iii. dies per hebdomadam in pane et aquâ. Et si mulier, præter dominum suum legitimum, alium habet virum, eodem sit digna."

The Canons of Edgar contain this provision:—
" We enjoin that a man abstain from concubinage, and love his lawful wife." Another canon of Edgar's, " De Modus Imponendi Pœnitentiam," agrees in its terms with those already referred to. Its language is this:—" Homo qui adulterat, vii. annos jejunet, iii. dies per hebdomadam in pane et aquâ; sit vir sit mulier."

It is unnecessary for our purpose to follow the ecclesiastical laws upon this subject in all their offensive details. Those who desire to consult the canons of this period will find that the penitentials and confessionals abound in particulars concerning the commission of such offences and the inclinations that suggest them, to be recounted in confession to the priest, which, if they are lawful to be written, are not decent to be read.

From the foregoing illustrations it will be perceived that in laws concerning such offences as are the subject of this chapter, several principles are to be traced, which, pervading all the ancient systems of jurisprudence, are yet most fully set forth in that of the Hebrews. Many distinctions are to be found in these examples, from which it is manifest that offences of this kind were regarded as the breach, not so much of a civil or conventional compact, as of a moral obligation. It is a remarkable proof of how far the legal constitutions of antiquity relied upon the sanctions of morality, to find that immoralities were punished as public crimes.

The precision with which the degrees of guilt are defined, if compared with the terms of what must be admitted to be the earliest of all laws, holds a peculiar significance. The following characteristics may be undeniably traced throughout them all, and these are, perhaps, the strongest evidence of the principles upon which such laws were framed.

In the first place, adultery with a woman bound by the social ties either of marriage or betrothal, is punished with greater severity than any other outrages of the same kind short of actual violation. A proof of the refinement of these ancient laws is to be found in the fact, that betrothal lent so deep a dye to a crime originally condemned for the protection of matrimony. For this seems to deal with the offence as a breach of the good faith which is the chief security of such contracts. It concerns an engagement, to the fulfilment of which neither party had conformed; and yet it invests such obligations with peculiar sanctity, and punishes their invasion capitally. Thus, it not only condemns the breach of social ties, but it also punishes the infringement of such moral obligations as those upon which conjugal rights are founded. And the spirit of these provisions seems to refer such rights to the mutual consent of the parties, and the acceptance of the responsibilities which such an engagement involves. Hence we find that in the Hebrew, the Greek, the Roman, and the Anglo-Saxon laws a much heavier punishment was imposed for the seduction of a woman betrothed, than for infringing the chastity of a woman bound by no such engagement.

Another point that deserves attention is the remedy provided for cases of seduction. Though the fault of the parents be mutual, the law did not forget the interests of the offspring. Its power was exerted to rescue the children from neglect and infamy, and prevented a man from defeating the purpose of marriage without making a due provision for its objects. The seducer of a maid was liable to endow her for his wife. If her father refused his consent, the seducer was bound to pay her dowry. The dowry seems to have been paid, not to the woman, but to her relations, who under certain circumstances were obliged to return it. To this custom we have some allusions in the narratives of antiquity. The dowry, therefore, seems to have answered to a settlement for the benefit of the woman and her issue, thus securing a provision for herself and her offspring. Seduction thence involved either compulsory marriage, or a compulsory provision for a woman according to her degree. These remedies, however, were only provided for the protection of a woman who was a maid. They do not seem to have been extended to one convicted of previous unchastity. They therefore afforded but little encouragement to habitual profligacy.

The advantages of such enactments, in remedying the evil rather than punishing the offence, are manifest enough to require no comment. Traces of the adoption of this principle are to be found in many ancient laws. It is conspicuous in the Anglo-Saxon codes. Perhaps nothing would tend more to diminish the number of suicides and child murders, that so often are resorted to by discarded women to hide the discovery of their shame, than to compel the seducer to marry his victim, under the severest penalties; or, where he had already a wife, to compel him to give a proportion of his estate for the benefit of his illegitimate offspring and its mother. Even where he had no estate, this principle might be carried out. An adequate portion of his earnings, according to his station in life, might be set aside for the same purpose, under some such compulsory process as that by which a bankrupt's estate is distributed amongst his creditors, still reserving to the woman the right of demanding marriage as soon as any existing impediments were removed.

## CHAPTER IX.

### LAWS RELATING TO MARRIAGE AND DIVORCE.

Mr. Selden, in his book "De Jure Nat. et Gent. juxta disciplinam Ebræorum," has collected many curious illustrations of the manner in which the obligations of marriage were regarded by the Jewish doctors. From these it appears, that the blessing, under which at the Creation the increase of all things living is expressed to be the will of the Creator, was by the Jews regarded as a command. Indeed, some of the Rabbinical writers go so far as to say, "that whoever neglects the precept to multiply the human race, is to be regarded as a homicide," inasmuch as abstinence from marriage tended to deprive the world of life. So another of the Rabbins says, "He who has not a wife is hardly to be called a man, since it is said in Scripture, Male and female created he them, and called their name 'Adam,' or man." The Jewish doctors, however, did not regard this injunction as obligatory upon females.

Treating on the Jewish laws, as illustrated by the Rabbinical comments, Selden appears to consider that the essence of the marriage contract consists in the consent of the parties, publicly attested, and followed by cohabitation, rather than to owe its obligation to the celebration of a religious ceremony at the nuptials. Of this latter, indeed, but slight and dubious traces are to be found in the Mosaic institutions; yet various formalities are mentioned as having been used at the betrothal. Maimonides observes upon this subject, that "before the law of Moses was given, if a man met a woman in public, and they both agreed to marry, he led her home before witnesses, and she became his wife."

The ceremonies with which such associations were attended from the earliest periods of antiquity, consisted, in the first instance, of a formal contract between the parties themselves, preliminary to cohabitation. The bride appears to have been in the gift of her parents. Where her parents were dead, the nearest relations, to whom had fallen the right of redemption, had the privilege of bestowing the hand of an unmarried girl in marriage. From this it appears, that a maiden was disqualified from engaging herself without the consent of her nearest kinsman. A widow, however, seems to have been at her own disposal. Indeed, amongst the Jews, a childless widow had peculiar claims upon her husband's kinsmen. She was entitled to demand marriage of her husband's brother. It is clear from what is mentioned in the book of Ruth, that her late husband's kinsmen were not entitled to redeem his property without at the same time marrying his widow. (Ruth vi. 5.) "Then said Boaz, What day thou buyest the field of the hand of Naomi, thou must buy it also of Ruth the Moabitess, the wife of the dead, to raise up the name of the dead upon his inheritance."

In the second place, it appears that in the case of a maiden, at least when residing at home, not only was the consent of her parents essential to the validity of a marriage contract, but at this time the friends of the bride imposed the conditions upon which their consent was to be obtained. We have an instance of this in the case of Rebecca, where Abraham's servant made her presents of jewels, and her parents and brother, at his solicitation, withdrew their stipulation that she should remain with them ten days at least. Thus it is manifest, that in these ancient days the consent of the parties, and the consent of the bride's nearest kinsmen, were essential to the validity of a betrothal. The marriage itself consisted simply in the performance of this contract. The narrative of Rebecca's marriage, in which the details are described with minuteness, not only in regard to what was actually done, but even what was said and thought, by the persons engaged in the transaction, does not make the slightest allusion to the performance of any nuptial rites. It does not even say that Isaac married her, or made her his wife. It seems to speak of cohabitation as the legitimate consequence of betrothal, without the imposition of any intermediate ceremony. The couple are dismissed from their first interview to their home in a very few words: "And Isaac brought her unto his mother Sarah's tent, and took Rebecca, and she became his wife." As if such a union were the state in which they were created to live, requiring only their consent to fulfil its obligations. The consent, however, required was a public one. In an age when concubinage was allowed, it was necessary that the obligations of the marriage contract should be clearly understood. The presence of witnesses, therefore, seems to have been essential to its validity. This, indeed, was the case with most contracts among the Hebrews. The circumstances under which they were evidenced, are mentioned in Ruth iv.: "Now this was the manner in former time in Israel concerning redeeming and concerning changing, for to confirm all things; a man plucked off his shoe, and gave it to his neighbour: and this was a testimony in Israel. And Boaz said unto the elders, and unto all the people, Ye are witnesses this day, that I have bought all that was Elimelech's, and all that was Chilion's and Mahlon's, of the hand of Naomi. Moreover, Ruth the Moabitess have I *purchased* to be my wife, to raise up the name of the dead upon his inheritance, that the name of the dead be not cut off from among his brethren, and from the gate of his place: ye are witnesses this day. And all the people that were in the gate, and the elders, said, We are witnesses."

Then it is related how the people gave Boaz their blessing. But, inasmuch as Ruth was not there, seeing that her mother-in-law had instructed her to remain at home until the business was concluded, the blessing of the people cannot be regarded as a religious ceremony in confirmation of the marriage. The ceremony then appears to have been complete. "So Boaz took Ruth, and she was his wife."

The consent of the bride's parents to the betrothal was usually purchased with a dowry. This was not, however, always paid in money or goods, but sometimes in personal services. Such was the bargain between Laban and Jacob, who served his father-in-law seven years for his wife. In the same way Saul promised David his daughter in marriage for services to be rendered in his war with the Philistines. The money to be paid by way of dowry appears to have been fixed at a certain sum. Thus, in Exodus, a payment is directed to be made, "according to the dowry of virgins." Corresponding regulations were adopted in the laws of the Greeks, as well as in those of the Anglo-Saxons, and those of the Middle Ages. In these institutions, certain sums were fixed as the penalty for injuries affecting the matrimonial prospects of unmarried women.

But dowry was used, not only to signify the price paid for a wife, but also the things or money with which she was endowed on her marriage. Formerly the dowry was given by the husband, or his family. In later times, the custom seems to have been reversed, and the dowry was given with the bride by her own friends. Thence dowry came to mean, not only what was the property of the wife in her own right, but also that interest to which she was entitled in her husband's estate.

The obligations of betrothal were regarded with peculiar sanctity, not only by the Hebrew laws, but also by most of the legislative systems of antiquity. The ancient laws most of them seem to have regarded betrothal as the foundation of the marriage contract. It bestowed upon the intended husband a right and interest in the person of his bride almost as extensive as that which followed its fulfilment by cohabitation.

This conclusion may be supported by many examples, which follow the discipline of the Hebrew institutions. The Anglo-Saxon laws, as well as those of the ancient Greeks and Romans, in conformity with the terms of the Levitical code, treat the pollution of a betrothed woman with much greater severity than where she was bound by no such engagement.

But as it was necessry that the fact of betrothal should be evidenced by witnesses, it is easy to conceive why particular qualifications should be required in those whose presence was requisite to confirm so important a ceremony. It is natural that the witnesses in the first instance should be chosen from among those who were not only well acquainted with the contracting parties, but who also would have a personal interest in the welfare of the match, since their family honour would be concerned in the fulfilment of its obligations. Thus it was that the presence of the nearest friends and relations was, in the earliest times, usual upon such occasions. But then, to prevent collusion, and to preclude the evasion of duties, the observance of which was essential to the welfare of society, it was manifestly desirable that the misplaced partiality of the friends of either party should have no opportunity of defeating the objects of the union; and thence we find that such contracts were sanctioned by the presence of the responsible officers of the community to which the parties belonged. Thus, in the case of Ruth and Boaz, it was witnessed by the elders of the city. Among the Anglo-Saxons, as the functions of the public officers were limited to particular occasions, and confined to special duties, we can understand how it came to pass that the witnesses of such a solemnity should be selected from the ministers of the national religion, with which the civil institutions of this country were then so closely interwoven. Thus we find that, by some of the Anglo-Saxon laws, it is directed that the marriage ceremony should be performed in the presence of the mass-priest. The laws of Edmund contain the earliest allusion to the use of a religious ceremony in this country: "At the nuptials there shall be a mass-priest by law, who shall, with God's blessing, bind their union to all prosperity." But, whatever may be the nature of the contract, whether social or religious, it cannot be a matter of surprise that, in Christian communities, so solemn an engagement should be consecrated with the sanctions of religion.

The relationship of marriage, under the Jewish laws, was maintained with conditions much less stringent than those adopted by Christian communities. In the early days of Jewish history, polygamy was lawful. But Josephus, although he admits that polygamy was practised by their forefathers, tells us that, in his day, it was esteemed disreputable among the Jews to have more than one wife at a time. Nor was the marriage bond regarded as indissoluble. Among the Jews, the power of discarding a wife rested very much with the will of the husband. And, although upon bargains of comparatively trivial nature the Jewish law abounds with special provisions, yet upon connections of this kind the obligations of the contract seem to have depended more upon the continuance of cohabitation than upon the permanent nature of the union. It is not, however, now necessary to discuss the religious obligation of such associations. Nor need we, for our present purpose, press an inquiry as to whether the institution of this state may not be referred to the same source as that of any other moral obligation. For whether it was from some tradition of the divine appointment of marriage in the persons of our first parents, or merely from a design to impress the solemnity of its obligation, the marriage rite in almost all civilized countries has been made a religious ceremony; "although," says Paley (in his Moral Philosophy), "marriage in its own nature, and abstracted from the "rules and declarations of Scripture, be properly a *civil* "contract, and nothing more." In a note upon this subject, archbishop Whately expresses his opinion in terms which, coming from so profound a writer, deserve great respect:—"Marriage," he says, "may be considered in two points of view; 1st, as a civil contract, referring to the legal rights and duties of the parties concerned and their offspring, which comes properly within the province of the civil government; and, 2ndly, as a religious engagement, which is a matter between each person's own conscience and his God. And in this it is best for the secular government not to interfere, especially when there are so many different religious persuasions. If the parties, of whatever religious denomination, were required (with due precautions against fraud) to make a regular contract before a magistrate, and have this duly registered by him,—they being, of course, left at liberty to go through any religious ceremony (before or after) that their conscience might dictate,—and if this contract were made universally the sole evidence of a legal and valid marriage, no one's conscience could be hurt, and we should escape at once and for ever all the anomalies, and grievances, and abuses of our patchwork legislation on this subject."

The "patchwork legislation," here alluded to, seems to have arisen, in a great measure, from a disposition to limit to each form of religion the power of marrying members of its own denomination. Each religious community viewed with jealousy any attempt to impose the obligation of its ceremonies upon members of another persuasion. For instance, in Ireland, where the marriage of two papists, if the ceremony be performed by a Romish priest, would be binding, the marriage of a protestant and a papist would, under the same circumstances, be invalid. So again, in Scotland cohabitation is held to constitute marriage. And such is the tenacity with which local customs are observed in Scotland, that what would be regarded a good marriage upon one side of the Tweed would be simply fornication on the other. This is sufficient to show how desirable it is to establish something like uniformity in the ceremonies with which such engagements should be attended; leaving it to the parties afterwards to consecrate their union with whatever religious sanctions they might think fit. Indeed, our Anglo-Saxon laws recognised very much this view of the subject. Yet, it may be remarked, that, although our earliest marriage laws require the attendance of a mass-priest, it is by no means clear that the ceremony was performed in the face of the church. If not, it must have been regarded not precisely as a religious ceremony, but as a civil contract to be solemnized in the presence of a minister of the national religion, whose functions, it must be remembered, were not then exclusively of a religious character.

In the laws of Æthelbright we find the following statute:—

"If a man buy a maiden with cattle, let the bargain stand, if it be without guile; but if there be guile, let him bring her home again, and let his property be restored to him."

Such a connection as this appears, therefore, to have been founded simply upon a civil contract. It was an arrangement, the validity of which depended upon the terms of the "bargain." This law proceeds:—

"If she bear a live child, let her have half the property, if the husband die first."

"If she wish to go away with her children, let her have half the property."

"If the husband wish to have them, let her portion be as one child."

A similar disposition, under different circumstances, occurs under the Bavarian law.

The law of Æthelbright continues thus:—

"If she bear a child, let her paternal kindred have the 'fioh' and the 'morgengyfe.'"

"If a man carry off a maiden by force, let him pay L. shillings to the owner, and afterwards *buy* the object of his will of the owner."

"If she be betrothed to another man in money, let him make 'bot' with xx. shillings."

"If she become 'gœngang' xxxv. shillings, and xv. shillings to the king."

The laws of Ine contain this provision:—"In case a man *buy* a wife, and the marriage take not place, let him give the money, and compensate and make 'bot' to his 'byrgea' as his 'borg-bryce' may be."

The buying of a wife purchased the consent of those who were entitled to dispose of her in marriage. It did not confer an unqualified right to her person. Contracts of this sort differed in some respects from an absolute purchase. For if the operation, not only of the Anglo-Saxon, but of other ancient customs, be considered, it will be perceived that the subject of the bargain was allowed to have an interest in the price.

The price or dowry did not in all cases go absolutely for the benefit of those to whom it was paid. There were circumstances under which the wife had a claim upon it. There is reason to suppose that the wife's relations held the dowry upon a sort of trust under which, on certain contingencies, she had a claim to some provision.

The custom of paying a dowry or marriage price for their wives generally obtains throughout the East. The practice of giving a consideration to the friends of the girl, instead of settling a dowry upon the girl herself, still prevails among the Kafir tribes. They probably derived it from their forefathers, whose traditions may be carried back to the time of Ishmael. Some documents on the Kafir laws, recently published by the order of Sir George Grey, throw a curious light upon the observance of this custom. In these documents it is stated that the transaction is not a mere purchase. The cattle paid for the bride are divided amongst her male relations, and are considered by the Kafir law to be held in trust for the benefit of herself and children, should she be left a widow. She is accordingly entitled to demand assistance from any of those who have partaken of her dowry; and her children can apply to them on the same ground for something to begin the world with. In case of a grievance, she can claim an asylum with her father, until her husband has given such redress as the occasion demands. In case this is refused, the father may detain both his daughter and her dowry.

Among the Kafirs, marriages are controlled by the ties of consanguinity. It is unlawful to marry any female who is a relative by blood. In the event of a daughter being married, the cattle derived from her marriage become the property of the eldest brother's house on the mother's side.

With the Zulu Kafirs, the wives are not liable to be dismissed for trifling causes. The usual grounds of divorce are adultery or an unbearable temper. Where the woman is in fault, the husband, on dismissing her, is entitled to a return of the cattle he has given for her. Such disputes are decided by the chief of the tribe. But if the woman has borne her husband a child, he is not entitled to recover her dowry. This exception is remarkable.

The power of divorce given by the Mosaic laws in later times fell into abuse. It was exercised upon frivolous grounds. It appears to have been as often adopted as a method for making way for a new wife as for the sake of getting rid of the old one. It was in fact used as a way of practising polygamy, and yet saving the expense of maintaining two wives at once. This seems to have become a common practice. The rabbi Akiba, in his Comments, says, "If any man saw a woman handsomer than his own wife, he might put his wife away, because it is said in the law, 'If she find no favour in his eyes,' &c."

Josephus, who lived in the days when Jesus Christ was upon earth, tells us in his autobiography, without any compunction, "About this time I put away my wife, who had borne me three children, not being pleased with her manners."

The following form of a writing of divorce is given by the Jewish writers:—

"I, A. B., with entire consent of mind and without any compulsion, have divorced, dismissed, and expelled thee, C. D., who wast heretofore my wife. But now I have dismissed thee so as to be free and at thine own disposal to marry whomsoever thou pleasest, without hindrance from any one from this day for ever. Let this be thy bill of divorce from me, and writing of separation and expulsion according to the law of Moses and Israel."

The terms of the Hebrew law are contained in Deut. xxiv.:—

"When a man hath taken a wife, and married her, and it come to pass that she find no favour in his eyes because he hath found some uncleanness in her: then let him write her a bill of divorcement, and give it into her hand, and send her out of his house.

"And when she is departed out of his house, she may go and be another man's wife.

"And if the latter husband hate her, and write her a bill of divorcement, and giveth it in her hand, and sendeth her out of his house; or if the latter husband die, which took her to be his wife;

"Her former husband, which sent her away, may

not take her again to be his wife, after that she is defiled."

If a man married a damsel, and suspected her previous chastity, by the Jewish law (Deut. xxii. 13) a method is provided for ascertaining the truth of his suspicions. If they proved to be correct, the damsel was stoned to death. If they proved groundless, the false accuser was punished with chastisement and a fine of one hundred shekels of silver, to be paid to the damsel's father, the husband being compelled to take her to wife without the power of subsequent divorce.

Herodotus affirms that throughout Egypt it was customary to marry one wife only. No instance, says Sir G. Wilkinson, in his Egyptian Antiquities, of two consorts is to be found in any of the sculptures which have yet been discovered.

But marriages were by the Egyptian law permitted between a brother and a sister; and this custom, Sir G. Wilkinson assures us, is fully authenticated by the sculptures of Upper and Lower Egypt.

Among the Athenians, it was lawful to marry a sister by the father's side, but not if born of the same mother. This distinction, however, was not observed in Egypt.

Although in Egypt it was the custom to have but one wife, concubinage with captives was allowed. These, with their offspring, appear to have been treated as a part of the family. The concubine ranked next after the lawful wife. Her children shared the inheritance. This custom still prevails amongst the Japanese, whose laws place the children of concubines upon an equality, as to hereditary rights, with the legitimate children of married women.

Pliny mentions an iron ring worn by those Egyptians who were betrothed. But the researches of Sir G. Wilkinson seem to show that the evidence of a ring having been used at the marriage ceremony is not conclusive. In fact, we have but scanty, if any, traces of what really were the formalities used on such occasions in Egypt.

The early Greeks appear to have indulged their passions unconfined by the restrictions of matrimony. In Greece, Cecrops is said to have been the author of this institution. However, with the growth of communities the necessity of domestic regulations was recognized, until at length marriage came to be esteemed very honourable in many of the Greek commonwealths. It was encouraged by many laws. The Lacedæmonians are remarkable for their severity against those who deferred marrying, as well as against those who wholly abstained from it. No man among them could live unmarried beyond a certain period without incurring a penalty. Polygamy was not commonly tolerated in Greece. Marriage was regarded as the association of one man with one woman. Whence, according to Potter's Greek Antiquities, the word γάμος was derived παρὰ τὸ δύο ἅμα εἶναι—from two becoming one.

When Herodotus relates that Anaxandrinos, the Spartan, had two wives, he remarks that it was contrary to the custom of Sparta. In this respect, most of the Greek cities agreed with the Lacedæmonians.

The time of marriage was not the same in all places. The Spartans were not permitted to marry until they had arrived at maturity. The Athenian laws are said once to have ordered that men should not marry until they had attained thirty-five years of age. Aristotle thought thirty-seven a good age; but Plato was content with thirty. Women married sooner than men. Some of the old Athenian laws did not permit them to marry till thirty-six. Aristotle, however, considered women marriageable at eighteen: Hesiod at fifteen.

Most of the Greeks regarded it as scandalous to contract marriage within certain degrees of consanguinity. Hermione, in the Euripides, speaks of the custom of brethren marrying their sisters with no less detestation than of sons marrying their mothers, or fathers their daughters. The Persians, however, were remarkable for such practices. Their Magi, the most sacred order among them, were the offspring of mothers and their sons.

The Lacedæmonians were forbidden to marry any of their kindred, whether in the direct degrees of ascent or descent. But this restriction did not apply to collateral relations. Nephews might marry their aunts, and uncles their nieces; but the marriages of brothers and sisters were utterly unlawful. Yet it was not reputed unlawful in several places for brothers to marry their half-sisters. The Lacedæmonians allowed marriages between those who had only the same mother and different fathers. The Athenians, on the other hand, we are told by Philo, were forbidden to marry sisters by the same mother, but not by the same father. The same custom also obtained in Chaldea in the age when Abraham left it; for he and Sarah his wife were thus related: "she is the daughter of my father but not of my mother, and she became my wife." Most of the Greek States required that their citizens should marry no one but citizens; foreigners being prohibited entirely from sharing with them the privileges of lawful matrimony. At Athens, if a foreigner married a freedwoman, he was liable to be called to account by an action before the Thesmothetæ. On conviction, he was sold for a slave, and his goods were confiscated. The same penalty was inflicted upon such as gave foreign women in marriage to the men of Athens under pretence that they were their daughters.

If an Athenian married any but a free-woman of the city, he was liable to a fine of a thousand drachms.

In conformity with the Hebrew laws, virgins were not allowed to marry without the consent of their parents. The mother's consent appears also to have been requisite. Thus Iphigenia, in Euripides, was not to be given in marriage to Achilles, until Clytemnestra had approved the match. Nor were men permitted to marry without consulting their parents.

When virgins had no fathers, their brothers disposed of them. Of this we have an instance in Creon promising his sister to any person who should destroy the sphinx that infested Thebes. And Orestes gave his sister Electra to his friend Pylades.

The Greeks had several forms of betrothal. One was:—"I give you this my daughter to make you father of children lawfully begotten." Upon the betrothal the terms of the arrangement were generally settled. In Xenophon, where Cyaxares betrothes his daughter to Cyrus, the dowry is mentioned:—"I give you, Cyrus, this woman, who is my daughter, with all Media for her dowry." In this instance the dowry seems to have been bestowed with the wife, contrary to the early Hebrew custom, in which the dowry was paid by the husband by way of purchase money.

The persons to be married plighted their faith to one another. The husband swore that he would be constant and sincere in his love; the wife that she would marry him, and make him master of all that she had. Ovid makes the next ceremony to the betrothal to be the virgin's oath to her lover, which from its language implies the consent of her father:—

"Promisit pater hanc, hæc et juravit amanti."

The ceremony of promising fidelity was kissing each other, or giving their right hands. The latter was the usual form of ratifying all agreements. It was the custom among the Thebans for lovers to plight their faith at the monument of Iolaus.

In early times, the Greeks appear to have purchased their wives, instead of receiving a dowry with them. For Aristotle uses it as an argument that the ancient Greeks were an uncivilized people, because it was their custom to purchase their wives. Of this custom there are instances to be found in Homer. In later times, however, we find Medea complaining in Euripides, of the misfortune of women, in that they were then obliged to purchase their husbands with a dowry, and yet to be subject to them.

To remedy the evils of mercenary matches, tending, as they did, to deprive poor women of the chance of marrying, both Lycurgus and Solon made laws restricting the amount of the dowry that a woman was allowed to bring to her husband.

Another custom resembling the Hebrew institutions was this. Where there was any orphan virgin without inheritance, he that was next in blood was obliged to marry her himself, or else to settle a portion upon her according to her quality. Such portions were regulated by special laws from 150 to 500 drachms. But if she had many relations equally allied, all of them contributed to make up the sum due for her portion. But if there were more than one virgin, their nearest relation was only obliged to marry or give a portion to one of them. In default of this, he was liable to an indictment before the archon, and to be condemned in a penalty of 1000 drachms.

It was usual for husbands to make a settlement upon the wife in return for her dowry, in case they should happen to be parted by death or divorce. Where this was not done, in case of divorce, the wife, unless the separation was occasioned by her own misconduct, was entitled to restitution of her dowry. The same obligation attached to the heirs upon refusal to maintain the wives of those whose estates they inherited.

It seems to have been regarded among the Greeks as a matter of right, that, on the dismissal of the wife, her portion should be returned. But if the woman departed of her own accord, she forfeited this right.

The payment of dowry was also attested by sufficient witnesses. Where this precaution had been omitted, the husband was not obliged to return the dowry, or to afford the wife a separate maintenance in case of separation. The dowry was repaid to the person by whom she had been endowed. The dowry appears to have been intended for the children's maintenance;

for when the woman's sons came of age, they enjoyed their mother's dowry while she was living, allowing her only a competent maintenance. Subsequent to the betrothal, but before the nuptials, it appears to have been usual with the Greeks to invoke the blessing of the gods, or rather of the goddesses, who were supposed to take an interest in the nuptials, and especially of Diana, from whose bonds of virgin purity they redeemed themselves by sacrifices. In reference to the Rabbinical comments concerning marriage as conferring a perfect right to manhood, it is curious to observe that marrying is termed by the Greeks τελειωθῆναι, to be made perfect. Married persons are called τελειοι, "perfect," and are said to be εν βίῳ τελείῳ (in a perfect state of life).

Before the nuptials, it was also customary with sacrifices and oblations to invoke the favour of various deities, to whom the fecundity of the female sex was attributed, in order to render the nuptials propitious.

The nuptials themselves appear to have been accompanied rather with social rejoicings than religious solemnities. On these occasions the gods of marriage were duly honoured with wine and dancing; after which the bride was led home to her husband's house, accompanied by her friends.

The nuptials were celebrated, not in a temple, but in a house, and this generally the house of the bride's parents. And the bride was conducted from her father's house to that of the bridegroom in the evening; that time, the Greeks say, being chosen to conceal her blushes. Torches were usually carried before her, the husband sitting by her side in a chariot. The axletree was burnt at their journey's end, to signify that the bride was never more to return to her father's house, having now become the head of a new family.

In many other particulars it will be seen the customs of the Greeks are closely conformed to the peculiarities of the Hebrew statutes upon these subjects.

The following Greek laws relating to marriage may be taken as illustrations:—

"No man shall have above one wife." One of Cecrops' laws.

"No Athenian is to marry any other than a citizen."

"If an heiress is contracted lawfully in full marriage by a father, brother by father's side, or grandside, it is lawful to procreate with her free-born children. But if she be not betrothed, these relations being dead, and she consequently an orphan, let her marry whom the law shall appoint; but supposing she is no heiress, and but low in the world, let her choose whom she pleases."

"If any one marry a stranger, as his kinswoman, to an Athenian citizen, he shall be infamous, his goods published for sale, the thirds of which shall fall to the impeacher, who shall make him appear before the Thesmothetæ, after the manner of those who are prosecuted with the action of Ξενια.

"No Athenian woman shall marry herself to an exotic family."

"Any one may make a sister by his father's side his wife."

"No heiress must marry out of her kindred, but shall resign up herself and her fortune to her nearest relation."

"If a father bury all his sons, he may entail his estate on his married daughters."

"If an heiress cannot conceive children, she may seek aid amongst the nearest of her husband's relations." This was one of Solon's laws.

"He that ravishes a virgin shall be obliged to marry her."

"A guardian shall not marry the mother of those orphans with whose estate he is intrusted." This also is one of Solon's laws.

"A bride shall not carry with her to her husband above three garments and vessels of small value." One of Solon's laws.

"They who are next in blood to an orphan virgin that hath no fortune shall marry her themselves, or settle a portion on her according as they are in quality. (The portions ranged from one hundred and fifty to five hundred drachms.) But if she hath many kindred, equally allied, all of them severally shall put in a contribution till they make up the respective sum. If there be many orphan virgins, their nearest relation shall either give in marriage or take one of them to wife; but if he do neither, the archon shall compel him. But if the archon does connive at the neglect, he himself shall be fined a thousand drachms, to be consecrated to Juno. Whoever breaks this law may be indicted by any person before the archon."

"That woman who brings her husband a fortune, and lives in the same house with her children, shall not claim interest money, but live upon the common stock with her children."

"An heiress's son, when come to man's estate, shall enjoy his mother's fortune, and keep her."

"He that promises to settle a dowry on a woman shall not be forced to stand to it if she dies without heirs."

"He who divorceth his wife must make restitution of her portion, or pay in lieu of it nine oboli every month. Her guardian otherwise may prosecute him in the Odeum, with the action called σιτου δικη, for her maintenance."

"If a woman forsake her husband, or he put away his wife, he who gave her in marriage shall exact the dowry given with her and no more."

"The woman who hath a mind to leave her husband must give in a separation bill to the archon with her own hand and not by a proxy."

As we have observed, under the Greek law of adultery, if a man did not put away his wife as soon as he discovered her infidelity, he was rendered infamous.

Roman marriages were of two sorts—*solemnes*, and *minus solemnes*. The former constituted legal marriages; the latter amounted merely to concubinage, to which the law attached certain incidental consequences.

The legal marriages among the Romans were contracted in three different ways, called "usus," "confarreatio," and "coemptio." "Usus," usage, or cohabitation, was probably the oldest form of marriage amongst the Romans. It obtained where a woman, with the consent of her parents or guardians, lived with a man for a whole year, without being absent for three nights: she thus became his lawful wife by a prescriptive use. The only ground of divorce which the law allowed her was the discontinuance of cohabitation during the first year of her engagement.

But the most solemn form of marriage was by confarreation, which was attended with a peculiar kind of sacrifice; the man and the woman each partaking of a cake made of salt, flour, and water. The ceremony was performed by the pontifex maximus, in the presence of at least ten witnesses.

By this form of marriage, both the wife and the children became entitled to particular privileges; the one having an interest in her husband's property, the other being eligible for pontifical offices. A marriage thus contracted could only be dissolved by another sacrificial solemnity, called "diffarreatio."

The third kind of marriage was called "coemptio." It seems to have been a sort of earnest paid by way of betrothal in consideration of future cohabitation. The right of purchase in marriage was not peculiar to the Romans. The custom was recognized generally by the nations of antiquity. It was common among the Germans and the Cantabri in Spain. This ceremony placed the Roman wife, in relation to her husband, in the same position as a daughter. Besides conferring marital rights over her property, it gave him the power of life and death over her person. With the Romans, the dowry, or marriage portion, was regulated by custom, according to the social condition of the woman.

"Contubernium" was the cohabitation of slaves. It did not confer the rights of lawful wedlock. Hence, under such connections, there was no process for adultery. This term "contubernium" is applied to all such connections as were not sanctioned by the Roman law.

Upon the same principle as that by which the Jews were confined to their own tribes, no marriage was held just and legal except between Roman citizens without a particular permission, which at first it was necessary to obtain from the people or senate, and afterwards from the emperors. Anciently a Roman citizen was not allowed even to marry a freed woman, much less a slave.

The children of a Roman citizen by a foreigner were deemed spurious.

Polygamy, or plurality of wives, was forbidden by the Roman laws.

Many of their laws were especially framed for the encouragement of marriage; bestowing privileges upon such as had as many as three children, and imposing fines upon those who had none. A parent could not disinherit a daughter for incontinence where he had neglected to provide her with an husband.

By the Roman law, an unmarried man was allowed to keep a concubine, but a man who had a wife was not entitled to do so.

Marriage contracts among the Romans were usually confirmed by articles drawn up in the form of a deed. In these documents were specified the amount of the dowry, and the instalments by which it was to be paid. On these occasions there was generally a feast, and the man gave his future bride a ring by way of pledge.

These instruments subsequently took the place of

a religious ceremony, which among the Romans fell into such disuse, that it gave rise amongst the lawyers to the maxim, "consensus non concubitus facit nuptias." This definition of the principles upon which marriage contracts were founded furnishes a key to the character of the Roman laws relating to divorce.

As consent was regarded as the essence of the contract, so it came to pass by degrees that the consent to cohabit was withdrawn upon frivolous grounds. To the want of consent were attributed all mistakes by which the purpose of marriage could be frustrated; such as consanguinity, sterility, or impotency, and such like causes.

In later times, mere dislike was esteemed a sufficient justification, either for the husband to dismiss his wife, or for the wife to forsake her husband.

By the laws of Romulus, a right to dissolve the marriage was allowed to the husband, but not to the wife. This power, however, could not be exercised without a just cause. A groundless or unjust divorce was punished with forfeiture of goods; of which one half fell to the injured wife, the other half was consecrated to Ceres.

A man might divorce his wife, after having formally consulted her relations about the complaint he had against her, upon the following grounds:—If she had violated the conjugal faith, or used poison to destroy her offspring, or brought upon her husband supposititious children; and, in some cases, even if she had counterfeited his keys, or drank wine without his knowledge. If a wife was guilty of infidelity, she forfeited her dowry; but if the divorce was obtained without any fault of hers, the dowry was restored to her.

These laws of divorce are supposed to have formed a part of the twelve tables. In many respects they resemble the laws both of the Greeks and the Hebrews.

The earliest instance of a Roman divorce is related to have occurred about the year B.C. 520, when Sp. Carvilius Ruga divorced his wife because she had no children.

In the later ages of the Republic, the same liberty of divorce was exercised by the woman as the man. Divorces were regarded as public acts. They were accompanied with various ceremonies, according to the manner in which the marriage had been celebrated.

In ancient times, marriages were dissolved with religious solemnities. In later times, the articles of marriage were torn up in the presence of seven witnesses; or the husband sent the wife a bill of divorcement, on which a set form of words was inscribed. Divorces were recorded in the public registers. If the marriage was dissolved without any fault on the part of the wife, her whole portion was restored to her, usually by three separate payments.

If the wife had committed adultery, she was prohibited from marrying the adulterer. In other cases, women were allowed to marry again after a period of ten months had elapsed. But, under any circumstances, second marriages were deemed dishonourable by the Romans. Polygamy they regarded with abhorrence. Sallust refers to it as a practice which rendered the barbarians the objects of scorn. By the edict of Diocletian, no one under the Roman jurisdiction was allowed to have two wives at once. The offender was liable to punishment by a competent tribunal. The Justinian Code forbade the Jews also to have two wives at once, according to the allowance of their own law.

By English jurists marriage is considered in no other light than as a civil contract. It is a contract which is evidenced in accordance with the provisions of a municipal law, as all contracts must be, though in its obligations and consequences it partakes of the responsibilities of a religious institution.

The legality of a civil contract depends in a great measure, if not entirely, upon the subject of the contract; the object is not always a recognised element in its construction or validity. But, in a matrimonial contract, the parties to it are alone the subject of obligation. Hence it is held that, in such contracts, disabilities follow the person, and render the parties liable, wherever they may go, to conform to the laws of the country of which they are subjects. But it is otherwise in a purely civil contract,—such a one, for instance, as concerns a bargain or a matter of merchandise or traffic. Here, if the contract is good under the laws of the country where it is made, for most purposes it is held to continue a valid obligation elsewhere. Where such a contract is binding in its inception, the parties to it cannot be released from its obligation simply by a change of residence.

This consideration is a strong argument in support of the proposition, that although marriage by writers of eminence is said to constitute only a civil contract, yet it is recognised by the law of England as an obligation involving principles to which the rules by which purely civil contracts are regulated are not altogether applicable.

The earliest Anglo-Saxon laws upon this subject that I have been able to discover are those of king Edmund. Upon this head the Anglo-Saxon institutions are remarkably silent. Nevertheless, such allusions as they furnish, though scanty, illustrate the customs of the age, and tend to shed some light upon the character in which such contracts were then regarded:—

"1. If a man desire to betroth a maiden or a woman, and it so be agreeable to her and her friends, then is it right that the bridegroom, according to the law of God, and according to the customs of the world, first promise and give a 'wed' to those who are her 'foresprecas,' that he desire her in such wise that he will keep her, accord ng to God's law, as a husband shall his wife: and let his friends guarantee that.

"2. After that, it is to be known to whom the 'foster-lean' belongs: let the bridegroom again give a 'wed' for this; and let his friends guarantee it.

"3. Then, after that, let the bridegroom declare what he will grant her, in case she choose his will, and what he will grant her if she live longer than he.

"4. If it be so agreed, then is it right that she be entitled to half the property, and to all, if they have children in common, except she again choose a husband.

"5. Let him confirm all that which he has promised with a 'wed,' and let his friends guarantee that.

"6. If they then are agreed in everything, then let the kinsmen take it in hand, and betroth their kinswoman to wife, and to a righteous life, to him who desired her, and let him take possession of the 'bohr' who has control of the 'wed.'

"7. But if a man desire to lead her out of the land, into another thane's land, then it will be advisable for her that her friends have an agreement that no wrong shall be done to her; and if she commit a fault, that they may be nearest in the 'bot,' if she have not wherewith she can make 'bot.'

"8. At the nuptials, there shall be a mass-priest by law; who shall, with God's blessing, bind their union to all prosperity.

"9. Well is it also to be looked to, that it be known that they, through kinship, be not too nearly allied; lest that be afterwards divided which before was wrongly joined."

We owe our laws of divorce to the civil or canon law. In ruder times, the marriage seems to have been dissolved by the dismissal of the wife for adultery without any formal ceremony. But as soon as the clergy began to exercise any influence in legislation, they managed to incorporate into the municipal laws many religious regulations. Such offences as related to marriage, and the disabilities affecting such unions, were, in the first instance, visited only with ecclesiastical censures. Whence it came to pass, that over the determination of such matters the church usurped jurisdiction, to the exclusion of the civil power.

By degrees the clergy began to define such offences by rules of their own, which varied from time to time, and were, for the most part, such interpretations of scriptural commands as their zeal or their cupidity dictated. These they designated canon laws; and by such arbitrary regulations they claimed the right of determining matters of which they had acquired the cognizance. But with respect to what is called the Canon Law, except so far as it is incorporated into, or is declaratory of, the common law of the country, it has been declared by the highest authority to be of no legal obligation whatever upon the laity.

Divorces were granted only by reason of the wife's adultery. The law did not regard the husband's irregularities with the same severity. Inasmuch as the Canon Law was avowedly based upon the Mosaic institutions, we may perhaps be justified in attributing this singularity to the Hebrew law, under which was allowed to the man a degree of license that was denied to the woman.

But according to Josephus, in his days the Jewish law upon marriages was interpreted with much greater strictness. He tells us distinctly that a man ought to have but one wife. His words are explicit (Cont. Apion, B. 2): "But then what are our laws about marriage? That law owns no other mixture of the sexes but that which nature hath appointed of a man with his wife, and this be used only for the procreation of children. It commands us also, when we marry, not to have a regard to portion, nor to take a woman by violence, nor to persuade her deceitfully and knavishly, but to demand her in marriage of him who hath power to dispose of her, and is fit to give her away by the nearness of his kindred; for, says the Scripture, a woman is inferior to her husband in all things. Let her therefore be obedient to him, not so that he should abuse her, but that she may acknowledge her duty to her husband; for God hath given the authority to the husband. A husband, therefore, is to lie only with his wife whom he hath married; but to have to do with another man's wife is a wicked thing, which if any one ventures upon, death is inevitably his punishment. No more can he avoid the same who forces a virgin betrothed to another man, or entices another man's wife."

"Now as to the incapacities for marriage. Disabilities under our law are of two sorts. First, those which are only canonical. These make the marriage voidable, and not *ipso facto* void. Of this nature are precontract, consanguinity, or relation by blood, and affinity, or relation by marriage, as well as some particular bodily infirmities. Such marriages, however, not being void *ab initio*, but voidable only by sentence of separation, are esteemed valid to all civil purposes, unless such separation is actually made during the life of the parties.

The other sort of disabilities are those which are created, or at least enforced, by the municipal laws.

These civil disabilities make the contract void *ab initio*, and not merely voidable; not that they dissolve a contract already formed, but they declare the parties to have been incapable of entering upon any such contract. To use the words of Blackstone, if any person under these legal incapacities come together, it is a meretricious and not a matrimonial union.

The civil law, which is partly of pagan origin, allows many causes of absolute divorce, and some of them pretty severe ones; as if the wife goes to the theatres or public games without the knowledge and consent of her husband. But adultery is, with reason, the principal cause for separation.

In England, up to a recent date, adultery was only a cause of separation from bed and board. For which the best reason that Blackstone can give, is that "if divorces were allowed to depend upon a matter within the power of either party, they would probably be extremely frequent."

It was perhaps partly for this reason that the common law only granted divorce for causes which existed before the marriage, and so rendered the parties incapable of contracting such an engagement. Hence it happened that a divorce had not, properly speaking, the effect of dissolving marriage, but amounted only to a declaration that no legal marriage ever existed. By consequence, the children of such unions were declared bastards. To retrieve this consequence, special acts of parliament were obtained. To such special interventions of the legislature persons who desired to be relieved from their marriage vows, upon the ground of adultery, were driven to have recourse.

The earliest regulations in this country concerning the degrees of consanguinity and affinity within which marriages were prohibited, refined a good deal upon the simplicity of the Levitical restrictions. It will be seen that not only kinship by blood or by marriage were impediments, but that also the doctrine of spiritual affinity, arising from the relation of persons standing as godfathers or godmothers to the object of their choice, was recognised as a disability to marriage. For the history of this doctrine, however, we must refer our readers to the learned opinion of Dr. Stephens, Q.C., on the 29th Canon of 1603 (published by Rivingtons).

The laws of Edward and Guthrum provide thus:—
"And concerning incestuous persons, the 'Witan' have ordained, that the king shall have the upper, and the bishop the nether, unless 'bot' be made before God and before the world, according as the deed may be, so as the bishop may teach. If two brothers or two near kinsmen commit fornication with the same woman, let them make 'bot' very strictly, in such wise as it may be allowed, as well by 'wer' as by 'wite,' or by 'lah-slit,' according as the deed may be."

The laws of king Ethelred declare the prohibited

degrees of affinity in the following terms: "And let it never be that a Christian man marry within the relationship of six persons in his own kin, that is, within the fourth degree, nor with the relict of him who was so near in worldly relationship, nor with the wife's relation whom he before had had. Nor with any hallowed nun, nor with his godmother, nor with one divorced, let any Christian man ever marry; nor have more wives than one, but be with that one as long as she may live, whoever will rightly observe God's law, and secure his soul from the burning of hell."

The laws of king Canute contain a similar provision: "And we instruct and beseech, and in God's name command, that no Christian man ever marry in his own family within the relationship of six persons, nor with the relict of his kinsman who was so near of kin, nor with the relative of the wife whom he had previously had, nor with his godmother, nor with a hallowed nun, nor with one divorced, let any Christian man ever marry, nor any fornication anywhere commit; nor have more wives than one, and let that be his wedded wife, and let him be with her alone as long as she may live, whoever will rightly keep God's law and secure his soul against the burning of hell."

## CHAPTER X.

### LAWS RELATING TO PARENTS AND CHILDREN.

The respect and obedience due to parents is a prominent principle in the early systems of jurisprudence. Upon this subject a variety of remarkable provisions occur in the laws of the Greeks and the Romans, as well as in those of the Egyptians. Amongst the most civilized nations of antiquity, the breach of filial duty entailed civil disabilities upon the offender, as well as severe punishment for the offence. In the Hebrew commonwealth such offences against social order were punished with death. These crimes, therefore, may be fairly classed among the subjects of municipal legislation. They were at least so regarded by the legislators of antiquity. Standing as it does at the root of domestic discipline, the relation of parent and child may properly be considered as the foundation of social order. Indeed, it is during the early period of life only that parental controul can be exercised with the advantages in which the force of affection and the power of compulsion are combined. It is only by such wholesome discipline that the untutored perversity of nature can be accustomed to the obligations of citizenship, under which the duty of acting for the benefit of others, as well as for personal advantage, is inculcated.

It is remarkable that the fifth commandment given to the Jews is the only one to the observance of which any reward is annexed: "Honour thy father and thy mother, that thy days may be long in the land which the Lord thy God giveth thee." But, upon the other hand, disobedience to this command is punished with a degree of severity which is the best proof of its guilt.

"He that smiteth his father, or his mother, shall surely be put to death. He that curseth his father, or his mother, shall surely be put to death." (Exod. xxi. 15, 17.)

"Thou shalt rise up before the hoary head, and honour the face of the old man, and fear thy God." (Lev. xix. 32.)

"If a man have a stubborn and rebellious son, which will not obey the voice of his father, or the voice of his mother, and that, when they have chastened him, will not hearken unto them: then shall his father and his mother lay hold on him, and bring him out unto the elders of his city, and unto the gate of his place; and they shall say unto the elders of his city, This our son is stubborn and rebellious, he will not obey our voice; he is a glutton, and a drunkard. And all the men of his city shall stone him with stones that he may die: so shalt thou put evil away from among you." (Deut. xxi. 18.)

According to Sir G. Wilkinson, filial duties were enforced by the Egyptians with marked severity. From the sculptures at Thebes Sir G. Wilkinson concludes that in Egypt much more was expected from a son than in any civilized nations of the present day; and that this was not confined to the lower orders, but extended to those of the highest ranks of society. The sons of the monarch filled the office of fan-bearer, which, although deemed an honourable post, entailed no ordinary show of humility. The king's sons walked on foot behind his chariot, bearing certain insignia over their father during the triumphal processions which took place in commemoration of his victories, and in the religious ceremonies over which he presided. In the education of youth they were particularly strict; and "they knew," says Plato, "that children ought to be early accustomed to such gestures, looks, and motions as are decent and proper; and not to be suffered either to hear or learn any verses and songs than those which are calculated to inspire them with virtue; and they consequently took care that every dance and ode introduced at their feasts or sacrifices should be subject to certain regulations." They particularly inculcated respect for old age; and the fact of this being required towards strangers necessarily argues a great regard for the person of a parent.

We are informed by Herodotus that they required every young man to give place to his superiors in years, and even, if seated, to rise on their approach. Nor were these honours limited to their lifetime. The memory of parents and ancestors was revered throughout succeeding generations. Their tombs were maintained with the greatest respect. Liturgies were performed by their children, or by priests at their expense. The laws concerning debt show that the legislators recognized and took advantage of this feeling. It was pronounced illegal for any one to borrow money without giving in pledge the body of his father or of his nearest relation. If the debtor failed to redeem so sacred a deposit, he was considered infamous; funeral obsequies and the right of burial, either in the tomb of his ancestors or elsewhere, were denied him. Nor could he inter any of his family so long as the debt was unpaid; the creditors being put in actual possession of his family tomb. Herodotus, however, mentions a law, that if a son was unwilling to maintain his parents, he was at liberty to refuse; but a daughter, on the contrary, was compelled to assist them, and on refusal was amenable to punishment. But Sir G. Wilkinson questions the truth of this statement, and thinks it inconsistent with the testimony of the sculptures that he had examined.

The following Greek laws are evidently based upon the same principle as that which distinguishes the Hebrew code. Social honour and domestic duty are treated as the foundation of civil obedience. "Let him be infamous who beats his parents, or does not provide for them."

But the obligation of maintaining parents was not enforced upon illegitimate children. This fact alone is sufficient to show how far the principles upon which the ancient laws of the Greeks were founded, tended to the discouragement of immorality. It will also be observed from the terms of the following law, that parents were bound to educate their children, and bring them up to some employment:—"No bastards, or such as have been brought up to no employ, shall be obliged to keep their parents." "He that is undutiful to his parents shall be incapable of bearing any office; and, further, shall be impeached before the magistrates."

Another law mentioned by Demosthenes is remarkable for its obvious reference to the very words of the sixth commandment:—

"If any one's estate, after his decease, shall be called in question, the enjoyer of it is obliged to prove the lawfulness of his parents' getting it according to the golden precept, *honour your parents.*"

"If any man, being found guilty of abusing his parents, frequent prohibited places, the Eleven shall fetter him, and bring him to trial at the Heliæan Court, where any one who is empowered thereto may accuse him. If he is here cast, the Heliæan judges shall inflict upon him what punishment they please; and if they fine him, let him be clapt up in gaol till he pays the whole."

Among the Greeks, parents appear to have enjoyed the power of disposing of the inheritance among their children, as well as that of adopting heirs where they were childless. They also gave their children names, and were bound to declare their legitimacy. The following laws, having these objects in view, show the rights of parentage:—

"They only shall be reckoned citizens whose parents are both so."

"He shall be looked upon as a bastard whose mother is not free."

But, nevertheless, from the time of Euclides the archon, bastards were allowed the right of inheritance:—

"Let one of spurious birth inherit either in sacred or civil things."

"That inheritance shall pass for good which is given by a childless person to an adopted son. Adoption must be made by persons living, not by their last testament."

"No one, unless the person who adopted him shall have a legitimate son, shall relinquish the family into which he is adopted to return to his natural."

"Parents may give their children what names they will, or change those they have for others."

Whenever parents came to enrol their children, whether genuine or adopted, in the public register of the φρατορες (or tribes) they were obliged to profess by oath that they were lawfully begotten of a free woman."

Demosthenes mentions a Greek law under which it is provided "that parents shall have full right to disinherit their children." "If through the infirmity of old age, or torture of a disease, any father be found crazed or distempered in his mind, a son may forthwith have an action against him, wherein if he be cast he may keep him in bonds."

In reference to the education of youth, one of the laws attributed to Solon provides, "The first institution of youth is to be in swimming, and the rudiments of literature; as for those whose abilities in the world are but mean, let them learn husbandry, manufactures, and trades; but they who can afford a gentle education shall learn to play on musical instruments, to ride, shall study philosophy, learn to hunt, and be instructed in gymnastic exercises."

Among the Romans, children were compelled to reverence their parent by a law which gave a father the power of life and death over his children. He could not only lawfully expose them when infants—a cruel custom, which prevailed at Rome for many ages—but even when his children were grown up, he might imprison, scourge, send them bound to work in the country, and also put them to death by any punishment he pleased, if they deserved it. Hence Seneca calls a father a domestic judge, or magistrate. Dionysius, however, relates that Romulus at first permitted this absolute right only in certain cases.

## CHAPTER XI.

#### THE CONSTITUTION OF THE SUPREME COURTS OF THE GREEKS AND EGYPTIANS.

In Egypt litigation was conducted in writing before the judicial assembly, whose functions seem to have included the power of deciding upon the facts as well as applying the law.

The proceedings consisted in the complaint, the plea, and the reply by the complaining person. Advocates were not allowed to plead for either party, "lest," says Diodorus Siculus, "the minds of the judges should be dazzled with that false eloquence which sometimes invests falsehood with the robes of truth, and hides truth under the garb of falsehood."

The Greeks had special forms of action for different kinds of crime and civil injury. Thus to some extent their judicial proceedings were necessarily reduced to writing. A Greek law is mentioned by Demosthenes under which it is required that evidence be declared in writing.

Another law, the terms of which have been preserved, provides that "eye-witnesses shall write down what they know, and read it."

The Greeks allowed hearsay evidence only where

the person from whom the statement emanated was dead, and therefore incapable of giving his testimony himself. In this case it was provided, in a Greek law preserved by Petit, "His evidence shall suffice that can give his ἀκοή, or what he heard from a deceased person or ἐκματυρία; i. e. an attestation received from one gone to travel, supposing the traveller hath no possibility of returning." Similar rules of procedure are adopted in modern courts of justice.

The system under which justice was administered both amongst the Egyptians and the Greeks seems to have been framed upon a Jewish model. The resemblance both in the formation of the courts and their peculiar functions in determining criminal cases, is especially remarkable in the supreme tribunals of each of these nations. The principal duty of the Egyptian kings was the administration of justice. This, therefore, was the science which they chiefly cultivated. In the discharge of their magisterial duties they were assisted by a court composed of thirty judges and a president. These were selected from the principal cities to form a body for dispensing justice throughout the whole kingdom of Egypt. None, says Diodorus, were chosen but those who were renowned for their wisdom and integrity. "He who was put at the head of them was the man most distinguished for his knowledge of the laws, and the one who was held in the highest esteem." They had also, he tells us, revenues assigned them, that, unembarrassed by domestic cares, and placed above the temptations of corruption, they might devote their whole time and attention to the study and administration of the laws.

This court decided such matters as did not fall within the immediate jurisdiction of the kings.

Amongst the Greeks, the highest court was the senate; or, at Athens, the Areopagus, whose name was taken from the place where it assembled. Aristides tells us it was the most sacred and venerable tribunal in all Greece. It was composed of the most honourable and distinguished citizens. Its numbers varied at different periods. In its character it was not unlike the assembly of elders amongst the Jews. All wilful murders and offences against the state came under the cognizance of this court.

By Solon's constitution the inspection and custody of the laws was committed to them. The public funds were disposed of according to their direction. The care of all young men in the city belonged to them. It was their business to appoint tutors and guardians to the youth of both sexes, and to see that they were properly educated. They had, also, the power of punishing such as led disorderly lives, and of rewarding the virtuous.

Idleness was an offence that more especially fell under their cognizance. Besides this, matters of religion, blasphemy against the gods, contempt of holy mysteries, and all sorts of impiety, the consecration of new gods, the erection of temples and altars, and the introduction of new ceremonies into divine worship, were referred to this court, which invariably sat in the open air.

The jurisdiction of this tribunal is defined by various laws. "The Areopagite Senate shall sit in judgment upon cases of wilful murder, of wounds given, wilfully setting houses on fire, and killing by poison."

Diodorus Siculus, who was evidently a great admirer of Egyptian institutions, after attempting to give a circumstantial account of the way in which Egypt became the source of laws and civilization to the nations with which it was brought into intercourse, with a curious acknowledgment of the obligations under which Egypt had placed the Greeks, proceeds thus:—" Having," he says, " now given an account of these things, it remains that we should declare how many wise and learned men among the Grecians journeyed into Egypt in ancient times to understand the laws and sciences of the country. For the Egyptian priests, out of their sacred records, relate that Orpheus Musæus, Melampodes, Dædalus, Homer the poet, Lycurgus the Spartan, Solon the Athenian, Plato the philosopher, Pythagoras the Samian, Eudoxus the mathematician, Democritus the Abderite, and Œnopides the Chian, all came to them in Egypt, and they show certain marks and signs of all these being there; of some by their pictures, and of others by the names of places, or pieces of work, which had been called after their names. And they bring arguments from every trade that is used to prove that everything wherein the Greeks excel, and for which they are admired, was brought over from Egypt into Greece. To these they add that Lycurgus, Solon, and Plato borrowed from Egypt many of those laws which they established in their several commonwealths; and that Pythagoras learned his mysterious and sacred expressions, the art of geometry, arithmetic, and transmigration of souls, in Egypt."

According to this author, the veneration with which the Egyptians regarded the sanctity of fixed laws was shown in the regulations under which even the conduct of their monarchs was controlled. We append his description of their mode of life. Nor is this without its resemblance to that which the Jewish constitution imposed upon its kings.

The Egyptians were the first who rightly understood the principles of government, perceiving that the true end of politics was the welfare of the state, and the happiness of the people. Even the social habits of their kings were regulated by prescribed rules. Sobriety and frugality were earnestly enjoined; but even their hours of rising, their devotions and daily sacrifices, the periods allotted to public business, the very food which they ate, and almost every action, were under the regulation of the laws.

It was different from other monarchies, where the prince acknowledges no other rule of his action but his arbitrary will and pleasure.

Everything was settled by ancient custom. They never sought, Diodorus tells us, to live in a way different from their ancestors. Old laws were reverenced; new ones were not wanted. No slave or foreigner was admitted into the immediate service of the prince. None, indeed, but those who were distinguished by their birth and attainments could approach the king's person, to the end that from men of such excellent education the king might hear nothing unbecoming his royal majesty, and have no sentiments instilled into him but such as were of a noble and generous kind.

From these particulars many resemblances may be traced between the Egyptians and the Jews, not only in the principles upon which justice was administered;

but in the manner in which the laws were executed. In this respect, the office of their kings and the functions of their supreme tribunals furnish a comparison, the accordance of which can scarcely be accounted for by chance. The same remark is singularly applicable to the supreme courts of the Greeks, whose original constitution appears to have been framed very much in conformity with the judicial system of the Jews.

In the patriarchal times, the elders or heads of tribes appear to have exercised magisterial functions. Before the time of Moses we read of no supreme council of the nation. Nor is any mention made of subordinate officers for the administration of justice, who were accountable for the discharge of their duties to a superior authority. There was then no general ruler of the people. Particular tribes acted as independent republics, each conducting its own internal administration, though they sometimes acted together for a general purpose in which their common interest was involved.

The constitution of Moses superseded the simpler system of the patriarchs. He was not only the lawgiver, but the chief magistrate of the Jews. When his judicial duties became too heavy for him, the more difficult questions were reserved for his decision; but for the administration of justice on matters of smaller importance, he appointed subordinate magistrates. These were constituted judges of tens, of fifties, of hundreds, and of thousands. This arrangement was well suited to the settlement of the people in tribes and families. It was also well adapted to the regulation of a marching army, whose host was distributed into the military division of thousands, hundreds, fifties, and tens.

But whatever may have been the reason for such an exact apportionment of judicial duties, it appears to have been the model of our own counties, hundreds, and tithings. Some of our legal antiquaries have supposed, and not without good reason, that the old Anglo-Saxon constitution of sheriffs in counties, hundreders or centgraves in hundreds, and deciners in decinaries, were introduced by king Alfred from the institutions of Moses. Moses also established a council or senate, consisting of seventy elders, to assist him in his deliberations. This constituted the supreme council of the nation. Its functions were subsequently restored in the institution of the Jewish Sanhedrim. But besides the judges, scribes were appointed to every city. Their duties seem to have answered to that of registrars and keepers of the public records.

The office of the judges was not hereditary. It was, however, held for life. Their authority was not inferior to that which was afterwards exercised by the kings.

As soon as the polity of the Hebrew commonwealth was settled by Moses, he commanded the Israelites to appoint judges and officers in all their gates throughout their tribes. (Deut. xvi. 18.) Their duty it was to exercise a magisterial supervision over the neighbouring villages. According to Josephus, these judges were seven in number. With these seven were associated two officers from the tribe of Levi; so that to each district was assigned a tribunal consisting of nine judges, seven of which were lay persons, and two Levites.

With respect to the manner in which the proceedings were conducted, it is manifestly essential that some uniformity should be observed in the method of its administration. To this end the proceedings in the Jewish courts were committed to writing, and preserved in archives or registries. Josephus informs us that there was such a repository at Jerusalem until it was burnt by the Romans. He states, also, that scribes or notaries were appointed for the purpose of recording judicial proceedings.

There is no reason to suppose that the parties were allowed the use of advocates. From casual expressions in the Scriptures it appears that causes were heard and judgment was executed in the morning. According to the Talmud, causes were prohibited from being heard at night. Nor could an execution be carried out upon the same day on which sentence was pronounced.

He who entered an action went to the judges and stated his complaint. If satisfied that there were sufficient grounds, the judges then sent officers with him to seize the offender and bring him to justice. In one respect the Jewish system differed from ours; for even in criminal cases the accused was allowed to give evidence in his defence. This seems but reasonable and just. For why should not the accused be allowed to state what he can in his defence, leaving it to his judges to attach to his testimony such credit as it may deserve? Before execution, it was usual with the Jews to administer to the criminal an intoxicating cup to deprive him of consciousness. But no one could be condemned by a judicial tribunal without a public trial. This agrees with one of the ordinances with which the twelve tables protected the security of Roman citizens, "No one shall be condemned before he is tried."

# CHAPTER XII.

## CONCLUSION.

TRADITION may conduct an institution from one period to another; history may trace its progress; but the principle that gave it life and destination must be sought for in the nature of the institution itself. To display the developement of a system, ample materials may be found within a narrow range. Its refinements are multiplied in proportion as the simplicity of its objects is forgotten. Indeed, they often overgrow and obliterate the design they profess to carry out, and attempt, by special provisions, to supersede the necessity of general principles. Such artificial regulations need not be traced to a remote age. They are usually the offspring of circumstance. Their application is changed at convenience. They become antique and curious, not so much from any merit of their own, as because their purpose is forgotten, and the object they had in view has been superseded by the habits of a subsequent age. But to ascertain the principles upon which judicial systems are founded, is a task of another kind. Their progress must be traced until the source from which they spring is eventually discovered.

In such an investigation history furnishes landmarks more or less perfect. So far as they concern the sources of jurisprudence, such illustrations lead, in a broken though not uncertain track, from the confines of modern civilization to the remotest periods of antiquity. But to establish their connection in reference to law, it is not only requisite to consult the history of its introduction, but the principle which first taught its necessity.

In conformity with this design, we have had recourse to evidence of various kinds, not confining the investigation to the circumstances under which the law was given, nor seeking its interpretation in the avowed design of its legislators, but seaching for its principles in the very nature of the thing itself. We have, therefore, in the first instance, not resorted to the primary institution of laws, but have been content to take examples from those legislators who have founded the most celebrated systems of antiquity, relying upon their acknowledgments and their method of legislation as the most independent proof of the principles by which, in endeavouring to establish a system, they considered its construction must be regulated and limited. The conclusions of such witnesses are the best testimony of the principles upon which they felt the necessity of acting. We have examined the methods of legislation adopted by the Greek and Roman philosophers. We have seen their repeated admissions that laws must be founded upon right and justice. We have their authority for the conclusion that right and justice are not to be determined by the arbitrary rules of convenience. Therefore, at the outset of this work we thought it the best opportunity to refer to those principles to which the philosophers of antiquity ascribed the authority of their legislation. That a moral obligation formed an essential element in the systems of the ancient lawgivers, is evident from the opinions of all those among their philosophers who attempted to reduce jurisprudence to any thing like a theoretical institution. Amongst them all the attainment of justice is avowedly their object. Amongst many the attainment of this object is avowedly referred to some superior power beyond the reach of those influences by which those who are subject to such obligations must be affected. They all refer the obligation of their institutions to a supreme power, as the necessary standard of right and wrong, and the only authority capable of discrimination between what is in itself just or unjust. Those who are liable to the penalties of the law, and the temptations by which the breach of it is induced, are necessarily liable to have their determination biassed rather by the circumstances under which the offence was committed than to decide upon the guilt of an offence by reference to a standard of right to the elements and the origin of which they are strangers. The principles of justice, therefore, were ascribed to a supreme power. Some referred it to a direct revelation from the gods; others maintained it was a supreme rule of conduct by which the gods themselves were governed; while, again, other philosophers defined the principle of justice as natural law, or the law of nature, ascribing to nature the divinity of a supreme power overruling and regulating the concerns of mortal beings.

How much they felt the necessity of some standard by which they could determine what was good from what was evil, what was just from what was unjust, is manifest from their own statements. They acknowledge the impossibility of determining these points without having some perfect standard of what is right and just in itself. This standard they describe as the law of nature. The law of nature they declare to be the law of creation, and ascribe its origin to the Divine Author of all things. The writings of some philosophers set forth this principle as the will of the sovereign Jupiter. Some treat the law of nature as emanating from the Divine mind. Some deify the principle itself, treating nature as a divine principle from which all human things had their origin, and by which they must regulated. But all agree in attributing to this principle an authority higher than that of a conventional obligation. We thence have the testimony of legislators, arguing upon laws, not from any preconceived principles, but from the nature of the subject with which they had to deal, that in order to establish any rule of conduct for the governance of mankind worthy the name of a law, such regulations must be founded, not upon the dictates of convenience, but upon some supreme principles of right and wrong.

With this acknowledgment of the necessity for a supreme power to ordain laws for the guidance of mortals, we have endeavoured to trace some of the most celebrated of the ancient systems to the laws of the Hebrews, because the divine authority of the Hebrew laws is more certainly established than that of any other human institutions. But as the Hebrew is the most ancient, as well as the most complete system of legislation of which any records have been preserved, it is not unreasonable to resort to this, not only for the traditions by which other legislative systems were moulded to a particular shape, but for the first principles of jurisprudence. The many resemblances between the earliest regulations adopted by other communities, and the laws of the Jews, are remarkable. The travels and the acknowledgments of their authors corroborate the evidence of their tradition. One evidence of the origin of these institutions is to be found in the terms of their provisions. Of their agreement with the Hebrew statutes, we have furnished many examples. But a still stronger proof of their derivation is to be found in the principles of their construction. Such evidence as this, though it does not lie so near the surface, yet, where it can be traced, furnishes the strongest testimony of the foundation of the system; because, though special coincidences may be attributed either to chance, or to the common instincts of humanity, yet the purpose and application of a law, where it extends beyond the immediate object of its provisions, must be attributed to the principles upon which the law itself is founded. So far, therefore, as the purpose and the application of the ancient laws is found to be in conformity with the Hebrew system, it is not unreasonable to conclude that they were founded upon the same principles. The reason for this arose either from necessity, or traditional knowledge. But from whatever cause the adoption of such principles may be explained, the resemblance of the most perfect legislative systems to the judicial code of the Jews presents many remarkable features for investigation. In such a comparison, nothing is more worthy of consideration than the religious element that pervades these institutions. This is to be discovered, not so much in the terms of their provisions, as in the method by which they were enforced, and the obligations by which the duties of obedience were inculcated. We find all the ancient lawgivers sought the sanction of a divine authority; some attributing their institution to one divinity, some to another; and some seeking for a rule of life in the responses of their oracles.

The origin of this may be traced, as we have endeavoured to show, to the source of the Jewish laws. The necessity of such a superintending principle, capable at once of bestowing temporal rewards and of inflicting future punishment after death, commended itself to those legislators upon whom had devolved the introduction, not of any special enactment, but of a general system of laws. This goes to establish the supposition that they not only copied Jewish institutions, but that they felt the necessity of confirming their statutes by the application of a moral principle which distinguished the Hebrew code. The evidence of this conclusion is to be found, not only in the sentiments of their philosophy, but in the laws themselves. To give their enactments something more than the transient force of compulsion, the ancients generally deified their legislators. Thus they insisted upon the moral obligation of their laws, which thence became part of a general system. Their laws were avowedly precepts for the guidance of mankind, sanctioned by an over-ruling providence.

Thence we find that the earliest legislative systems

were closely associated with the religious institutions of the state. The observance of the one was the sanction of the other. The elements of the one contained the principle of the other. Therefore it was that instruction in the national religion became the basis of public education. The national religion was the authority from which municipal regulations derived their obligation. Hence the system under which religion was inculcated may be traced to a political purpose. The methods by which the observance of such ordinances was kept alive, are hardly less remarkable than the nature of the rites themselves. Their import may be established, where their imitation cannot be commended, since the corruptions of time disfigured the ordinances, where they could not obliterate the purpose of their institution. In proof of this, we need only refer to the subject of oaths. For, on the occasion of solemn conventions, we discover not only a direct appeal to a divine power, but in many cases this appeal was confirmed by the same ceremonies as those which were practised by the Jews, and derived their sanction, if not their obligation, from the ordinances of the Levitical institutions. This, though a singular instance, may suffice to illustrate one general principle that pervaded the political systems of the ancients. The means that they adopted to inculcate their authority obviously had reference to considerations of a religious character. These they reckoned to be the foundation of public education. It was upon these principles alone that they taught the necessity of moral obligations, and the authority of municipal institutions. And this undoubtedly is the great object of all public education, namely, to teach those who would otherwise be beyond the reach of such incentives to duty, what obligations they are under to their Maker, and what duties they owe to the community to which they belong. Whatever goes beyond this is not included in the purposes of an education such as that which a community for its own sake is bound to bestow. It belongs rather to the sphere of private industry and enterprise. It is the duty of the State to teach its subjects the nature of the obligations which it will compel them to observe. The object of public education is not to fit a man for a particular calling, but to teach him his duty to himself and to society, in whatever position he may be placed. Beyond this, it is manifestly unjust to impose upon the community the burden of contributing to the advancement of those whose means or whose indolence do not entitle them to enjoy such advantages; advantages which not unfrequently are beyond the reach of those whose position compels them to pay for the children of others what they could ill afford for their own.

Among the ancient communities, the national religion necessarily became the vehicle of public instruction; since their deities, amongst their other attributes, held the destiny of public affairs, as well as presided over the various functions of life.

The requisite machinery for imparting these doctrines was furnished by their religious institutions. The obligation of providing such means of education was recognised as an essential part of their political systems. Thus, whatever may have been the reasons for it, the national religion was made the foundation of all public education by the most famous legislators of antiquity. It seems, indeed, to accord with every maxim of prudence and good government that this should be the case. It is at least a lesson inevitably conveyed by the political systems of antiquity which have been commonly regarded as most worthy of admiration. If, then, universal experience has demonstrated a principle supported by every consideration of prudence and political security, it is difficult to perceive upon what grounds its adoption should be rejected in modern times. The necessity of such a rule holds good now as much as ever. Since the national religion of a country is the foundation of its political constitution, it is only reasonable and right that it should be the basis of public education. In a Protestant country, the Protestant religion should furnish the elements of public instruction. In a Catholic country, we may concede that the teaching of the Catholic religion would so far tend to the immediate security of the State, since thence its existing institutions derive their authority. But in a Protestant country, whose institutions are founded upon the Protestant religion, it appears to be subversive of public security, and of every constitutional principle, to inculcate, at the expense of the State, the doctrines of a religion that openly denies its authority and professes allegiance to a foreign power. But the adoption of this system by the nations of antiquity gave their legislation peculiar advantages. The consequence of it was, that their institutions were conformed to a recognised principle, by which the force and interpretation of their laws was regulated. The dictates of convenience ceased to be regarded as rules of conduct. At the first institution of almost every system of laws, from the time of Solon to the laws of Alfred, the principles, if not the provisions, of the Hebrew code have been resorted to as the basis of legislation. But as the necessity for special regulations increased, the spirit of those institutions has been lost sight of. The Hebrew laws, indeed, are adapted with peculiar consideration to the various circumstances of life. Without disguising the standard of justice upon which these statutes depend, they abound in equitable qualifications sufficient to temper the hardship with which the exercise of a general principle might occasionally fall upon an individual. Law, to be just, or even to be intelligible, must, in a civilized country, assume the form of a system, and every alteration must be considered, not on its own merits merely, but strictly with reference to some universal standard of justice.

There is probably no greater obstacle to the reform and consolidation of laws in this country than the abnegation of such a principle. Yet nowhere is it set forth in such comprehensive terms as in the Mosaic laws, to which our legal institutions owe their origin. It is from the absence of any general principles upon which laws should be framed that arise the almost insuperable obstacles which so long have prevented the codification of the various fragments of legislation which from time to time occasion has dignified with the name of laws. What is it that has distinguished our greatest lawyers, but the power and the courage to reconcile our laws to some general principles of right and justice? What is it that has rendered famous the decisions of our most celebrated judges, but the clearness with which the principles of justice have been eliminated from a mass of judicial decisions, in which such elements are only casually to be met with, because the most simple and perfect standard of right and wrong had ceased to be recognised?

A system founded upon such a principle as this, would leave no room for the distinctions between law and equity, because the operation of the law would require no machinery to modify the harshness or the injustice of its application. The very existence of such a tribunal is an acknowledgment that the law is imperfect or unjust, otherwise any interference with its jurisdiction would be at once superfluous and wrong. But in the Hebrew laws, as well as in those systems which were founded upon the Hebrew model, not only are their provisions avowedly referred to the principles of morality and right, but they abound also in equitable qualifications, modifying their application according to circumstances. This object is accomplished, even in the face of the most severe statutes, without infringing the principles of justice that dictated their provisions. In no instance is this more conspicuous than in the laws relating to bloodshed and violence. The moral guilt attending such transgressions is never permitted to pass without an atonement; nevertheless the punishment is modified according to the degree of guilt. However innocent may have been the motives of the transgressor, the breach of the law is never suffered to escape with impunity.

Those offences against the law which are made the subject of retribution, furnish many examples of the manner in which this principle was applied. These, as we have seen, are chiefly of a criminal nature. They consist, for the most part, of crimes involving personal violence, or outrages affecting personal rights, including assaults, adulteries, and personal injuries. Among these, murder is the most prominent, and is the subject of capital punishment. The manner in which murder was distinguished from manslaughter, and the circumstances that justified homicide, are remarkable illustrations of what may be termed the equitable adjustments of the Mosaic Code. How far these peculiarities were preserved in the subsequent systems of the Greeks and the Romans, has been already shown by certain proofs of their adoption, not only in practice, but in principle. Provisions of the same kind were adopted by the Anglo-Saxon codes, in terms of similar import to those contained in the Hebrew laws. The laws relating to cities of refuge, and to the right of avenging bloodshed, have also left many traces of their adoption in the provisions concerning chance-medley, and accidental homicide. The punishment of false witness, by inflicting upon the criminal a punishment corresponding with the consequence of his perjury, is another singular instance of the strictness with which the principles of the Mosaic laws were copied by the legislators of antiquity. The same observation applies to the distinction observed in the Greek and Roman institutions concerning the right to slay a thief by night, where in the day time it was only lawful in self-defence.

But to dismiss now this part of the subject, we may pass on to the laws of restitution. These properly concern civil injuries rather than criminal offences. Upon wrongful acts of this nature the spirit of the Hebrew laws presents a marked contrast with those of its provisions that concerned criminal acts of violence. In regard to crimes, it treats the offender as primarily liable to public punishment, though such penalties might sometimes be averted by restitution or private amends. Upon the other hand, when dealing with civil injuries, it treats them in the first instance as the subject of restitution; but after restitution had failed, the offender became liable to criminal punishment for having committed a wrong, and for having refused to make amends for it.

By a comparison of their judicial systems, we have endeavoured to show that the principles of the Mosaic Code were adopted by the legislators of antiquity, and that thence many peculiarities to be discovered in the structure of modern institutions may be attributed to a Jewish model. In no respect is this coincidence more remarkable than in the laws of retribution. However severely an injury is condemned, the motive of the offender was always regarded as an ingredient in his guilt. By this means wilful crimes were distinguished from accidental offences. The punishment was awarded, in many instances, according to the circumstances under which the offence was committed.

In the earlier examples which we have given, this is perhaps more apparent than in the later ones, until we arrive at last at a period in which policy or interest had by degrees obliterated almost all trace of the principle upon which the law was originally founded. The various circumstances under which the penalties of retribution might be escaped, lead to the consideration of a class of offences in regard to which the provisions of the law more formally adopted the equitable spirit of its principles. For even by the act of the offender, such transgressions were suffered to be withdrawn from the penalties that attended the breach of the law. On making timely amends to the person injured, the offender was permitted to avert the consequences of a public crime. Thus civil injuries fell within the province of the laws prescribing restitution. For it was the policy of the ancient legislators to treat in the first instance as civil offences such injuries as were capable of being settled between the parties by compensation, without prejudice to the public welfare.

The simplicity with which this object may be accomplished, is conspicuous in the earlier laws of Europe. A departure from this principle, however, is to be observed in the shape that more modern institutions have assumed. This, probably, may be accounted for in the peculiar state of society that arose from the feudal system. At this time, one man was permitted to have a property in another. Hence, for an injury done to his servant, the lord was entitled to demand compensation. This method of redress was often also attended with a fine to the king, and sometimes with a pecuniary penalty to the clergy. So that the compensation originally intended for the benefit of the person injured, was by degrees diverted from its object, until at length private injuries became, generally, the subject of public fines. To enforce these penalties, imprisonment and other punishments were resorted to, until at length what was recognised, in the first resort, as the proper subject of restitution, was transferred at once to the harsher jurisdiction of the criminal code. Thus the character of the institutions established in the middle ages, upon the principles of the Hebrew laws, was gradually conformed to the tyrannical spirit of a system that consulted chiefly the interests of those who were lords of the soil.

The evils of this system reached its height with the introduction of penances by the Romish church, and tended more to subvert the principles of law than perhaps any other of its theological dogmas. The church, indeed, acknowledged the existence of a supreme standard of right, the violation of which it punished with penances; but it assumed a divine authority for granting absolution for the breach of the law, where the law itself allowed no remission of the guilt attending its transgression. The priest virtually arrogated to himself the right of declaring that the breach of a divine command did not necessarily incur the guilt which the law had declared to consist in its transgression. Thus it violated the very principle it professed to establish. For we have the distinct declaration of Scripture, that "sin is the transgression of the law." In the Mosaic Code a distinct penalty is attached to every offence, the guilt of which is not to be removed without some atonement. But by granting absolution for past transgressions, and still more so by granting it for future disobedience, the necessity of this doctrine is totally denied. And that the church of Rome professes not only to forgive past transgressions, but also those which are to be committed hereafter, admits of the fullest pooof.

In the seventh preceding chapter, those offences

which fell immediately within the laws of restitution have been more particularly referred to. They will be found to consist chiefly of thefts, trespasses, and injuries to the property of others. There are, however, other subjects, involving moral duties, which fall partly within the province assigned to the laws of restitution, and partly within the limits of those statutes which have restitution for their object. These are mostly offences involving the breach of domestic duties and the invasion of the rights conferred by such obligations. These offences, as we have seen, have been almost universally treated as public crimes. The exception to this rule is to be found in cases of seduction, where the injury could be redressed by marriage, without prejudicing the claims of any other person who had lawfully an interest in the woman. Under other circumstances, offences of this sort were followed by criminal punishment.

In no respect have the principles of the Hebrew Code been more faithfully followed by subsequent legislators than in this.

Although in this country adultery has been withdrawn by modern usage from the grasp of criminal laws, yet from the terms of our earlier codes it cannot be doubted that even here it was originally treated as a public crime. How this change came to pass, it is not difficult to perceive. It may be traced to the influence of the clergy. At first the church exercised a jurisdiction over such offences concurrent with that of the criminal laws. The church imposed fines and penances. By degrees the authority of the clergy superseded the power of the laws, and transferred these offences to the exclusive jurisdiction of the spiritual courts. But then, again, the supremacy of the law prevailed, and having left the church to enforce its sentence with spiritual penalties, at length denied the authority of ecclesiastical sentence in anything but matters spiritual. So that the power of the church was confined to the conscience, and was not permitted to affect the civil rights of the subject. Thus such injuries escaped the restraint of criminal punishment altogether, and were left to be redressed by compensation. To enforce this, the parties were driven to resort to the remedies provided by the civil courts.

But if the laws restraining wrongful actions are worth examination, the original construction of those regulations by which private rights and duties are maintained no less deserves attention. For it is apparent that where the provisions of the Hebrew laws in restraint of wrongs have been imitated, its principles have been adopted with equal subservience in that class of enactments by which rights are conferred. Examples of this are furnished in the laws relating to inheritances, to adoption, to boundaries, to the obligations and rights of marriage, and to the duties involved in the relationship of parent and child. But besides these, there were many institutions that sprang from a state of society peculiar to the Jews; yet, in the earlier systems of jurisprudence many special provisions have been traced which are almost identical with the terms of the Hebrew statutes. We have instances of this in the laws relating to usury and landmarks, but more especially in the laws relating to religion. These are the more remarkable, since they affect the general principles of the institutions in which they are found.

The elements, then, of a judicial system may be divided into two classes; namely, those by which rights are conferred, and those by which wrongs are prevented. But it is manifest that the existence of the one is the foundation upon which must rest the provisions of the other. Rights must be defined before wrongs can be ascertained, because wrongs are the infringement of rights. Therefore the principle upon which rights are founded must pervade those institutions by which wrongs are restrained. Hence it is important to trace the recognition of those principles by which the codes of the earliest legislators were distinguished. Even by those writers who attribute the origin of jurisprudence to the laws of nature it is conceded that natural law, for its due fulfilment, requires a moral sense of right and wrong; and that this natural law or moral obligation must form an essential ingredient in every system of jurisprudence, is amply attested, not only by the writings but by the customs of antiquity. As to the opinions of the philosophers, their own arguments have been given in the first chapter to prove their conviction that the law of nature was derived from the Creator of all things. And since the breach of moral laws is presumptively attended by future as well as present retribution, besides attributing to their laws the direct sanction of a divine authority, the ancient legislators evidently sought to enforce their systems by an appeal to the terror of future punishment and to the hope of future reward. Hence they made their religious institutions the basis of civil government. A religious element, therefore, found its way into the construction of their secular laws, since these derived no small part of their authority from the religious institutions of the state. This design is more conspicuous in the Hebrew polity than in that of any other nation. Therefore, where the principles that distinguish the Jewish system are adopted by subsequent legislators as the authority and sanction from which their institutions derive their obligation, it surely strengthens the proof of their origin to be able to show that if, in the one case, religious institutions were adapted to secular purposes, in the other the laws relating to religion were so constituted as to controul and regulate the secular laws by provisions that display the same peculiarities as those which for particular purposes were embodied in the Jewish system. For this shows not only that the principles upon which the Jewish laws were based were acknowledged by subsequent legislators to be the only authority from which judicial institutions could derive any moral obligation, but also that the authors of subsequent systems felt that those principles were best applied by the method pointed out in the model they either copied or adopted. If they copied them, it shows that they believed that the Jews possessed the wisest laws. If they, from the result of their own reasoning, endeavouring to frame a system from the best materials within their reach, constructed institutions in conformity with the provisions of the Hebrew constitution, they must have arrived at the conclusion that such institutions were the most perfect that could be framed for the governance of a community. In either case, the existence of similar institutions in a subsequent age, and in different countries, is a tribute not only to the superiority of the Jewish system, but it shows that it contains in itself the principle of all that mankind have regarded as just legislation.

The most prominent features, therefore, of the religious institutions of the ancient communities whose laws have become celebrated, have been compared with the Jewish system. The comparison furnishes many points of resemblance. The coincidences we have mentioned are the most prominent, if not the most conclusive, evidence of the source from which they originated. Of these amongst others, we may refer to the duties and office of the priests, to the regulations affecting their families, and their hereditary rights—to the laws relating to religious worship, to the sanctity of the altar, and the protection it afforded to criminals—to the manner of offering sacrifices—to the customs concerning oaths—to the observance of sacred days, as well as to other particulars; and the various allusions to these subjects, taken from Greek and Roman authors in corroboration of their origin. These, however, have been considered in detail in a previous chapter. It has been seen, also, how these principles were inculcated. Many special laws have been noticed under which public instruction in the religion and the laws of the country was provided for by the State as an essential part of its political institutions. At the same time, these systems took notice of many subjects that custom has led us to suppose do not belong to the province of laws. They enforce moral obligations with remarkable rigour, and compel, by positive enactments, the observance of social duties. For example, they prescribe the obligations of marriage, and regulate the permission of divorce very much in conformity with the terms of the Mosaic ordinances. They do not, however, avowedly acknowledge them.

But in the laws of the middle ages, although they were for the most part founded upon the ruins of the Roman system, yet almost all their codes are prefaced by some reference to the Divine laws. Thus they claim the sanction of a Divine authority, at least so far as their general principles are concerned.

In the Anglo-Saxon laws, the Mosaic institutions are more prominently referred to than in any others. Many of these codes, as we have seen, are introduced with a recapitulation of the Hebrew laws, and by reference to these the obligation of their subsequent provisions is expressly enforced. So much so, indeed, that the power of the church was invoked to inculcate their observance by the imposition of spiritual punishments. Indeed, the methods by which their authority was strengthened are no less remarkable than the importance that was manifestly attached to their Divine obligation. The breach of the law was not only rendered liable to spiritual punishment, but the ministers of religion were invested with the duty of instructing the people in the principles of the law as a necessary lesson of morality. By this means the church and the state gathered mutual strength from their union. The church inculcating the most solemn obligations for those institutions, the application of which was enforced by the secular tribunals, not as the only authority for their existence, but as the authorized means for carrying them into execution, where their moral obligation had failed to secure their observance. By this means the laws became the basis of public education, embodying not only the principles of the constitution, but also the rule of conduct which it imposed upon its citizens, giving them not only certain regulations to which it could compel them to conform, but also certain motives of action, the observance of which tended to supersede the restraint of municipal regulations. In this consists the superiority of such institutions, that they not only restrain the outward actions of men, but they regulate the motives by which those actions are controuled.

In the Hebrew laws, then, we have a model embodying principles which universal experience has acknowledged to be the essential foundation of all moral rules of conduct. These principles were, by the ancients, justly ascribed to a Divine author. To us they are more completely conveyed by the express revelation of the Scriptures. Here are signified, in unequivocal terms, the great principles of right and justice. Each individual is held accountable for his motives, as well as for his actions. The duties of obedience, by which the motives are to be regulated, are here enunciated. But inasmuch as a man's actions affect others, it is manifest that the motives by which his actions are prompted, concern those who may be injured by his actions. Therefore, it is a matter of interest to them that the motives of others should be duly regulated as well as restrained by law. For this constitutes exactly the difference between acting upon duty and a right principle which benefits all, and acting from motives of convenience which may injure many. Therefore, it seemed a matter of no small importance to trace the systems which the wisest legislators have imposed to regulate the conduct of men up to the same source as that by which the motives of men can be controuled, and thus to SHOW THE OBLIGATIONS WHICH LEGISLATION OWES TO THE SACRED SCRIPTURES.

www.ingramcontent.com/pod-product-compliance
Lightning Source LLC
Chambersburg PA
CBHW021953220426
43663CB00007B/804